It is rare to find a book that offers the reader a seamless, yet powerful, integration of Black liberation theory; intersectional feminism; and illustrations of the stark, intergenerational, and persistent effects of the sexual assaults that have been perpetrated on Black women's bodies from the moment they were hauled onto slave ships 400 years ago. Yet *The Cultural Betrayal of Black Women and Girls: A Black Feminist Approach to Healing From Sexual Abuse* does all of these things, and eloquently. Any therapist who works with women of African descent, any woman of African descent healing from trauma, any ally to these women, should be reading this book, because it is transformative, and what Jennifer Gómez has to say matters.

—**Laura S. Brown, PhD, ABPP,** independent intersectional feminist practice, Seattle, WA

In *The Cultural Betrayal of Black Women and Girls: A Black Feminist Approach to Healing From Sexual Abuse*, Jennifer M. Gómez, PhD, brilliantly articulates a widely known phenomenon that often goes unnamed—that the trauma following sexual abuse is exacerbated when those we trust, those from our own cultural group, are our perpetrators. Dr. Gómez reviews how cultural betrayal sexual trauma complicates nearly every part of surviving sexual abuse, from our freedom to seek safety from family members, our church homes, or the legal system to our ability to seek medical and therapeutic care even decades after the abuse has ended. This book is a must-read for anyone who works with Black women and girls who have experienced sexual trauma and wants to offer culturally competent trauma therapy that contributes to our holistic healing. Equally important, Black survivors of cultural betrayal sexual trauma will benefit from this book, seeing the complexity of their abuse and their pain named and validated. Finally, Dr. Gómez encourages all of us to think beyond the individual to consider how each and every one of us can strive for radical healing in our communities and in the world.

—**NiCole T. Buchanan, PhD,** Professor of Psychology, Michigan State University, East Lansing, MI; Fellow of the Association for Psychological Science and the American Psychological Association

The Cultural Betrayal of Black Women and Girls

The Cultural Betrayal of Black Women and Girls

A Black Feminist Approach to Healing From Sexual Abuse

Jennifer M. Gómez

 AMERICAN PSYCHOLOGICAL ASSOCIATION

Copyright © 2023 by the American Psychological Association. All rights reserved. Except as permitted under the United States Copyright Act of 1976, no part of this publication may be reproduced or distributed in any form or by any means, including, but not limited to, the process of scanning and digitization, or stored in a database or retrieval system, without the prior written permission of the publisher.

The opinions and statements published are the responsibility of the author, and such opinions and statements do not necessarily represent the policies of the American Psychological Association.

Published by
American Psychological Association
750 First Street, NE
Washington, DC 20002
https://www.apa.org

Order Department
https://www.apa.org/pubs/books
order@apa.org

Typeset in Charter and Interstate by Circle Graphics, Inc., Reisterstown, MD

Printer: Gasch Printing, Odenton, MD
Cover Designer: Gwen J. Grafft, Minneapolis, MN

Library of Congress Cataloging-in-Publication Data

Names: Gómez, Jennifer M., author.
Title: The cultural betrayal of Black women and girls : a Black feminist approach to healing from sexual abuse / by Jennifer M. Gómez.
Description: Washington, DC : American Psychological Association, [2023] | Includes bibliographical references and index.
Identifiers: LCCN 2023006328 (print) | LCCN 2023006329 (ebook) | ISBN 9781433838880 (paperback) | ISBN 9781433838897 (ebook)
Subjects: LCSH: Sexual abuse victims--Psychology. | African American women--Violence against. | Women, Black--Violence against. | Rape culture. | Men, Black--Psychology. | Psychic trauma--Treatment. | Racism--Psychological aspects. | Feminist theory. | BISAC: PSYCHOLOGY / Psychopathology / Post-Traumatic Stress Disorder (PTSD) | SOCIAL SCIENCE / Gender Studies
Classification: LCC HV6556 .G635 2023 (print) | LCC HV6556 (ebook) | DDC 362.883089/96073--dc23/eng/20230421
LC record available at https://lccn.loc.gov/2023006328
LC ebook record available at https://lccn.loc.gov/2023006329

https://doi.org/10.1037/0000362-000

Printed in the United States of America

10 9 8 7 6 5 4 3 2

To all the Black women and girls who did not live long enough to experience healing from the spirit-crushing violations of cultural betrayal rape, sexual assault, sexual abuse, sexual trauma, sexual harassment, molestation, trafficking, and child sexual abuse pornography. I write this book in the hopes that those of us who remain and are yet to come will create a world in which others are not subjected to the same suffering and death. For those dearly departed, I write in honor and remembrance of your everlasting souls.

Contents

Foreword: A Love Song for Black Women and Girl Survivors of Sexual Abuse—
  Thema Bryant — ix
Preface — xi
Acknowledgments — xv

1. What's Racism Got to Do With It? Black Women and Girls, Sexual Abuse, and Liberation — 3
2. Black Women and Girls: Racism and Intersectional Oppression — 21
3. The "Rape Problem" and Secondary Marginalization Against Black Women and Girls — 35
4. Cultural Betrayal Trauma Theory: Framework, Evidence, and Future Directions — 47
5. Culturally Competent Trauma Therapy: Holistic Healing — 77
6. Radical Healing in the Black Community — 113
7. Institutional Courage to Change the World — 133

   Conclusion: What Does It All Mean? From Micro- to Macrolevel Change — 169

References — 177
Index — 217
About the Author — 235

Foreword
A Love Song for Black Women and Girl Survivors of Sexual Abuse

Our beings and bodies are sacred, worthy of safety, care, respect, and soft places to land. We survive anti-Black racism, misogynoir, violence, and intersectional oppression. These interpersonal, collective, and historical traumas have taken so much from us—emotionally, cognitively, socially, spiritually, physically, and even financially. Yet we are still here—some crawling, some soaring, and all breathing. The violations we have survived did not wait until adulthood to visit us. Objectification, sexualization, and adultification desecrate girlhood for many of us.

This important work, *The Cultural Betrayal of Black Women and Girls: A Black Feminist Approach to Healing From Sexual Abuse* by Jennifer M. Gómez, is a love song to the survival of Black cis and trans women and girls. For love to be liberating, it must see and affirm survivors holistically and historically. In these pages, Dr. Gómez calls upon psychologists and other mental health providers to adopt courageous compassion, which means sharing concern and outrage at the realities of sexual violence as well as concern and outrage for the injustices that contextualize the trauma and recovery process for Black women and girls. The integration of theory, empirical scholarship, and cultural wisdom honors multicultural/intersectional feminist psychology in content and orientation.

There has been a growing body of research on the cultural context of sexual abuse, including attending to prevention, risk factors, protective factors, and coping strategies. The framework of cultural betrayal contributes a much needed, and historically overlooked, aspect of our understanding of the experience of Black survivors. Violation within Black families and communities dismantles a major source of our strength, healing, and capacity to navigate oppression: connection.

The racial inequities documented in the physical and mental health fields, as well as the criminal (in)justice system, are significant barriers to healing and justice. The American Psychological Association issued an apology in 2021 for the role of psychology in promoting, perpetuating, and failing to challenge racism. Implementing change to eradicate structural racism includes attending to the ways practitioners, researchers, educators, and consultants have ignored the impact of oppression. This love song enriches the field by helping us to move from erasure and marginalization to centering the experience of Black women and girls. The gift of this work is to see not only the trauma but also the triumph, thriving, and cultural resources embodied by Black survivors.

I join my voice in this chorus as not only an African American trauma psychologist but also an African American trauma survivor. By singing together, we build collaborative spaces where truth telling is welcome and recognized as necessary on the path to liberation. As a womanist, and multicultural feminist psychologist, I recognize the importance of community care as an ethic that has sustained Black women across the generations. To provide transformative care means not only do we work for the restoration of Black women and girls, but also the transformation of the institutions and systems that are intended to protect and nourish them.

—*Thema Bryant*

Preface

You have to act as if it were possible to radically transform the world. And you have to do it all the time.

–Angela Davis, personal communication, 2016

How can we radically transform the world? That is the question. Answers for me come during a discussion I had with colleagues in 2019, when I came up with the idea of *dreamstorming*. As an extension of brainstorming, in dreamstorming I envision liberation and engage in fantasy for what has never been but what I do believe could be (brown & Imarisha, 2015): a truly free world. We're not yet *There*. But it would not be life if we were not fighting to transform *There* into existence now.

BLACK FEMINISM AND CULTURAL BETRAYAL TRAUMA THEORY: RHETORICALLY DISMANTLING WHITE SUPREMACY

> Our assignment isn't just to help people navigate up the racial hierarchy, but to dismantle the hierarchy altogether. (Rinku Shen, personal communication, 2018)

To bring us closer to *There*, I am deliberately imploding the concept of universality by centralizing Black women and girls in this book. With a Black feminist lens (e.g., Collins, 1991/2000), I dismantle an oppressive cognitive framework that creates a dichotomy between the universal and the particular, where the universal is static Whiteness (Henrich et al., 2010) and the particular, in this case, is the "exotic Black female other." In my attempts at imploding such insidious, implicit, and explicit White supremacy in research and clinical practice (Buchanan et al., 2021), I hope this book will be a reflection of an *Us* that is centered, unapologetic, and without toxic comparison (e.g., Collins, 1991/2000).

The original impetus for this book is cultural betrayal trauma theory (CBTT). I first began preverbally thinking about CBTT when I was still a ballet dancer at Dance Theatre of Harlem under cofounder and then artistic director Mr. Arthur Mitchell (Dance Theatre of Harlem, 2023). I noticed how amid all the hierarchy and elitism in the dance world, Black dancers were proactively friendly with one another—even when we did not know each other personally or work in the same space. This connection seemed to indicate a silent bond predicated on the assumption that as Black people in a largely White dance world, we had solidarity with each other. After retiring from ballet, I found Jennifer J. Freyd's humanizing research with betrayal trauma theory (Freyd, 1996): The adult who was raped as a child by their parent is not pathological; instead, they are psychologically and behaviorally responding in ways that make perfect sense given their parent's violence against them. With my dancer experiences combined with Freyd's betrayal trauma theory research, my thoughts that would become CBTT started to grow (Gómez, 2012).

Thus far, I have spent a decade theory building and empirically testing CBTT across diverse marginalized populations—building from the seminal and groundbreaking Black feminist and womanist scholarship and advocacy of so many who have come before me: Thema Bryant, Tricia Bent-Goodley, Anna Julia Cooper, the Combahee River Collective, Audre Lorde, bell hooks, Alice Walker, Kimberlé Crenshaw, and so many others. While building that research, I have known I wanted to write an academic book about CBTT, sexual abuse, and Black women and girls. Over the years, however, I realized I did not want my only contribution to be documenting abuse and its negative effects. I additionally want my research to influence measurable changes within individual, interpersonal, and structural healing processes. And incredibly importantly, I want to better situate that my work builds upon that of brilliant Black feminist, womanist, and race scholars who, for decades, have produced phenomenal theoretical and empirical research, including many of the concepts I put neatly together into a scientifically testable theory.

Though CBTT was the original kernel from which the book was born, *violent silencing* has become the theme: how Black women and girls endure external and internalized demands for denial under the guise of Black solidarity (Gómez & Gobin, 2020b) and within the threat of violence and rejection. In the backdrop of violent silencing, I dive into the frustrating complexity of a problem as big as sexual abuse in the Black community—specifically Black males abusing Black women and girls. As such, complexity is the subject matter (Butler, 2021), not a diversion or obstacle to overcome. I incorporate multiple and interlocking oppressions, abuse, violence, and individual, cultural, and within-group differences. As the opposite of reductionism, my goals are to think, write, and live within these and other complexities. In doing so, I implicitly encourage readers to not be satisfied with simple answers, thoughtless research, therapy by numbers, and comfortable learning that never challenges them. After all, the fallacy of so-called mastery of disciplinary scholarship and practice is fool's gold: shiny but irrelevant and uninteresting. Instead, centering true learning and self-examination fosters intellectual and soulful creativity in ourselves and our work, and shows how both can positively affect the world.

MY SOUL SELF

> The cost of liberty may be our lives: our physical safety, our psychological security. At times, the fight for liberty is a literal matter of life and death. However, the price of repression and silence is higher: It is our very souls. (Jennifer M. Gómez, personal communication, 2021)

The choice between fighting for freedom versus remaining silent is an unfair one. The costs of each are high. Nevertheless, for me, I consistently choose my soul. I picture inside myself a place where there is no bigotry, no gaslighting, no abuse, no rape, no racism, no sexism, no intersectional oppression, and no harm. There, in that place, I am truly me, with my soul being my truest self. It is from my soul self that I write this book.

COURAGEOUSLY RADICAL HOPE

> I'm just a soul whose intentions are good, oh lord, please don't let me be misunderstood. (Nina Simone, 1977)

With a book project that spans history, disciplines, research, clinical application, community organizing, and ultimately institutional courage (Freyd, 2014b) for a better world, I necessarily feel insecure and uncertain: *Does anything I do matter? Could this book even make a difference? What if this writing harms people?* In grappling with that question on October 7, 2021, in my Study 53 at the Center for Advanced Study in the Behavioral Sciences (CASBS) at Stanford University, I wrote the following:

> It feeling impossible to make change isn't a reason to give up. Instead, it feeling impossible is the precise reason to keep going: so that someday, it will no longer be impossible. It will just be: a more equal, more equitable, more peaceful, more caring world for everyone.

Throughout writing this book, I have revisited that passage each time I felt too overwhelmed to work toward the day when the world will just *be*. Remaining grounded in my own experiences of much of what I cover in this book, I continue to persevere because within the world's senselessness and depravity are the souls that remain. Thus, there is beauty in the fight for what's right. And with that beauty is solidarity, freedom, and hope: radical hope that, despite all the evidence to the contrary, the world, and each of us in it, is worth saving.

Salud to you, me, and we, who are doing our parts to unabashedly dreamstorm a liberatory world into reality for generations to come.

In solidarity,
Jennifer M. Gómez

Acknowledgments

First and foremost, I thank those closest to me who have provided the freedom, space, support, belief, and love in me as a person and a scholar: Jennifer J. Freyd, Christina Gamache Martin, Jacob Levernier, Laura K. Noll, Erik L. Knight, Kathleen Best, Lola Gavrilovic, Rebecca L. Calcott, Kathryn Iurino, Lauren Vega O'Neil, Chris Martin, Kate Beauchamp, Rose Maier Hartman, Joshua J. Hartman, Heather Wallace Solisz, Jason Hubbard, Kellie Geldreich, Leslie E. Roos, Junaid Salim Merchant, and Cheri and Erik Toberman. And to my dearly departed grandmother, Anna Cook Gómez, who remains with me.

Next, I would like to share gratitude for the spaces and the people that have ultimately made this book possible through their support across years: to the man and the place that gave me hope and saved my life in my younger years, Mr. Arthur Mitchell and the Dance Theatre of Harlem; to my first entry into higher education with the Bridges to the Baccalaureate Grant from the National Institutes of Health at San Diego Mesa College and San Diego State University, including Emilio Ulloa, Audrey Hokoda, Dina Miyoshi, Jaye Van Kirk, and Yoshito Kawahara; to my graduate advisor, Jennifer J. Freyd, who gave me the space and encouragement to develop cultural betrayal trauma theory (CBTT) in graduate school; to my Jegna as a graduate student through the Association of Black Psychologists, Marva Lewis; to the Center for Community Counseling, especially my clinical supervisor, Melissa Thomas; to my first academic home upon earning my PhD, the Merrill Palmer Skillman Institute for Child and Family Development (MPSI) at Wayne State University; to RacismLab at University of Michigan Institute for Social Research, especially principal investigator Margaret Takako Hicken; to the Ford Foundation Fellowships Program, administered by the National Academies of Sciences, Engineering, and Medicine, which has made my research with CBTT and my career in academia possible through providing both material funding and a community of brilliant scholars, including Koritha Mitchell, Victor Ray, Rashawn Ray, and Alyasah A. Sewell; and to additional funders for making CBTT research possible: Wayne State University, Stanford University, the Michigan Center for Urban African American Aging Research (with Co-PI Samuele Zilioli; funded by National Institute on Aging, PI Robert Taylor), and the National Science Foundation (principal investigator: Oliver Hill). To my CBTT collaborators, I am grateful for our work together: Robyn L. Gobin, Lars U. Johnson, Jennifer J. Freyd, Rebecca L. Howard Valdivia, Courtney Ahrens, Breanne Helmers, Samuele Zilioli, M. Colleen McDaniel, Logan Zelenak, and Sasha Shen Johfre (formerly Sasha Johnson-Freyd).

Thanks to the Center for Advanced Study in the Behavioral Sciences (CASBS) at Stanford University that, with the 2021–2022 CASBS fellowship, provided me with the time, cross-disciplinary collegiality and learning, funding, and beauty to write this book, and to the CASBS fellows who generously shared their time, wisdom, expertise, support, and hearts to make both the book and the book-writing experience intellectually and personally transformative: Aisha M. Beliso-De Jesús, Scott L. Cummings, Jennifer A. Richeson, Laurence Ralph, Megan Finn, Estelle Freedman, Manuel Pastor, Teresa L. McCarty, Kevin Mumford, Julie Livingston, Jules Naudet, Michael Bernstein, and Lise Guilhamon.

Thanks to American Psychological Association Books, including my acquisitions editor, Stevie Davall; my development editor, Molly Gage; the editorial team; and five masked reviewers of the book proposal and book: Thank you for respecting and trusting me and my vision for this book. Thanks to Thema Bryant: Having admired your work and your humanity from afar for a decade, I am honored you have chosen to write the foreword for this book. Thanks to my informal reviewers who provided feedback on book draft writings: Tricia Bent-Goodley, Patrick R. Grzanka, Helen Neville, Robyn L. Gobin, Lauren Vega O'Neil, Nelson O. O. Zounlome, Jorge Delva, Annmarie Caño, Scott L. Cummings, Steven J. Ondersma, Jennifer J. Freyd, Anita Hardon, Dawn Belkin Martínez, and Erik L. Knight. And to Jeffrey Todahl, Alison Deleget, Preston Warren Dugger, III, Pratyusha Tummala-Narra, and Brooklyn Mack for lovingly reminding me to keep myself and my voice in this book. You each collectively gave me the opportunity and the support to write the best book I possibly could and to share it with the world.

Thanks to the students I have had the honor of advising, mentoring, and collaborating with both within and outside of my HOPE research laboratory: Daeja Marzette, Zunaira Jilani, Logan Zelenak, Lama Hassoun Ayoub, Rebecca L. Howard Valdivia, Nokwanda Ndlovu Grava, Melissa L. Barnes, M. Colleen McDaniel, Breanne Helmers, Zenaida Rivera, Alexis Adams-Clark, and Sarah J. Harsey.

With far too many to name (see the References), I must thank the brilliant scholars and activists whose work across fields, contexts, and time profoundly shaped my thinking and my spirit, while teaching me how I want to exist in the world. Without your groundbreaking, courageous work over centuries, a book like mine would not be possible.

And finally, I would like to extend my deepest gratitude to courageous Black women and girls who have endured cultural betrayal sexual trauma, including Drew Dixon, Sherri Sher, Jane Doe (from the University of Oregon; Read, 2015b), my research participants, my therapy clients, my loved ones, and many more. It is us whom I do the work for and with. I live in solidarity with you.

The Cultural Betrayal of Black Women and Girls

1 WHAT'S RACISM GOT TO DO WITH IT?

Black Women and Girls, Sexual Abuse, and Liberation

> **CHAPTER AT A GLANCE**
>
> In this chapter, I provide the landscape for the book: defining cultural betrayal trauma theory, detailing the scope and format of the book, providing a Black feminist primer to aid readers in how to get the most from the book, and stating my goals for both the book and society.

The colored woman of today occupies . . . a unique position in this country. . . . She is confronted by both a woman question and a race problem, and is as yet an unknown or unacknowledged factor in both.

—Anna Julia Cooper, 1892, As Cited In K. Taylor, 2017, p. 5

It is telling that a book written by a Black woman in the 21st century could open with another Black woman's quote from the 1800s: a quote that remains frighteningly poignant and disturbingly true in many ways. Perhaps because

---
https://doi.org/10.1037/0000362-001
The Cultural Betrayal of Black Women and Girls: A Black Feminist Approach to Healing From Sexual Abuse, by J. M. Gómez
Copyright © 2023 by the American Psychological Association. All rights reserved.

of the resonance in the above quote by Anna Julia Cooper, I have created this book as an odyssey that I hope can contribute to actual, tangible, individual, interpersonal, cultural, and structural positive change in the lives of Black women and girls. My ambitious anchor is that *everyone needs to know everything*, meaning that trauma researchers and clinicians need to understand structural racism, intersectional oppression, and the context of Black women and girls being erased from the "rape problem" discourse in the Black community. Race scholars need to know about cultural betrayal, trauma, abuse, violence, and mental health. The clinicians need grounding in the trauma, race, and Black feminist research while knowing about the White supremacy within the psychology profession and, relatedly, the need for radical healing within and outside of formal therapy. The dominant and mainstream researchers need to grasp the importance of Black feminist theorizing, as well as the empirical research that can stem from such theorizing. Change agents, which we all should be, need to be knowledgeable of and empowered by institutional courage (Freyd, 2014b), with actionable steps for making structural, systemic, and lasting societal change. Most important, the Black women and girls who do and do not occupy the aforementioned professional positions need to have aspects of themselves reflected in this work—a mirror of the intersectional oppression, the violence, and the pain, right alongside the self-determination, the self-valuation (Collins, 1991/2000), the hope, and the freedom that we as Black women and girls can and often do possess.

In this introduction chapter, I first provide the societal landscape of the present time, and then I define cultural betrayal trauma theory (CBTT). Next, I discuss the contextual predicaments of conducting CBTT research within the context of structural inequalities. Following that, I provide the scope and format of the book, with descriptions of each chapter. I then detail how readers can get the most out of the current book by providing a primer on Black feminist tradition and related ideologies, including the role of premises and emotionality in this work. Finally, I conclude with thoughts on my goals for both the book itself and the world in which we live.

SOCIETAL LANDSCAPE

> We are living in contradictory realities. (Laurence Ralph, personal communication, 2022)

Our current reality is filled with absurdity of the worst kind (P. J. Williams et al., 2021). With Whiteness being a set of power relations (Mills, 1997), the combined structural and direct harm of COVID-19 and anti-Black violence (e.g., Cokley et al., 2022; Poteat et al., 2020) manifests in at least two distinct ways. First, there is repetitive, persistent, and arrogant everyday discrimination (McClelland et al., 2016) that many White people—particularly those with additional institutional power—often engage in by denying racism while perpetrating the same individually and structurally. The epistemic violence (e.g., Dotson, 2011) associated with silencing marginalized individuals is simultaneously deeply personal and truly systemic (R. L. Calcott, personal communication, March 12, 2022). Second, the contemporary context includes the disproportionate death of Black people from COVID-19 (Wrigley-Field, 2020), government-sanctioned racist murder of Black people (Dreyer et al., 2020), and ubiquitous dehumanization and degradation of the Black community (for a discussion, see Gómez, 2022d).

Additionally hopeful, however, is the awareness and mobilization against these societal ills (e.g., Dreyer et al., 2020; Fisher et al., 2017), including from the American Psychological Association (APA) Council of Representatives in their resolutions *Apology to People of Color for APA's Role in Promoting, Perpetuating, and Failing to Challenge Racism, Racial Discrimination, and Human Hierarchy in U.S.* (APA, 2021a) and *Role of Psychology and APA in Dismantling Systemic Racism Against People of Color in U.S.* (APA, 2021b). While these statements were met with understandable mistrust (e.g., Association of Black Psychologists, 2022), action within APA continues, with Black feminist trauma psychologist Dr. Thema Bryant as the President (Tan, 2022). With that recognition and action, importantly, comes the possibility for change (Gómez & Freyd, 2014).

INTRODUCTION TO CULTURAL BETRAYAL TRAUMA THEORY

> A theory in the flesh means one where the physical realities of our lives—our skin color, the land or concrete we grew up on, our sexual longings—all fuse to create a politic born out of necessity. (Gloria Anzaldúa and Cherríe Moraga, 1981, p. 23)

Created, expanded upon, and tested within societal inequalities, CBTT (e.g., Gómez, 2012, 2019c; Chapter 4, this volume) provides a theoretical anchoring for the current book. Based on scholarship, research, and activism within Black feminism (e.g., Collins, 1991/2000), structural racism (e.g., Mills, 1997), and intersectional oppression (Combahee River Collective, 1977, as cited in K. Taylor, 2017; Crenshaw, 1991; Chapter 3), I specifically created CBTT with Black people in mind (Gómez, n.d.-a, n.d.-b, 2015b, 2015e, 2016, 2018, 2019b, 2019c, 2019i, 2019k, 2022a; Gómez & Freyd, 2019; Gómez & Gobin, 2020a, 2020b, 2022; Gómez & Johnson, 2022; McDaniel et al.,

2022), though this framework has and can be used in culturally congruent ways with other marginalized populations (e.g., Gómez, 2017, 2019a, 2019e, 2019j, 2019k, 2021a, 2021b, 2021d; Gómez & Freyd, 2018; Howard Valdivia et al., 2022).

According to CBTT in reference to the Black community (e.g., Gómez & Gobin, 2020a), anti-Black racism engenders (intra)cultural trust, or solidarity, within the Black community. As such, abuse perpetrated by a Black person against another Black person includes a cultural betrayal because it is a violation of this (intra)cultural trust. This abuse, known as *cultural betrayal trauma*, is associated with abuse outcomes, such as dissociation, and cultural outcomes, such as internalized prejudice. Moreover, (intra)cultural pressure—including violent silencing as a cultural mandate to not disclose cultural betrayal trauma—further harms survivors.

In the current book, I focus specifically on cultural betrayal sexual trauma, or sexual abuse within the Black community. Though cultural betrayal sexual trauma occurs across genders (e.g., Gómez & Johnson, 2022), for brevity and to centralize Black women and girls, the term *cultural betrayal sexual trauma* in the current book refers only to Black male–perpetrated sexual abuse against Black women and girls. As such, this book can serve as a companion to work that centralizes the experiences of Black people of other genders.

THE MEANING OF CBTT

> Black women's oppression made them more open to the possibilities of radical politics and activism. (Keeanga-Yamahtta Taylor, 2017, p. 8)

In CBTT, I make complexity the subject, allowing for layered harms to be identified and addressed. As a basis for research, CBTT is a kind of radical scholarly activism (Gómez, in press) against both raceless, contextual-less work and the scientific racism predicated upon dehumanizing Black people across genders as genetically and socially inferior (e.g., Washington, 2006; Winston, 2020). As such, CBTT itself is an act of self-determination in which I, a Black woman, centralize Black women and girls through lenses of oppression, abuse, vulnerability, strength, and hope.

CBTT provides a framework for understanding Black women and girl survivors of cultural betrayal sexual trauma, including the roles of cultural and societal contexts. For example, with CBTT, we can systematically investigate how cultural betrayal sexual trauma for Black women and girls can result in protecting the perpetrator(s) in the aftermath of the abuse by not reporting to the police (e.g., Slatton & Richard, 2020). CBTT additionally grapples with deeply entrenched myths and erasure of Black women and girl survivors due to both intersectional oppression (e.g., racism and sexism; Chapter 2) from the dominant society (e.g., Davis, 1985; Gómez, 2019k; McGuire, 2010) and secondary marginalization within the Black community (C. J. Cohen, 2009; Chapter 3).

CBTT also amplifies the need to be in solidarity with Black men as our brethren, while often tolerating the costs of privileging Black men as the primary victims of racism (Combahee River Collective, 1977, as cited in K. Taylor, 2017). Moreover, CBTT details the (intra)cultural trust and support that make our Black lives so connectedly rich and giving. With mind and heart centering on the humanity of Black women and girls, CBTT helps determine what research questions to investigate (e.g., internalized prejudice as an outcome of trauma), what questions to avoid (e.g., no White comparison groups), what harm to tackle clinically (e.g., beyond fear present during the abuse), what context to pull from (e.g., structural racism, intersectional oppression, [intra]cultural pressure), and what levels of intervention to employ (individual, group, community, structural).

PREDICAMENTS

> By naming sexist oppression . . . it would appear that we would have to identify as threatening a group we have heretofore assumed to be our allies: Black men. . . . If we cannot entertain the idea that some [Black] men are the enemy . . . then we will never be able to figure out all the reasons why, for example, we are . . . raped by our neighbors. (Barbara Smith, "Notes for Yet Another Paper on Black Feminism, or, Will the Real Enemy Please Stand Up?" as cited in hooks, 1984/2015, p. 76)

CBTT, and by extension this book, is situated within this predicament of wanting and needing solidarity within and across the Black community while acknowledging the cultural betrayal sexual trauma and the accompanied violent silencing that tear us apart from our community and ourselves. Within societal reckonings against anti-Black racism (e.g., Black Lives Matter Global Foundation Network, Inc., n.d.) and sexist sexual abuse (#MeToo; e.g., Burke, 2021), I write this book from under the spotlight of high-profile perpetrators of cultural betrayal sexual trauma (e.g., R. Kelly [Gómez, 2019k]; Russell Simmons [Gómez & Gobin, 2020b]) and courageous Black women survivors (@RapedAtSpelman as cited in Gómez, 2016; Dick & Ziering, 2020; A. Hill, 1997; Feminist Campus Team, 2017).

WHITE SUPREMACY, BLACK FEMINISM, AND THE BOOK

> Racism has become an accepted topic in feminist discussions not as a result of black women calling attention to it (this was done at the very onset of the movement), but as a result of white female input validating such discussions, a process which is indicative of how racism works. (bell hooks, 1984/2015, p. 52)

I experience dis-ease knowing that Whiteness has given validity to the Black experiences I describe in this book. What began 10 years ago as ceaseless rejections has turned into exaltation in many elite, and often tightly guarded, spaces. As I share this work across the United States and abroad, I understand that the same racism and intersectional oppression that is presently granting credence to this work also maintains White domination. In addition to the within-group focus, my critical consciousness of the White supremacist world in which I live continues to inform my work with CBTT and this book. In this way, my own identity politics, as defined by Black feminists (e.g., the Combahee River Collective, 1977, as cited in K. Taylor, 2017), has provided me with a way to examine my own experiences and that of my Black sisters through research, scholarship, clinical work, and activism. As such, I have written this book as an exercise in disrupting my own internalized inclination to cater to the White Read (Bowleg, 2021; Chapter 5). The White Read is an interpretation of how a homogenous White audience will interpret one's own writing. Catering to the White Read distorts the work by privileging a homogenous White population as both the primary and the most important audience of one's own work. Instead, I center Black women, girls, and our perspectives in ways that neither ask permission of Whiteness nor run comparisons with Whiteness to justify our existence and legitimacy.

Additionally in this book, I am engaging in a cultural shift in dominant psychology, from rote memorization to critical thinking that complicates constructs as opposed to providing easy answers. In the tradition of Ladson-Billings (2021; Chapter 5), this book builds upon critical theoretical and empirical research that promotes asking different questions and thus sparking different solutions from across disciplines, including psychology, Black feminist studies, law, social work, sociology, philosophy, political science, anthropology, and women and gender studies.

Importantly, I conceptualize the work of this book as a starting place, not a seminal conclusion. Though I have tried to create a work with equality and equity in process and outcome (Cummings, 2021a; Chapter 7), I have no doubt that in the years following publication, I will reread, rethink, reassess, and reframe concepts I have laid out here. As lifelong learners, I invite readers to do the same. Critical interrogation that furthers our lives and our work requires taking what is known and building on it for a better, brighter, more equitable future.

SCOPE AND FORMAT OF THE BOOK

> Sexism as a system of domination is institutionalized, but it has never determined in an absolute way the fate of all women in this society. (bell hooks, 1984/2015, p. 5)

The primary audience for this book is academic, research, and clinical psychologists, as well as researchers and clinicians from social work, sociology, gender and feminist studies, public health, psychiatry, anthropology, Africana studies, and other allied professionals in fields interested in understanding the impact of cultural betrayal sexual trauma against Black women and girls within the context of racism and intersectional oppression. The secondary audience includes graduate and undergraduate students involved in academic, research, and/or clinical training in psychology, social work, psychiatry, and allied fields (see primary audience disciplines above). Additional audiences include Black women and girls who have experienced cultural betrayal sexual trauma; Black people who want to contribute to shared community healing across genders; people who have been sexually victimized who are not Black women or girls; anyone who wants to better understand and support Black women and girls who have been sexually victimized; and race, feminist, and other activists engaged in fights for societal equality related to anti-Black racism, sexism, intersectional oppression, and violence against women and girls.

Chapter Overview

> Offering subordinate groups new knowledge about their own experiences can be empowering. But revealing new ways of knowing that allow subordinate groups to define their own reality has far greater implications. (Patricia Hill Collins, 1991/2000, p. 222)

Each chapter opens with a Chapter at a Glance section that provides a brief statement of the scope of the chapter, followed by an introductory paragraph (a) framing the chapter. Next, the critical visioning section relays the background and CBTT lens for a tension engendered by White supremacy that is germane to one or more topics of the chapter; after that, my self-reflexive critical visioning on the tension is a pedagogical tool that provides examples of my positionality, standpoint (e.g., Collins, 1986, 1991/2000), and underlying premises of the chapter, as well as the complexity of the thought process endemic in my theoretical, empirical, and clinical work with Black women and girls. Following detailing basic and/or applied theoretical and empirical research and scholarship, Chapters 2, 4, 5, 6, and 7 include sections with examples of what the content of the chapter could actually be like in reality. This section serves to ground each chapter in Black women and girls' humanity while providing tangible skills to readers. To protect their privacy, I use pseudonyms in all true stories from real people. Lastly, Chapters 2, 3, 4, 5, 6, and 7 each close with summary bullet points that highlight the chapter's main takeaway messages. All in all, I have created each chapter to have practical implications and tangible knowledge that is grounded in the literature reviewed and described.

As in the current introduction chapter, quotes are peppered throughout the book to serve as guideposts—orienting readers to upcoming content, situating the work within such content, and highlighting brilliant scholars and activists. In using these quotes to frame my writing, I am rejecting a singular, individualization of my work in favor of contextualizing my contributions within the past and present collective We (Collins, 1991/2000). This rhetorical strategy can illustrate how my scholarly expertise and outsider-within stance (Collins, 1991/2000) are in connection with others' work and activism that has been done across disciplines, contexts, and time periods. Using these quotes additionally provides a meta-message for the whole book: The concepts I am discussing and naming, such as cultural betrayal, are placed within and atop more than 150 years of Black women's (and some others') scholarship and activism; as such, we can call upon the strength, wisdom, perseverance, soul, spirit, and heart of our lineage.

Though they each could be read as stand-alone chapters based on the interest of the reader, I have written the book with each chapter building on the prior content. I have also deliberately woven an arc that begins with structural oppression and violence, extends through individual and interpersonal healing, and ends with structural change, freedom, and liberation through institutional courage (Freyd, 2014b). Specifically, critical race perspectives on racism (Chapter 2) explain why the rape problem in the Black community (Chapter 3) is typically understood as that of White women's false accusations against Black men and boys. The Black feminist concept of intersectional oppression (Chapter 2) and secondary marginalization (Cohen, 2009; Chapter 3) further elucidates how Black males' perpetration of sexual abuse against Black women and girls is occluded from dominant White feminist and antiracist movements. Built within this multifaceted context, CBTT provides a scientifically testable framework for examining cultural betrayal sexual trauma, including community response to (intra)cultural pressure in the form of violent silencing—a theme of the book (Chapter 4). Taken together, the basic research from Chapters 2 to 4 inform culturally competent trauma therapy while indicting the White supremacy within the medical model (Chapter 5). Understanding that healing cannot and should not ever be relegated to the confines of the four walls of therapy, radical healing that promotes critical consciousness, hope, freedom, and liberation is possible for Black women and girl survivors of cultural betrayal sexual trauma, as well as Black families and communities (Chapter 6). The entire book culminates in furthering us toward a truly peaceful and equitable world through specific structural healing and change through institutional courage (Freyd, 2018; Chapter 7). The Conclusion provides a capstone of lessons learned from the book.

Fundamentally, the framing of the book makes explicit links between the harmful aspects of Black women's and girls' context—racism, intersectional oppression, secondary marginalization (C. J. Cohen, 2009), cultural betrayal sexual trauma, (intra)cultural pressure, and violent silencing (e.g., Gómez, 2019c; current book)—and levels of healing—individual, interpersonal, and structural (Figure 1.1). This is distinct from dominant approaches in psychology that conceptualize sexual abuse as an individual harm that requires individual-level intervention for survivors. Conversely, in addition to individual healing, this book directly names and targets the implicated contextual harms to engender cultural, institutional, and structural change. This shift in focus

FIGURE 1.1. Centering Black Women and Girls: Individual, Interpersonal, and Structural Healing

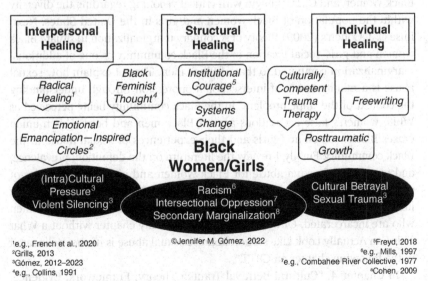

[1] e.g., French et al., 2020
[2] Grills, 2013
[3] Gómez, 2012–2023
[4] e.g., Collins, 1991
©Jennifer M. Gómez, 2022
[5] Freyd, 2018
[6] e.g., Mills, 1997
[7] e.g., Combahee River Collective, 1977
[8] Cohen, 2009

Note. Copyright 2022 by J. M. Gómez. Reprinted with permission.

can promote radical transformation into a more peaceful and equitable world for Black women and girls.

Chapter by Chapter

> Black women's experiences cannot be reduced to either race or gender but have to be understood on their own terms. (Keeanga-Yamahtta Taylor, 2017, p. 2)

In Chapter 2, "Black Women and Girls: Racism and Intersectional Oppression," my critical visioning centers on understanding how inequality has manifested in Black women-led the Black Lives Matter (Black Lives Matter Foundation, Inc., n.d.) and #MeToo (Burke, 2021) movements. Next, I use Mills's (1997) theory of a "racial contract" as foundational to understanding anti-Black racism, including White supremacy and structural racism. Then, I pull from Black feminist scholar and activist work on intersectional oppression (e.g., Combahee River Collective, 1977, as cited in K. Taylor, 2017; Davis, 1985), with a focus on Crenshaw's (1991) theories of structural, political, and representational intersectionality. Based on Cole's (2009) and Grzanka's (2020a) work, I then detail how intersectionality can be incorporated into the field of psychology. I close with an example of political intersectionality (Crenshaw, 1991) in antiracism and anti-sexual violence initiatives on college campuses. The goal of this chapter is to provide an accessible foundation of the multiple and oft-interlocking systems of oppression against Black people.

In Chapter 3, "The 'Rape Problem' and Secondary Marginalization Against Black Women and Girls," I begin with critical visioning regarding the diversity within the population of Black women and girls in the United States. Next, I use C. J. Cohen's (2009) theory of secondary marginalization to situate Black women and girls' social location in the Black community as one of additional marginalization compared to that of Black men. Then, I explain how sexual abuse is a manifestation of intersectional oppression through understanding the context of the "rape problem" in the Black community being perceived as White women's false accusations against Black men and boys. This framing erases Black women and girls and their experiences of sexual abuse in the Black community. Finally, I review the literature on the definition, prevalence, and outcomes of sexual abuse for Black women and girls, with attempts of specifications for those additionally marginalized—Black trans*women, Black immigrant women, Black Latinas, Black Muslim women, and Black women who are incarcerated. Of note, Chapter 3 is the only chapter without a What This Can Actually Look Like section because sexual abuse is further delineated in the following chapter on CBTT.

In Chapter 4, "Cultural Betrayal Trauma Theory: Framework, Evidence, and Future Directions," I open with critical visioning on how CBTT can be used as a tool of oppression against Black people. Next, I provide a brief explanation of betrayal trauma theory (e.g., Freyd, 1996), followed by a detailed description of CBTT, including the framework, definitions, and examples of key constructs: (intra)cultural trust, cultural betrayal, cultural betrayal trauma, (intra)cultural pressure, including violent silencing, (intra)cultural support, abuse and cultural outcomes, and posttraumatic growth. Next, I provide an explanation of the 10 postulates of CBTT, under the three classes of premises, counterhypotheses, and outcomes. I then review the general evidence across populations of CBTT, with a specific focus on the findings within Black populations. Following detailing an example of cultural betrayal sexual trauma for a Black female undergraduate, I delineate key theoretical and methodological future directions for CBTT research. As such, this chapter is likely the most empirically dense of the book.

In Chapter 5, "Culturally Competent Trauma Therapy: Holistic Healing," I engage in critical visioning regarding the potential of replacing the medical model in conceptualizations of psychological distress while abolishing the White Read (Bowleg, 2021). I then explicitly detail the humanity of Black women and girls, alongside our therapeutic responsibility to them as clients. Next, I critique the medical model by interrogating its cultural premises, past criticisms, and lackluster evidence, offering alternative conceptualizations of mental health. Following detailing diverse outcomes of trauma (e.g., Bryant-Davis, 2005), I explain individual and structural cultural competency in therapy. Then, I highlight processes and practices of trauma therapy, including working with and through emotional intensity and complexity; engaging in critical self-reflection; collaborating with clients throughout the therapeutic process; bearing witness to clients' traumatic experiences, oppression, and pain; holding hope for clients and their futures; centralizing individual and structural cultural competency in therapy; and engaging in self-care. Next, I review relational cultural theory (e.g., Miller, 1976) and the liberation health framework (Belkin Martinez, 2014) as models for culturally competent trauma therapy for Black women and girls. From my work as a student clinician, I close by providing clinical case examples on respecting client autonomy, self-care, power-with collaboration with clients, client-perpetrated discrimination in therapy, and social justice advocacy in clinical work. This chapter is the most clinically rich of the book.

In Chapter 6, "Radical Healing in the Black Community," I open my critical visioning by engaging in self-reflexivity to discuss the threat of violent silencing that I, and we, experience as Black women and girls who discuss cultural betrayal sexual trauma. I then describe the psychological framework of radical healing in communities of color (French et al., 2020). Next,

I discuss how radical healing can manifest on the individual level physiologically, emotionally, and behaviorally. In detailing radical healing in the Black community, I draw on principles from restorative justice (e.g., Zehr, 2005), including discussing the role of hatred for the perpetrator(s) of cultural betrayal sexual trauma. Then, I provide tips for how to respond well to disclosure, discuss adapting Emotional Emancipation Circles (Grills, 2013; Myers, 2013) for group-level healing from cultural betrayal sexual trauma and (intra)cultural pressure, and explain the role of Black men in preventing cultural betrayal sexual trauma. Next, I discuss sexist oppression and abuse within the Black family and potential strategies for peaceful and equal family life. Drawing upon Black classical musician Nina Simone (2008), I then query how individuals can define what is free for themselves, followed by two examples from a Black woman survivor using a form of journaling known as *freewriting* to self-discover freedom and liberation within themselves. With this chapter speaking directly to Black women and girl survivors, it can be useful for Black women researchers, clinicians, and students who have experienced cultural betrayal sexual trauma. Additionally, professionals can incorporate this chapter into their work with colleagues, research teams, clinical staff, coalitions, students, and clients to provide institutional support for structured reflection (Delker, 2019) and self-care (Gómez, 2019g).

In Chapter 7, "Institutional Courage to Change the World," I privilege Black feminist emotionality in institutional change work in my critical visioning section. I then briefly review the literature on institutional betrayal (C. P. Smith & Freyd, 2014), institutional cowardice (L. S. Brown, 2021), and institutional courage (Freyd, 2014b), including adapting steps of institutional courage for the benefit of Black women and girl survivors of intersectional oppression and cultural betrayal sexual trauma. Next, I provide vignette examples of institutional betrayal, institutional courage, and dreamstorming (see the definition in the Preface) a world of peace and equality across health care, universities, and the nonprofit sector. Then, I provide a real example of institutional courage in community–lawyer collaborations on community benefits agreements (CBAs) in the Los Angeles city redevelopment processes (Cummings, 2021a), including lessons for academic, research, and clinical psychologists and allied professionals. Next, I describe four ways in which work toward institutional change can be inhibited through White mediocrity, functions of inequality, difficulty in measuring progress and success, and problems with power as domination. I close with a capstone of perseverance for change that can transcend generations. Built upon the knowledge gained from the previous chapters, Chapter 7 focuses on the practical, tangible, and doable strategies for promoting structural healing and systemic change across institutions and society.

In the final chapter, "Conclusion: What Does It All Mean? From Micro- to Macrolevel Change," I give a grounded summary of humanizing Black women and girls, with a final lesson on the need for freedom in the process of change. I then provide a table of example solutions by chapter topics. I close with a recognition of how the ubiquity of structural inequality, though overwhelming, also gives us ample opportunity to succeed in change-making in every aspect of our lives. As such, I use the conclusion chapter to highlight hope that structural healing and societal change are in fact possible.

GETTING THE MOST OUT OF THE BOOK: A BLACK FEMINIST PRIMER

> Black women intellectuals have laid a vital analytical foundation for a distinctive standpoint on self, community, and society, and, in doing so, created a Black women's intellectual tradition. . . . Black feminist thought—its definitions, core themes, and epistemological significance—is fundamentally embedded in a political context that has challenged its very right to exist. (Patricia Hill Collins, 1991/2000, pp. 5–6)

In the Black feminist tradition of privileging Black feminist perspectives (Preface), my default audience for the book is Black women. Through reclaiming the Black feminist intellectual tradition, I privilege Black women's "independent, viable, yet subjugated knowledge concerning our own subordination" (Collins, 1991/2000, p. 13). This is contrasted with dominant mainstream psychological work in which the implicit audience is rich and White, with all cultural outsiders needing to do the labor of culturally translating the work for ourselves. In this book, the onus of responsibility for any cultural translation falls onto cultural outsiders, who will disproportionately be White people; I am deliberately making this decision to centralize and validate the perspectives of Black women and girls with neither apology nor second-class comparison with White people and their worldviews.

Knowledge Validation Process

> Epistemological choices about who to trust, what to believe, and why something is true are not benign academic issues. Instead these concerns tap the fundamental question of which versions of the truth will prevail and shape thought and action. (Patricia Hill Collins, 1991/2000, pp. 202–203)

Collins (1991/2000) provided the groundwork for an Afrocentric feminist epistemology in the knowledge validation process—that is, the process in which purported knowledge becomes conceptualized as valid. This knowledge validation process (Collins, 1991/2000) centers wisdom through experience, as opposed to detached knowledge, such as memorizing decontextualized facts, as "knowledge without wisdom is adequate for the powerful, but wisdom is essential to the survival of the subordinate" (Collins, 1991/2000, p. 208). This process has three tenets (Collins, 1991/2000): (a) the importance of dialogue and connectedness in knowledge generation; (b) the ethic of caring, also known as "talking with the heart," in which unique expression that can represent the group and appreciation of emotions belong in knowledge-sharing (Chapter 7); and (c) the ethic of personal accountability, by where each person is responsible for the information they put forth. These tenets are evident throughout the book at both minute and metalevels, including my own standpoint from lived experience (Preface), the use of quotes representing a connectedness and dialogue with scholars and activists, the emotion-filled tone of my writing, and my ethical accountability to myself, other Black women and girl survivors, and my readers across races, genders, and experiences.

The process of knowledge validation I employ in the current book stems from different epistemological assumptions than that of dominant psychology, including the cultural assumptions and underlying premises upon which the work is built. Historically, White, male, culturally dominated academic spaces have subjugated, rejected, and/or attempted to erase Black feminist scholars' work stemming from Afrocentric feminist epistemologies (Collins, 1991/2000). In writing this book by using such epistemologies, I am trusting that the dominant epistemic community, including APA, is ready for such contributions in the mainstream.

Premises

Black feminist thought consists of specialized knowledge created by African-American women which clarifies a standpoint of and for Black women. . . . Black feminist thought encompasses theoretical interpretations of Black women's realities by those who live it. (Patricia Hill Collins, 1991, p. 22)

I use my standpoint as a Black woman in tandem with literature that understands racism and interlocking oppressions as systemic and impactful. Specifically, themes of Black feminist standpoints are evident throughout the current book and include the legacy of struggle, interlocking of oppressions (e.g., racism and sexism), self-definition, Black activism, sexual politics, and empowerment and resistance (Collins, 1991/2000). Moreover, ethical trauma and inequality research requires knowledge of the theory and cultural assumptions that such work depends on (Gómez, 2020a). In addition to standpoint engendering such knowledge, those working from marginalized perspectives may perhaps be more likely to understand the cultural premises underpinning their own work and that of the dominant field out of necessity (Conclusion): The cultural translation required to understand and engage in dominant work can further foment a deeper understanding of the problems inherent in such work, as well as provide directions for their own work.

Worldview

> To write the books one wants to read is both to point the direction of vision and, at the same time, to follow it. (Alice Walker, 1983, p. 8)

In the current book, I am writing in ways where ideas, research, and scholarship are not diametrically removed from real people and their lives (hooks, 1989). Therefore, I am operating from premises related to Black feminism, critical race perspectives, and nonpathologizing frameworks from across disciplines. In addition to the above from Black feminism, I write from the assumption that the humanity and perspectives of Black women and girls carry inherent value and knowledge that should be privileged, particularly in endeavors that include us (e.g., Combahee River Collective, 1977, as cited in K. Taylor, 2017). Additionally from Black feminist (e.g., Collins, 1991/2000) and critical race (e.g., Crenshaw et al., 1995) perspectives, I take as fact that structural racism—as well as interlocking oppressions that include racism—exists, while being endemic and impactful in each and every system, field, structure, community, and individual in the United States. As such, there can be no discussion of mental health (Chapter 5), for instance, without explicitly incorporating the role that White supremacy historically and contemporarily plays in every aspect of mental health's conceptualization and its manifestation in society. Finally, my nonpathologizing stance indicates that the locus of the harm resides in the abuse itself and the context of inequalities (e.g., Gómez, Lewis, et al., 2016). Therefore, Black women and girl survivors are not pathological when they are suffering and/or thriving but rather reacting naturally to the violent and oppressive circumstances they face. The job of the reader includes using the above premises to legitimate the arguments I make in the book while taking the opportunity to interrogate the similar and different assumptions underlain in their own work.

Centering Black Feminist Perspectives

> Rather than rejecting our marginality, Black women intellectuals can use our outsider-within stance as a position of strength in building effective coalitions and stimulating dialogue. (Patricia Hill Collins, 1991, p. 36)

I understand the harm of presenting disparate information as equally factual, given one side is critical of systems of domination and violence, while the other refuses to acknowledge such harm exists at all, much less in those systems (Conclusion). Therefore, I do not present views, such as race-neutral paradigms versus critical race perspectives, as if they are simply different ways of understanding humanity, each having its strengths and limitations. I instead use critical transdisciplinary scholarship to name, legitimate, and interrogate systems of oppression and abuse, in order to identify more equal and equitable avenues of change. This rhetorical stance is not meant to make cross-group coalitions more difficult. On the contrary, I hope this approach provides the basis for freedom, equity, and equality within such coalitions by beginning with foundational truth that engenders actual structural change instead of nonperformative lip service (Ahmed, 2012). The reader's role is to engage in critical reflection (Chapter 5; for a review, see D'Cruz et al., 2007) to continually reject White domination through centering and recentering, as necessary, Black women and girls and our perspectives.

Emotionality

> Struggle is rarely safe or pleasurable. (bell hooks, 1984/2015, p. 30)

As previously mentioned, an ethic of caring demands that emotions are present in our work (e.g., Collins, 1991/2000; Chapter 7). Furthermore, awareness of emotions provides feedback to ourselves, with emotion suppression rarely serving us fully. The potent content of the book may give rise to feelings of discomfort, defensiveness, denial, overwhelmed-ness, insecurity, and more. This can occur for multiple reasons, including that topics that are often swept under the rug, such as rape and discrimination, are discussed openly in ways that ground the harm done to human beings: ourselves, those we love, and individuals we do not even know.

Additionally difficult is the breadth of the book, including the transdisciplinary scholarship on which I built the book, thus dismantling disciplinary boundaries in favor of centering Black women and girls. With a goal of "everyone knowing everything" as stated at the beginning of the current chapter, there will necessarily be spaces of epistemological distance between what the reader knows—including how they have come to know it—and what is being discussed. That reality can make certain chapters more appreciable and digestible than others based on the worldview and disciplinary lens the reader begins with. Furthermore, that reality can interrupt professional self-concepts of those who consider themselves experts, while amplifying imposter syndrome for those who already feel they are not good enough for academia.

My challenge to readers and myself is to continuously harken back to the reasons for doing the work we do (for further discussion, see Gómez, 2020e).

Our work is not about the arrogance or toxic insecurity that can reify our fragile egos. Instead, for example, I myself do this work with and for those who unfairly, unjustly, and repeatedly are discriminated against, oppressed, abused, and violated, with the explicit goal of being able to contribute to healing and fundamental change across all levels of society. Provided we remain open to using critical epistemologies through critical thinking and reflection, this book can get us closer to understanding the inequality contexts of Black women and girls and what that means for our experience of cultural betrayal sexual trauma, therapy, radical healing in the community, and institutional change. Therefore, we must not allow uncomfortable emotions to stop us from growing, learning, and contributing to a transformed world.

Transformation in Process

> The white fathers told us: I think, therefore I am. The Black mother within each of us—the poet—whispers in our dreams: I feel, therefore I can be free. Poetry coins the language to express and charter this revolutionary demand, the implementation of that freedom. (Audre Lorde, 1984, p. 38)

Finally, amid the weight of the pain exposed in the current book, my want for us is that we additionally experience poetry, validation, relief, hope, motivation, joy, healing, connection, solidarity, strength, wisdom, freedom, and even liberation. Not for nothing, our work moves mountains in people's lives—including our own—every single day. We must choose to experience that uplifting reality over and again.

CONCLUDING THOUGHTS

> If any real efforts are to be made to free Black people of the constraints and conditions that characterize racial subordination, then theories and strategies purporting to reflect the Black community's needs must include an analysis of sexism and patriarchy. Similarly, [White] feminism must include an analysis of race [racism]. (Kimberlé Crenshaw, 1989, p. 166)

My ultimate goal for this book is to use transdisciplinary research, scholarship, and activism to paradoxically make the book itself obsolete. By providing readers with a single book for interrogating anti-Black racism, intersectional oppression, cultural betrayal sexual trauma, violent silencing, culturally competent trauma therapy, radical healing in the Black community, and institutional, structural, and societal change, my hope is to engender transformation at individual, interpersonal, and structural levels. Given this goal will not be achieved in my lifetime, I wish for the book to benefit Black women and girls by providing a road map for understanding, addressing, preventing, and ultimately healing from cultural betrayal sexual trauma.

My aspirations are grounded in the knowledge that large-scale change occurs in one person, one soul, and one spirit at a time. As such, each and every life matters (for a discussion, see Gómez in Asmelash, 2022). Given it is people who cocreate policy, culture, and society, hope comes from so-called small, individual wins because they foment large-scale policy, cultural, and societal change. Needed for individual and structural change is to abolish the apparent structural needs for violent silencing: the anti-Black racism, the intersectional oppression, the secondary marginalization, the cultural betrayal, and the sexist abuse. Therefore, in embarking upon the odyssey that is the current book, what Robyn L. Gobin and I stated in the summer of 2020 remains true (Gómez & Gobin, 2020b, para. 29):

> Today, in a time where Black solidarity is so desperately needed, we hope we can all throw out the silent oath of secrecy we have and replace it with true solidarity that, by definition, includes the needs of all of us—including Black women and girls.

2 BLACK WOMEN AND GIRLS
Racism and Intersectional Oppression

CHAPTER AT A GLANCE

In this chapter, I give a primer on structural racism, intersectional oppression, and intersectionality that provides the foundation for the rest of the book on Black male-perpetrated sexual abuse against Black women and girls, cultural betrayal trauma theory, culturally competent trauma therapy, radical healing in the Black community, and structural healing through institutional courage.

While being black has been the most powerful social attribution in my life, it is only one of a number of governing narratives or presiding fictions by which I am constantly reconfiguring myself in the world.
—Patricia Williams, 1991, p. 256

https://doi.org/10.1037/0000362-002
The Cultural Betrayal of Black Women and Girls: A Black Feminist Approach to Healing From Sexual Abuse, by J. M. Gómez
Copyright © 2023 by the American Psychological Association. All rights reserved.

The duel systemic societal harms of the COVID-19 pandemic and violent racial injustice (e.g., Cokley et al., 2022; Poteat et al., 2020) have reexposed centuries-long oppression and violence that affects Black people in the United States (e.g., Akbar, 2017; Alexander, 2010; Archer, 2021; Beliso-De Jesús, 2022; Belkin Martinez et al., n.d.; Branch & Jackson, 2020; Centers for Disease Control and Prevention, 2020; Crenshaw et al., 1995; Dreyer et al., 2020; Hannah-Jones, 2021; Iruka et al., 2022; Kendi, 2016; D. D. King et al., 2022; Laurencin & McClinton, 2020; McGoron et al., 2022; Obasogie, 2021; Ralph, 2020; V. Ray, 2022; Roberts, 2022; Yip, 2020; Zilioli et al., 2022). These systemic harms, however, are not unilaterally distributed across racial lines (e.g., Bowleg, 2020), as Black women and girls endure intersectional oppression, including the unique amalgamation of racism and sexism (Combahee River Collective, 1977, as cited in K. Taylor, 2017; Crenshaw, 1989; Gómez & Partridge, 2022; Hassoun Ayoub et al., 2022; hooks, 1981/2015, 1984/2015). It is within these interlocking oppressions that sexual abuse flourishes.

In the current chapter, I open with critical visioning regarding how we understand inequality in social justice movements. Then, I introduce scholarship on anti-Black racism (e.g., Mills, 1997), intersectional oppression (e.g., hooks, 1981/2015), and Crenshaw's (1991) theories of intersectionality to frame the contextually oppressive experiences of Black women and girls. Next, I provide an application for examining intersectionality within the field of psychology. I then detail what such intersectional oppression can actually look like in the lives of Black women and girls. Finally, I close with summary bullet points of the main takeaway messages from the current chapter.

CRITICAL VISIONING: UNDERSTANDING INEQUALITY IN MOVEMENTS

> The colored girl . . . is not known and hence not believed in; she belongs to a race that is best designated by the term "problem," and she lives beneath the shadow of that problem which envelops and obscures her. (Fannie Barrier Williams, 1905, as cited in F. B. Williams, 1987, p. 150)

Mirroring the civil rights and White feminist movements (e.g., hooks, 1981/2015, 1984/2015; Taylor, 2017), the Black Lives Matter (https://blacklivesmatter.com/about/; K. Taylor, 2016) and Me Too (Burke, 2021) movements provide a spotlight on each group's most privileged members—Black cisgender, heterosexual men and boys and White cisgender, heterosexual, and upper-class women, respectively. Evidence of this can be found in Black Lives Matter events, which frame racialized police brutality as a problem solely affecting Black men and boys (Alicia Garza, as discussed in K. Taylor, 2017). Black women have responded to this political and representational intersectionality (Crenshaw, 1991; as discussed in the current chapter) through campaigns, such as #SayHerName (Crenshaw & Ritchie, 2015), that amplify police violence against Black women and girls. In parallel, there are rich White women who publicly take credit for the #MeToo movement (e.g., Carlson, 2021). These cases illustrate how social justice movements can reproduce inequalities (Polletta, 2012; Strolovitch, 2008) by where secondary marginalization with the Black community (C. J. Cohen, 2009) and White womanhood elide Black women and girls within social justice movements (e.g., Crenshaw, 1991).

Cultural Betrayal Trauma Theory Lens

With cultural betrayal trauma theory (CBTT; Gómez, 2019c), I integrate anti-Black racism and sexual abuse together as two branches of intertwined contemporary social issues. I conceptualize this as not a solitary or even a new endeavor but rather one that builds upon Black feminists' work (e.g., Combahee River Collective, 1977, as cited in K. Taylor, 2017; hooks, 1981/2015, 1984/2015). With CBTT residing on the shoulders of this and similar work (e.g., C. J. Cohen, 2009), the occlusion of the issue of sexual abuse against Black women and girls is both painful and predictable. As such, CBTT as a theoretical and empirical tool for studying sexual abuse in the Black community serves as an intervention against this elision by identifying and interrupting political intersectionality (Crenshaw, 1991), including Black women and girls' exclusion from White feminist and antiracist efforts.

The Tension and My Critical Visioning

> The fight for social justice cannot be relegated to a hypocritical battle to make things better over there. We must work simultaneously to change the status quo here. (Jennifer M. Gómez, 2015a, para. 7)

The tension is if and how best to address the political intersectionality (Crenshaw, 1991) in the Black Lives Matter (https://blacklivesmatter.com/about/) and #MeToo (Burke, 2021) movements. My first worry in identifying this subjugation and elision is that I myself will engage in the erasure of Tarana Burke, Alicia Garza, and other Black and Brown women who addressed this problem. Specifically, both Burke (2021) and Garza (as detailed in K. Taylor, 2017) have discussed their fights against the public prioritization of the aforementioned White women and Black men, respectively, in the movements they created and cocreated, respectively. Thus, highlighting this problem could appear to criticize Black women leaders who are already tackling the problem. Conversely, not discussing the dominant society's privileged co-optation of these movements from Black women leaders paints a dishonest picture of the movements themselves. Importantly, an absence of interrogation of these problems can keep knowledge and wisdom that could be used to address political intersectionality (Crenshaw, 1991) hidden.

My critical visioning is to identify and historically contextualize the in vivo political intersectionality (Crenshaw, 1991) happening in and around these movements. White women's privileged co-optation (e.g., K. Taylor, 2017) of the #MeToo movement (Burke, 2021) continues a century-long legacy of such stealing and subsequent shapeshifting of Black women's activism (e.g., hooks, 1984/2015). Resistance against this co-optation remains central and increasingly mainstream (Gómez, as discussed in Asmelash, 2022). Black men's centeredness in the Black Lives Matter movement also mirrors the same in the previous civil rights movement (e.g., hooks, 1981/2015, 1984/2015; K. Taylor, 2017) and is particularly relevant for CBTT on several fronts. First, privileging Black men as the paragon of Blackness has meant that issues that affect roughly half of Black people (e.g., women and girls) remain marginalized within and outside the Black community (e.g., Crenshaw, 1991). Second, in the case of cultural betrayal sexual trauma, Black men's centrality to the understanding of the Black experience within the context of misogynoir (Bailey, 2016) has meant that Black women and girl survivors endure violent silencing within (intra)cultural pressure. Black women and girls' health and well-being can be compromised through the process of privileging and protecting Black men and the Black community over themselves. Thus, in building upon work that uses intersectional approaches in social justice (e.g., M. Brown et al., 2017; Fisher et al., 2017), I use this book to provide strategies for dismantling and disrupting the (intra)cultural pressure itself and its parent, intersectional societal inequality.

ANTI-BLACK RACISM

> When White people say "justice," they mean "just us." (Black folksism, as cited in Charles W. Mills, 1997, p. 110)

Within a critical race perspective (e.g., Crenshaw et al., 1995), Mills (1997) identified White supremacy as a unifying political system under which other multi-axes of oppression flourish. In that way, racism is not an anomaly; rather, it stems from White European humanism in which only White Europeans are granted practical and epistemic humanity (Mills, 1997). The racial contract, which exists structurally and interpersonally between White people, indicates a set of power relations that are enforced through ideological conditioning

(Mills, 1997). Such conditioning means that White people on average remain ignorant of their role in and how they benefit from the racial contract (Mills, 1997) while having "an appalling lack of knowledge concerning the reality of" Black life (M. L. King, 1968, p. 2). While residing at the top of the racial hierarchy, White people's ignorance, evasion, and self-deception create a distance between what White domination conceptualizes as "objective reality" versus the actual experiences of Black people (Mills, 1997). Furthermore, the racial contract prescribes the scope of and caveats to the American social contract of equal opportunity, ensuring that human rights are limited to White people's rights. In doing so, the racial contract capitalizes on abstract notions of people of color's subpersonhood to justify actual oppression in the present.

A clear example of this manifestation of abstract subpersonhood comes in the form of the continued use of the Graduate Record Examinations (ETS, 2022) despite the evidence that it unjustly bars qualified students of color from admission in psychology doctoral programs (e.g., Gómez, Caño, et al., 2021), while exhibiting weak criterion-related validity (Gómez, Caño, et al., 2021) and no demonstrable construct validity (Boykin, 2022; Gómez, 2022d). As such, the racial contract upholds White domination, enforces White domination, and rewrites itself as needed to make White domination acceptable within changing cultural norms (Mills, 1997). It is this theory of the "racial contract" that justifies a current book that uses race as a unifying group characteristic.

RACE, RACIALIZATION, AND STRUCTURAL RACISM

> Anti-Black racism is systemic in the United States, a society whose founding and economic success was based on the institution of Black slavery. Developing a view of Black people as less than human helped justify a system of slavery and the enormous profits made from it. (Shantel Gabrieal Buggs et al., 2020, pp. 289–290)

As opposed to a biological factor, race is a social construct that "refers to a characterization of a group of people believed to share physical characteristics, such as skin color, facial features, and other hereditary traits" (Cokley, 2007, p. 225). As alluded to by the theory of the "racial contract" (Mills, 1997), racialization determines opportunity based on race through oppressive societal systems categorizing individuals based on phenotype (Adames & Chavez-Dueñas, 2017). On violently colonized land that is presently known as the United States of America, Black people have been subjected to racism and related harm for 400 years (e.g., Hannah-Jones, 2021).

Distinct from individual prejudice and unconscious bias (e.g., Eberhardt, 2020), structural racism (Bonilla-Silva, 2021) is a "system of dominance, power, and privilege based on" racialization and is perpetuated by "maintaining structures, ideology, values, and behavior that have the intent or effect of leaving non-dominant-group members relatively excluded from power, esteem, status, and/or equal access to societal resources" (Harrell, 2000, p. 43). As the mechanism by which White domination shape-shifts, cultural racism perpetuates structural racism by promoting institutionalized racialized norms that can be difficult to detect (Dressler et al., 2005; Hicken et al., 2018; V. Ray, 2019). Examples of cultural racism reifying structural racism over time are numerous and include the institution of slavery being abolished on plantations while remaining legal within prisons in which Black people are overrepresented (Alexander, 2010) due to the cultural racism that pairs Blackness with criminality (Hetey & Eberhardt, 2018) and pathology (Obasogie, 2021). Structural and systemic racism (Last, 2020) systemically reproduces itself across diverse American institutions, including the university (e.g., Gómez, 2014), mental health care (e.g., Gómez, 2015d), the community (e.g., Akbar, 2017), the criminal justice system (e.g., Rucker & Richeson, 2021), policing (e.g., Bryant-Davis et al., 2017; Gómez & Freyd, 2014; Obasogie, 2021; Ralph, 2020), and the prison industrial complex (e.g., Alexander, 2010). Far from inconsequential, racism can be traumatic (Bryant-Davis & Ocampo, 2005) and costly to Black people's mental and physical health (e.g., Gómez, 2015d; Hicken et al., 2018; Wrigley-Field, 2020).

INTERSECTIONAL OPPRESSION

> We clung to the hope that liberation from racial oppression would be all that was necessary for us to be free. (bell hooks, 1981/2015, p. 1)

As hooks (1981) intimated in the above quote, it can be enticing to believe the lie that a united Blackness translates into racism being the singular harm that affects us all as Black people. Moreover, because of said racism, White feminist activism is additionally poorly situated to privilege the experiences of Black women (e.g., hooks, 1981/2015). From Black feminism (e.g., Collins, 1991/2000; Combahee River Collective, 1977, as cited in Taylor, 2017; Combahee River Collective, 1995), Black women have been publicly identifying intersectional oppression since at least the 1850s (e.g., Mary McLeod Bethune, Zora Neale Hurston, Toni Morrison, Barbara Smith, Alice Walker, and Ida B. Wells, as cited in Collins, 1991/2000; Anna Julia Cooper, Amanda Berry Smith, Mary Church Terrell, and Sojourner Truth, as cited in hooks, 1981/2015). Moreover, in 1977, the Combahee River Collective (K. Taylor, 2017) "described oppressions as 'interlocking' or happening simultaneously, thus creating new measures of oppression and inequality":

> Black women could not quantify their oppression only in terms of sexism or racism . . . or homophobia. . . . They were not ever a single category, but it was the merging or enmeshment of those identities that compounded how Black women experienced oppression. (p. 4)

Crenshaw's (1991) theories of intersectionality are a contemporary extension of the Black feminist tradition regarding intersectional oppression. Within law, Crenshaw (1989) identified how discrimination against Black women has not always been legally substantiated due to intersectionality. Specifically, race discrimination was viewed in terms of sex and class privilege, while sex discrimination was understood through race and class privilege. Thus, all people within a race (e.g., all Black people) and all people within a sex (e.g., all women) are expected to be discriminated against in the same way. However, Black women are subjected to discrimination that is both similar and different to their ready-made comparators—Black men and White women (Collins, 1991/2000; Crenshaw, 1989)—because of intersectional oppression.

Intersectionality

> When feminist theory and politics that claim to reflect women's experiences and women's aspirations do not include or speak to Black women . . . how can the claims that "women are," "women believe," and "women need" be made when such claims are inapplicable or unresponsive to the needs, interests and experiences of Black women? (Kimberlé Crenshaw, 1989, p. 154)

Similar to Black feminism that predated her work (e.g., Collins, 1990; Combahee River Collective, 1977, as cited in K. Taylor, 2017), Crenshaw's (1991) theories of intersectionality described interlocking systems of oppression, while also providing a landscape for understanding how oppression and power can reside within one individual, as is the case for Black men who have both racist oppression and gender privilege and White women with both race privilege and sexist oppression. In this way, privilege is central to understanding intersectional oppression because it is these dynamic processes that help situate a given individual within complex social and structural systems (Case, 2015, 2017). Therefore, this intraindividual and within-group dialectic (Gómez, 2019g) of oppression and privilege affects if and how equity needs are or are not addressed (e.g., C. J. Cohen, 2009). Thus, the umbrella term of *intersectionality* is explicitly a critical interrogation of power, including how power operates, how power dominates, and for whom power serves. As such, theories of intersectionality are intertwined with social action (e.g., French et al., 2020; Grzanka, 2020a).

Structural Intersectionality
Because of their intersectional identity as both women and of color within the discourses that are shaped to respond to one or the other, women of color are marginalized within both. (Kimberlé Crenshaw, 1991, p. 1244)

Centered on women of color's experience of violence and abuse, Crenshaw (1991) proposed three types of intersectionality: structural, political, and representational. In reference to Black women, structural intersectionality is how racism and sexism together affect Black women, in four distinct ways: discrimination that is similar to that faced by Black men, discrimination that is akin to that endured by White women, double discrimination of combined effects of racist and sexist discrimination, and unique amalgamated discrimination of gendered racism (Crenshaw, 1989).

Political Intersectionality
As foreshadowed in the Critical Visioning section of the current chapter, political intersectionality is "how both [White] feminist and antiracist politics have, paradoxically, often helped to marginalize the issue of violence against women of color" (Crenshaw, 1991, p. 1245). As is further detailed in the What This Can Actually Look Like section of the current chapter, political intersectionality (Crenshaw, 1991) results in a kind of cultural homelessness for Black women, in which our lack of prototypicality of privileged group members—Black men, White women—result in the erasure of ourselves and our experiences of violence and oppression (Hames-García, 2000; Purdie-Vaughns & Eibach, 2008).

Representational Intersectionality
Finally, representational intersectionality (Crenshaw, 1991) is another form of intersectional disempowerment in which our representation erases the true social location and experience of Black women (e.g., hooks, 1981/2015). An example of representational intersectionality within the academic context during the COVID-19 pandemic is when women faculty as a class of people are presumed to be all White mothers who are sexistly overburdened in the home, thus erasing the Black women faculty who do not have children but are nevertheless exploited with the intersectionally oppressive expectations of caretaking in the work setting (e.g., Gómez, 2021g). Finally, as discussed in a panel on CBTT (Wilson et al., 2021), the *On the Record* documentary (Dick & Ziering, 2020) about Black women survivors of prominent Black man Russell Simmons, underscores the issues raised by intersectionality: Who gets to be

considered "Black"? What are "Black issues"? Who benefits from Black solidarity? Who is violated and silenced in the name of such solidarity?

Extending Intersectionality Within Psychology

> Intersectionality is not . . . a scientific theory of identity that is falsifiable. (Patrick Grzanka, 2020a, p. 249)

Crenshaw's (1991) theories of intersectionality, as well as the concept of intersectional oppression generally (e.g., Combahee River Collective, 1977, as cited in K. Taylor, 2017), can be useful in psychology (Rosenthal, 2016) and across multiple disciplines (M. Brown et al., 2017; Cole, 2020; Crenshaw, 2012, 2019; Fisher et al., 2017; Grzanka, 2019). Nevertheless, the intersectional framework provides a quandary for psychologists who rely on quantitative methods to test scientific theories, even though (a) theorizing from a Black feminist framework is valuable in and of itself; (b) all research has frames that betray the worldview of the researchers, with the most prevalent being paradigms that obfuscate both inequality and the general lived experience of marginalized individuals (e.g., Burstow, 2005; Zuberi & Bonilla-Silva, 2021); and (c) intersectionality itself provides a useful lens from which to engender research (e.g., Cole, 2009; Grzanka, 2020a).

Importantly for psychologists and other social scientists, intersectionality can be used as the starting framework for creating research questions and designing studies. Specifically, this work follows Hicken and colleagues' (2018) recommendation that research should begin with conceptual and empirical models of oppression. Therefore, such work begins with the reality that racism and intersectional oppressions both exist and affect individuals, groups, and their experiences of other harms, such as sexual abuse. As intersectionality provides a lens for understanding both oppression and privilege (Cole, 2009), such contextual frameworks should be used with all populations, not just those that are marginalized by single or multi-axial oppressions. As the opposite of hiding oppressive institutional violence in plain sight (Ahmed, 2012), "intersectionality is about exposing those very claims" (of injustice), "highlighting when and where the injury is happening" (Grzanka, 2020a, p. 249). Given that the injury stems from the unequal and violent context, not the individual, substantive structural change is warranted to promote individuals' and the collective's healing (Grzanka, 2020a).

Intersectionality and Research

> The notion that systems and identities are co-constitutive is not a falsifiable claim in the scientific sense. One can use intersectionality or intersectional framework to posit falsifiable hypotheses about structural dynamics. This distinction is

more than semantic, however. Insomuch as intersectionality "theory" is rooted in women of color's lived experiences and standpoints (Collins, 1986), the falsifiability of intersectionality is not up for debate because to falsify intersectionality would be to claim that individuals do not experience harm in multiple, overlapping ways. However, intersectionality can be used in scientific contexts to develop questions that lend themselves to relatively traditional scientific and clinical practice. For example, are these participants experiencing intersectional discrimination, or is one dimension of their identity superordinate in this context? (Patrick Grzanka, 2020a, p. 250)

Cole (2009) provided psychology researchers with three questions for engendering scientific research within the framework of intersectionality. The first question is: "Who is included within this category?" This question is relevant for examining sexual abuse against Black women and girls. Specifically, when determining that we are conducting research with Black women and girls to understand their experiences of cultural betrayal sexual trauma, who is included? Who is excluded from study? This question is in line with representational intersectionality (Crenshaw, 1991), involving intersectional invisibility (Coles & Pasek, 2020; Purdie-Vaughns & Eibach, 2008; Wilkins-Yel et al., 2019) in which Black women are without metaphoric homes with Black men or White women, respectively. Within Black women and girls themselves, this question foments attuning to within-group diversity, including those who are secondarily marginalized (C. J. Cohen, 2009), such as Black transwomen and Black Muslim women.

Cole's (2009) second question is: "What role does inequality play?" This question relates to Grzanka's (2020a) push for identifying contextually where the harm occurs, presently and historically. In line with Hicken and colleagues (2018), the foundation of the research is predicated on historical and current manifestations of inequality, with research questions stemming from that context. For instance, racism against Black males plays a role in the issue of White women's false accusations against Black men and boys being privileged over Black women and girls' experience of sexual violence that is perpetrated by Black males.

Cole's (2009) final question is: "Where are there similarities?" Potentially provocative, this question must not lead to elision of differences in intersectional oppression across groups. Instead, it serves to identify similarities in social and institutional oppression and power (e.g., Collins, 1991/2000) that can serve coalition work to dismantle overlapping inequalities, such as that within the Women's March (Fisher et al., 2017).

Grzanka (2020a) built upon Cole's work with an additional three questions, which he deliberately numbered 4, 5, and 6. The fourth question is: "How can I address constructs and systems, not only identities?" Much of the research undertaken in psychology under the guise of intersectionality operationalizes identities, such as race and gender, and not the structures of oppression that give these identities contextual meaning, such as racism and sexism. With this question, Grzanka (2020a) pushed for work to center the axes of oppression, including intersectional oppression, thus locating the harm externally (within oppression) as opposed to internally (within the individual).

Related to Cole's (2009) final question on similarities, Grzanka's (2020a) next question is: "How is social power operating in this situation?" Social power is distinct from typical conceptualizations of power in psychology, such as statistical power to detect a significant effect in an experiment. Instead, it has to do with how people exist in the world both independently and interconnectedly due to differences in institutional and social power (e.g., professor vs. student; clinician vs. client; White man vs. Black woman). Beyond enumerating disparities between oppressed and privileged groups, this question contextualizes intersectional oppression and secondary marginalization (C. J. Cohen, 2009) as fundamental to psychological processes and behaviors.

Social Justice in the Field of Psychology
> If you've just described something, then how have you done social justice work? Where's the advocacy? Where's the change? . . . Where's the transformation of business-as-usual in the discipline? (Patrick Grzanka, 2020b, 12:54–13:07)

The sixth and final question for psychology researchers is: "What role can psychologists play in addressing this social problem?" (Grzanka, 2020a). Harkening back to intersectionality fundamentally being about dismantling systems of oppression (e.g., Cole, 2009), Grzanka (2020a) presupposed two things. The first is that so-called psychological problems are better conceptualized as social problems, given the locus of pathology is in the intersectionally oppressive environment. Equally as important is the second presupposition, in which Grzanka (2020a) placed responsibility on psychologists, including researchers and clinicians, to be working toward transformative social justice through roles as public intellectuals, scholar–activists, and advocates in coalition.

WHAT THIS CAN ACTUALLY LOOK LIKE

> For White women, if you ever find yourself in a space where you sound like an ignorant White man or you do things that are like ignorant White men, then rethink it. There's a call now that if you're coming to serve on an all-White-men panel, don't go. So stop it with the all-White-women panels and summits around sexual violence and sexual assault. (Jennifer M. Gómez, 2019m, as cited in Gómez, 2020f)

Examples of resource organization and allocation (Ray, 2019) demonstrate how political intersectionality (Crenshaw, 1991) in particular slows down progress while erasing Black women and girls. We can take the example of a university that has two committees: Committee 1 addresses racism and is organizing a workshop that will inform their work, and Committee 2 addresses sexual abuse and is planning programming for a summit during April as Sexual Assault Awareness Month (https://www.nsvrc.org/saam). Political intersectionality (Crenshaw, 1991) occurs when Marva, a Black woman faculty member, asks how the problem of sexual abuse against Black women will be incorporated into Committee 1's workshop and is told that such inclusion is "beyond the scope of the workshop because sexual abuse is not a race issue." Political intersectionality is mirrored when Marva then brings the topic to Committee 2 and is told that "once we solidify efforts to address campus sexual violence, we can consider adding a section on race in future years." In both responses, representational intersectionality (Crenshaw, 1991) is at play: Black women are considered not representative of Black people or women. As a result, their needs are conceptualized as neither Black enough nor woman enough to be addressed by either committee. The respective sexism and racism underlying this erasure are self-evident and systemically work together to intersectionally oppress Black women. This reality highlights the importance of Hames-García's (2000, 2011) theory of multiplicity: For Black women, what it means to be Black is informed by what it means to be a woman, while simultaneously, what it means to be a woman is informed by what it means to be Black. Complicating identity, including the intersectional oppressions that inform identity, are necessary conceptualizations as we pursue efforts to be inclusive in our understanding of multiple simultaneous identities and interlocking oppressions.

SUMMARY BULLET POINTS

1. Equity, equality, and inclusion must be sought after within social justice initiatives themselves, with history informing our understanding of present-day co-optation, inequality, and erasure.

2. The theory of a "racial contract" identifies White supremacy as a unifying political system under which multiple axes of oppression exist.

3. The racial contract is both structural and interpersonal in nature, with White people's ignorance creating distance between their perceived reality and that of Black people's.

4. Racialization and racism give meaning to the social construct of race.

5. Structural racism is a system of dominance that excludes people of color from equal access to resources, with cultural racism providing the ideological justification for such exclusion.

6. Identified by Black feminist activists and scholars for over 150 years, the concept of intersectional oppression describes how multiple axes of oppression, such as racism, sexism, classism, and homophobia, together affect Black women.

7. Coming from legal studies, the concepts of structural, political, and representational intersectionality explain how intersecting oppressions result in Black women's exclusion and erasure within social justice efforts, including civil rights and violence against women.

8. Structural intersectionality refers to the existence and impact of multiple systems of oppression, political intersectionality explains the absence of attention to Black women's needs related to violence in antiracist and antisexist initiatives, and representational intersectionality describes how Black women's misrepresentation leads to erasure.

9. Within psychology, intersectionality provides a framework for incorporating intersectional oppression, power, and privilege into scientific research.

10. The concept of intersectional oppression/intersectionality provides the foundation for understanding the existence and impact of Black male–perpetrated sexual abuse against Black women and girls.

3. THE "RAPE PROBLEM" AND SECONDARY MARGINALIZATION AGAINST BLACK WOMEN AND GIRLS

CHAPTER AT A GLANCE

In this chapter, I provide the context of Black male-perpetrated sexual abuse against Black women and girls, with specific foci on (a) Black women/girls' lower status within the Black community through secondary marginalization, (b) sexual abuse as an instantiation of intersectional oppression, (c) the inverted "rape problem" in the Black community (White women's false rape accusations against Black men versus some Black men sexually abusing Black women and girls), and (d) definitions and statistics regarding sexual abuse against Black women and girls.

Racism has always nourished itself by sexual coercion. . . . The fictional image of the black man as rapist has always strengthened its inseparable companion: the image of the black woman as chronically promiscuous . . . their claims of rape will always lack legitimacy [within oppressive society].
    −Angela Davis, 1978, as reprinted in Davis, 1981, pp. 40–42

https://doi.org/10.1037/0000362-003
The Cultural Betrayal of Black Women and Girls: A Black Feminist Approach to Healing From Sexual Abuse, by J. M. Gómez
Copyright © 2023 by the American Psychological Association. All rights reserved.

Intersectional oppression (e.g., Crenshaw, 1989) negatively affects the lives of Black women and girls, including their experience of sexual abuse within the Black community. Moreover, secondary marginalization (C. J. Cohen, 2009) and the inverted "rape problem" in the Black community provide the context for sexual abuse against Black women and girls. I deliberately detail these contexts before introducing the sexual abuse literature to further illustrate that such contexts are foundational for understanding sexual abuse, outcomes, and healing for Black women and girls. As such, I open with critical visioning regarding conceptualizing Black women and girls in ways that explicitly include those additionally marginalized by factors outside of racism and sexism, such as homophobia, Islamophobia, ableism, and more. Next, I introduce C. J. Cohen's (2009) theory of secondary marginalization to identify Black women's social location within the Black community. I then discuss sexual abuse itself as a manifestation of intersectional oppression for Black women and girls, while detailing the historical context of both White and Black male–perpetrated sexual abuse against us. With these contexts as the foundation for understanding sexual abuse, I then provide definitions, prevalence, and outcomes of sexual abuse for diverse Black women and girls; I further link outcomes to the classic trap presented in cultural betrayal trauma theory (CBTT; e.g., Gómez & Gobin, 2020a): Societal oppression combined with an unsupportive Black community leaves Black women and girl survivors in a no-person's land of isolation and rejection. Finally, I close with a list of bullet points that summarizes the takeaway messages of the current chapter.

CRITICAL VISIONING: DIVERSIFYING "BLACK WOMEN AND GIRLS"

> Any attack against Black people is a lesbian and gay issue. . . . Any attack against lesbians and gays is a Black issue. . . . There is no hierarchy of oppressions. (Audre Lorde, 1983, p. 9)

In preparing to discuss the experiences of Black women and girls, a definition of the population of interest is warranted. Knowing the population also helps with interpreting the findings and can guide future directions: What do we know? For whom? Who is included? Who is missing? (Cole, 2009). At first glance, the population of Black women and girls is self-evident: Black women and girls, in this context, are those in the United States. However, upon further interrogation, the answer to who are Black women and girls is not so straightforward.

Although all Black women and girls endure intersectional oppression related to anti-Black racism and sexism, there are additional axes of oppression that intersect, such as anti-Mexican racism (e.g., Feagin, 2001; Orozco, 2012), nationalism (discrimination against immigrants; e.g., Nkimbeng et al., 2021), classism (e.g., K. Taylor, 2017), homophobia and heterosexism (e.g., Blumenfeld, 1992), Islamophobia (Nation of Islam; Talhami, 2008), ageism (e.g., Cohen, 2001), ableism (e.g., Annamma et al., 2013), and transphobia (violence against Black transwomen; e.g., Fitzgerald, 2017; Joseph, 2020). What this means is that a Black woman or girl's intersectionally oppressive and violent experiences are not uniformly relegated to anti-Black racism and sexism. Furthermore, other identities, such as those within the LGBTQ community (e.g., queer), may provide additional cultural meaning, both in relation to and distinct from the tied oppression (e.g., multiplicity; Hames-García, 2000, 2011). Moreover, structural categories, such as *Black* and *girl*, may not match individuals' subjective identities. Important for the current chapter, differing inequality affects the incidence, meaning making, and outcomes of sexual abuse.

Further complicating matters is the ease of privileging race and racism over other forms of identity and oppression. The current book, for instance, has Blackness as a defining group feature of the selected population of women and girls. This is contrasted with Audre Lorde's (1983) argument against hierarchies of oppression, in which she states that oppressive experiences can be neither separated nor rank-ordered because people are simultaneously Black and lesbian/gay, for instance. Despite being in line with intersectionality studies (e.g., Combahee River Collective, 1977, as cited in K. Taylor, 2017), this stance nevertheless muddies how we understand the population of Black women and girls. Specifically: *Is a framing around Blackness even appropriate, given it reifies a rank-ordering in which race and racism are conceptualized as the predominant defining features of people's lives?*

Cultural Betrayal Trauma Theory Lens

I created CBTT (Gómez, 2012) as a Black feminist, critical race framework that is predicated on the existence and impact of structural inequality. Nevertheless, CBTT to date has not meaningfully incorporated multiple inequalities theoretically or empirically. That notwithstanding, there has been initial work in this area. First detailed publicly at a talk I gave to the Motor City Singers Space community event in Detroit (Gómez, 2019b), I have been theorizing that Black male–perpetrated sexual abuse against Black women and girls contains two contextual aspects: (a) cultural betrayal based on the "Black to Black" nature of the violence and (b) oppression, with such sexist abuse being conceived as manifestations of sexism and misogynoir (Bailey, 2016).

Additionally, I am constantly theoretically and methodologically grappling with how to incorporate intersectionality (e.g., Crenshaw, 1991) and multiple cultural betrayals into this work, including delineating the pros and cons of additive versus interactive versus cumulative conceptualizations of cultural betrayal. Despite these efforts, the extant theoretical and empirical work so far with CBTT is underwhelming in these domains.

The Tension and My Critical Visioning

The tension is centered on how to equitably organize the current chapter. On the one hand, a chapter on sexual abuse against Black women and girls that excludes inequality-related diversity is incomplete at best, while prescribing a normative hierarchy of Black woman-ness at worst. On the other hand, a chapter that separates sections into categories, such as *Black Women/Girls*, *Black Queer Women/Girls*, and *Black Muslim Women/Girls*, can read like an incoherent circus sideshow. It would also fail to do justice to all the diverse Black women and girls since there is neither time nor space to go into depth on how varying, multiple intersecting oppressions affect their experiences of sexual abuse.

My critical visioning has several arms, with the first being to directly name and correct the homogenous misperceptions that both outsiders and ourselves have about who Black women and girls are. Such naming can prime us to complicate our thinking on the diversity within and across Black women and girls (e.g., Cade Bambara, 1970). Next, while I do understand and appreciate Lorde's (1983) and others' (e.g., hooks, 1984/2015) call to not reify hierarchies of oppression, in this chapter and book, I use Black philosopher Charles W. Mills's (1997) theory of the "racial contract" to understand White supremacy as a dominantly oppressive political system. Key to not stating that racism is the only form of oppression, Mills (1997) argued that racism as a unifying oppression can explain why other coalitions for equality, such as women who endure sexism, typically do not successfully unite across races due to racism (e.g., Combahee River Collective, 1977, as cited in K. Taylor, 2017; hooks, 1984/2015). Within the lens of the "racial contract" (Mills, 1997), I frame women and girls as Black, while diving into the aforementioned diversity to the extent that has been done in the field. This knowledge base then provides future directions in conceptualizing "Black women and girls" that can meaningfully appreciate and incorporate diversity, intersectional oppression, cultural betrayal and oppression, and multiple cultural betrayals into theoretical, empirical, and clinical work.

BLACK WOMEN AND GIRLS' SOCIAL LOCATION WITHIN THE BLACK COMMUNITY

> The assertion of racial community sometimes supports defensive priorities that marginalize Black women. Black women's particular interests are thus relegated to the periphery in public policy discussions about the presumed needs of the Black community. (Kimberlé Crenshaw, 1989, p. 163)

From the lens of structural intersectionality (Crenshaw, 1991), we can understand how Black women and girls are simultaneously subjected to at least racism and sexism in ways that affect our lives, including our experience of abuse. Furthermore, political intersectionality (Crenshaw, 1991) identifies how the issue of violence against Black women and girls—including that perpetrated by Black men and boys—"fall into the void between concerns about women's issues and concerns about racism" (p. 1282). Given that power does not operate categorically between The Privileged and The Oppressed (C. J. Cohen, 2009; Gómez, 2019g), what is Black women and girls' positioning within the Black community?

In line with Hames-García's (2000) discussion of the opaque interests of nondominant members of marginalized groups, C. J. Cohen's (2009) theory of marginalization "incorporates the reality of difference as it exists among marginal groups" (p. 36), while examining impactful "intracommunity patterns of power and membership" (p. 36). As one pattern of power within the marginalized group, Cohen (2009) elucidated secondary marginalization, which is the regular management of more marginal group members by relatively more privileged members. This means that within the Black community, cisgender, heterosexual Black men, for instance, enjoy higher status. As such, secondary marginalization occurs through Black men oppressively dictating how Black women and girls should behave.

An example of secondary marginalization (C. J. Cohen, 2009) as this dynamic of oppressive power within the Black community came in summer 2020 from Russell Simmons, famed hip-hop pioneer and alleged serial rapist of Black women across decades (Dick & Ziering, 2020). In an interview, Simmons (2020, 19:17–19:33) stated,

> I want my daughters to have proper boundaries, because toxic femininity is when one perhaps may not put up those boundaries and may regret it later. So I want my daughters to know how to say no, and I want my daughters to put up boundaries and be strong and be leaders.

On its face, such a statement is an absurd manipulation of the construct of toxic masculinity (Salam, 2019), which is made even more shocking when being employed by a man who has at least 20 women disclosing the sexual abuse he perpetrated against them (Dick & Ziering, 2020). However, conceptualized through the theory of marginalization (C. J. Cohen, 2009), such behavior, though still harmful, is somewhat predictable.

As a rich, famous, powerful, and influential Black man, Simmons enjoys high status within the Black community. Though many supportive behaviors can be chosen by Black men (Gómez & Gobin, 2020b), Simmons instead engages in sexist secondary marginalization against Black women and girls by dictating how we should behave, while conveniently eliding his own alleged sexually abusive behavior. The result is further oppression and exclusion of Black women and girls' needs that is cloaked within a race–rape culture in which Black women and girls are erroneously made responsible for the abusive behavior of some Black men. Furthermore, Black men's simultaneous high status within the Black community and low status in American society are conceptually and behaviorally reified and preserved—with Black men's societal oppression being used as currency for both protection and immunity within the Black community. Unfortunately, these dynamics of power and secondary marginalization can be internalized by the oppressed: Black women and girls.

THE "RAPE PROBLEM": SEXUAL ABUSE AS A MANIFESTATION OF INTERSECTIONAL OPPRESSION

> "We'll know we've reached equality when the Black man can rape just like the White man can rape." That can't be where we're trying to go. (Jennifer M. Gómez, 2019b)

Violence against Black women is central to Crenshaw's (1991) theory of structural intersectionality. Nevertheless, and contrary to the topic of the current book, the "rape problem" in the Black community is not considered to be cultural betrayal sexual trauma—that is, Black male–perpetrated sexual abuse against Black women and girls. Instead, the rape problem is predominantly framed as White women falsely accusing Black men and boys of rape, resulting in an array of human rights violations, including lynching and imprisonment (Blee, 2008; Bones & Mathew, 2020; Crenshaw, 1989; Richie, 2003; Wells-Barnett, 1895/2021). Therefore, the rape problem is often understood as an issue of Black men and boys being falsely accused by White women—not Black men and boys sexually abusing Black women and girls. This frame is not entirely inaccurate, as there remains prejudice against Black men and boys as inherently aggressive and sexually violent (A. Phillips, 2018; Thompson, 2013; Wong et al., 2013; Zounlome et al., 2021) due to enduring racism against Black men.

The Role of Racism Against Black Men

> Racism is linked to patriarchy to the extent that racism denies men of color the power and privilege that dominant men enjoy. When violence is understood as an acting-out of being denied male power in other spheres, it seems counterproductive to embrace constructs that implicitly link the solution to . . . violence to the acquisition of greater male power. (Kimberlé Crenshaw, 1991, p. 1258)

A singular focus of sexist domination and violence within the Black community as simply an outcome of discrimination against men (for a discussion, see Crenshaw, 1991) further centralizes the Black male experience while relegating Black women and girls to the margins. As Crenshaw (1991) pointed out in the above quote, solutions that preserve and extend Black males' power, such as those that mirror White men's freedom to dominate and oppress, will likely not eradicate sexual abuse in the Black community at all. Unequivocally, the reality of racism against Black men cannot be used to defend or permit such sexual abuse in the name of antiracism while Black women and girls remain largely unprotected, unsupported, and even violently silenced as we endure cultural betrayal sexual trauma.

The "Rape Problem": Against Black Women and Girls

> As we grew older we became aware of the threat of physical and sexual abuse by men. (Combahee River Collective Statement, 1977, as cited in K. Taylor, 2017, p. 17)

Rooted in White supremacy (e.g., Bent-Goodley et al., 2012), sociocultural dynamics help explain why the dominant discourse on rape does not include this Black male–perpetrated cultural betrayal sexual trauma against Black women and girls. Put simply, Black women have not been prioritized when addressing women's or Black people's struggles for liberation and equality (e.g., Lindsey, 2022). Within the backdrop of secondary marginalization (C. J. Cohen, 2009), this erasure occurs within the historical and contemporary contexts of Black feminist activists and scholars naming and advocating against the sexual abuse and oppression of Black women and girls (e.g., Burke, 2021; Cade Bambara, 1970; Combahee River Collective, 1977, in K. Taylor, 2017; Anna Julia Cooper and Sojourner Truth in Crenshaw, 1989; Gómez, 2015h; Gómez, Gobin et al., 2021; Gómez & Partridge, 2022; A. Hill, 2021; hooks, 1981/2015, 1984/2015; Lindsey, 2022; Lorde, 1983; Rosa Parks in McGuire, 2010; A. Walker, 1982). Nevertheless, in incidence and community and societal response, sexual abuse as a manifestation of intersectional oppression remains relatively hidden.

From chattel slavery (e.g., Davis, 1981; Hine, 1989) onward (e.g., Hlavka & Mulla, 2021; McGuire, 2010; West, 2006), White men, including the police (e.g., Jacobs, 2021), rape Black women and girls largely without systemic recourse in the criminal justice system and elsewhere. Unlike some White women being conceptualized as "good women" who should not be raped, Black women endure sexualizing intersectional oppression that conceptualizes us as animalistic, sexually wanton, and subhuman (e.g., Collins, 1991/2000; Crenshaw, 1991; Davis, 1981; Tillman et al., 2010; Zounlome et al., 2019). Consequently, Black women are conceptualized as inordinately strong (e.g., Slatton & Richard, 2020; Zounlome et al., 2019), while we are simultaneously not considered to be legitimate victims of rape (Davis, 1985; Slatton & Richard, 2020). Moreover, the criminal justice system further positions Black women and girls below their Black male counterparts. Therefore, guilty verdicts against Black men who perpetrate cultural betrayal sexual trauma are additionally rare (e.g., Crenshaw, 1991). Therefore, Black women and girls remain societally unprotected from abusive men—White and Black.

DEFINITIONS AND PREVALENCE OF SEXUAL ABUSE

> I didn't sleep that night, I held my pillow tight. Now trust me when I say, you have been told. I'm telling you never to touch me no more. (Aaliyah, 2001)

Black male–perpetrated sexual abuse against Black women and girls is an instantiation of intersectional oppression that is predicated upon both our secondary marginalization (C. J. Cohen, 2009) within the Black community and the inverted rape problem of White women's false rape accusations against Black men. Situated within these contexts, sexual abuse includes molestation, child sexual abuse pornography, sexual harassment, sexual assault, rape, gang rape, and sex trafficking that a person(s) enacts through abuses of power, physical force, coercion, grooming, and/or incapacitation of the victim(s). Sexual abuse can occur across the life span and in multiple relational dynamics: family, marriage, romantic relationships, and friendships, as well as between coworkers, teachers and students, friends of friends, neighbors, acquaintances, and strangers.

Importantly, sexual abuse is about power, not sex. As such, perpetrators of sexual abuse use sexual language to enact violent power and domination over others in ways that reproduce inequalities for those subjected to sexism, racism, classism, ageism, homophobia and heterosexism, ableism, and/or nationalism (Armstrong et al., 2018). Consequently, sexual abuse is not *sex* in the traditional sense because sex, by definition, is consensual and in many cases is also sexually, physically, emotionally, and spiritually pleasurable. As such, the harm of sexual abuse can be particularly pernicious because it violates the victimized person's body and psyche through acts that are both culturally meaningful and societally weaponized against women and girls. Therefore, understanding the distinction between sexual abuse and sex is important, as it can focus prevention efforts away from *sex*, such as the clothing or perceived sexual behavior of Black women and girls (e.g., Davis, 1981).

Intersectional oppression places Black women and girls at risk for sexual abuse within our households, communities, and social spheres (Richie & Eife, 2021), with complex trauma—multiple victimizations—being common (Herman, 1997). New research suggests that over 80% of Black young women endure some form of sexual abuse, including sexual harassment (Gómez & Johnson, 2022), with approximately one in three Black women experiencing contact sexual abuse, excluding sexual harassment (Gómez & Johnson, 2022; Green, 2017; S. G. Smith et al., 2017; West & Johnson, 2013). Moreover, over 20% of Black women experience attempted or completed rape (S. G. Smith et al., 2017), with 13% of Black young women indicating a history of sex trafficking (Gómez & Johnson, 2022).

With sexual abuse being about power and domination (e.g., Armstrong et al., 2018), I hoped to highlight the experiences of sexual abuse against oft-erased and secondarily marginalized Black women. Specifically, I searched for prevalence rates of Black women additionally marginalized by transphobia and nationalism, as well as diverse Black women underrepresented in the dominant literature: Black Latinas, Black Muslim women, and Black women who are incarcerated. Disappointingly, the research with these populations was sorely lacking.

I was unable to find specific statistics regarding Black transwomen, though over half of transwomen across races endure contact sexual abuse in their lifetime (S. G. Smith et al., 2017). Though some Black immigrant women's experiences of sexual abuse have been highlighted (e.g., Crenshaw, 1991; Hislop, 2020), I was similarly unable to find specified rates in this diverse subpopulation of Black women. I also could not find research with Black Latinas and Black Muslim women specifically. Though unable to find rates on Black women specifically who are incarcerated, some work suggests that up to 82% of women across races who are incarcerated endured sexual assault in their lifetime (Karlsson & Zielinski, 2020). Moreover, quantitative and qualitative research suggests an established link between sexist violence and the incarceration of Black women (Dichter, 2015; Lynch et al., 2012; Power et al., 2016; Richie, 2012; Richie & Eife, 2021), despite an absence of increased criminal behavior (Gross, 2015; Ritchie, 2017).

This relative dearth of information across multiple populations is yet another instantiation of intersectional oppression against diverse Black women and girls. As I myself am guilty of such erasure, I plead with each of us to better and more fully incorporate intersectionality into our research, including into whom our research studies include and how we interpret the generalizability of our findings (Cole, 2009; Grzanka, 2020a). Put simply, examining incarcerated women without attention to race or Black women in comparison with (non-Black) Latinas, for example, serves to erase culturally diverse and multiply marginalized Black women and girls.

OUTCOMES OF SEXUAL ABUSE

> There is also a more generalized community ethic against public intervention, the product of a desire to create a private world free from the diverse assaults on the public lives of racially subordinated people. The home is not simply a man's castle in the patriarchal sense, but may also function as a safe haven from the indignities of life in a racist society. (Kimberlé Crenshaw, 1991, p. 1257)

The contexts of racism against Black men and intersectional oppression against Black women and girls affect the meaning and outcomes of sexual abuse (Bent-Goodley & Gómez, in press). As an ostensible ingroup protective cultural script, racial loyalty (e.g., Bent-Goodley, 2001; Slatton & Richard, 2020; Tillman et al., 2010) demands that Black women and girls shoulder the responsibility for the Black community by protecting Black men—even sexually abusive Black men—at all costs. Consequently, Black women and girls suffer, with sexual abuse being linked with elevated incidence of posttraumatic stress, depression, substance use, sexual health concerns, and suicidal behavior (e.g., Bryant-Davis et al., 2009; Gobin & Allard, 2016; Gobin & Gómez, 2020; White & Satyen, 2015). These outcomes are neither abstract nor decontextualized. They are real harms that occur in the context of the classic trap highlighted in CBTT (e.g., Gómez & Gobin, 2020a): Societal oppression makes the larger society dangerous, while cultural betrayal, (intra) pressure, and violent silencing remove safety from the marginalized ingroup. At its most harmful, this leaves Black women and girls who experience cultural betrayal sexual trauma between the rock of oppression and the hard place of an unsupportive Black community (for an artistic representation, see Gómez & Johnson-Freyd, 2015). Thus, despite the long history of Black women's resistance against rape (e.g., Davis, 1981; Lindsey, 2022; McGuire, 2010), the necessary attention to the health and well-being of Black women and girls both within the Black community and in society at large is lacking (e.g., Stabile & Grant, 2022).

SUMMARY BULLET POINTS

1. The population of Black women and girls is heterogeneous—culturally and intersectionally.
2. Black women and girls are subjected to both intersectional oppression in society and secondary marginalization within the Black community.
3. Black male–perpetrated sexual abuse against Black women and girls is an instantiation of intersectional oppression, as the issue is relegated to the margins in favor of highlighting the rape problem of White women falsely accusing Black men and boys of rape.
4. To the extent that racism and sexual coercion are linked, increasing Black men's domination in society is not an appropriate prevention measure against Black male–perpetrated sexual abuse against Black women and girls.
5. Sexual abuse is not synonymous with sex, as sexual abuse uses sexual language to enact violence that reproduces inequalities, whereas sex is characterized by consent and pleasure.
6. Occurring across the life span, sexual abuse includes molestation, child sexual abuse pornography, sexual harassment, sexual assault, rape, gang rape, and sex trafficking that a person(s) enacts through abuses of power, physical force, coercion, grooming, and/or incapacitation of the victim(s).
7. Within the contexts of racism against Black men, secondary marginalization and intersectional oppression against Black women and girls, and the inverted rape problem of White women's false accusations against Black men, sexual abuse is relatively common in the lives of Black women and girls and affects our mental, behavioral, and physical health.
8. The context of the dueling rape problems—White women's false accusations against Black men and Black men's sexual abuse against Black women—places Black women and girl survivors between the rock of oppression and the hard place of an unsupportive Black community; this trap provides the foundation for understanding the latter within the context of cultural betrayal trauma theory.

4 CULTURAL BETRAYAL TRAUMA THEORY

Framework, Evidence, and Future Directions

CHAPTER AT A GLANCE

In this chapter, I provide a detailed analysis of cultural betrayal trauma theory (CBTT), with foci on (a) the socioecological context of Black male–perpetrated sexual abuse against Black women and girls—known as one form of cultural betrayal sexual trauma, (b) CBTT's theoretical framework, (c) CBTT's empirical evidence generally and within Black populations specifically, and (d) CBTT's future theoretical and methodological research directions.

The effort to politicize violence against women will do little to address the experiences of Black . . . women until the ramifications of racial stratification among women can be acknowledged.

—Kimberlé Crenshaw, 1991, p. 1282

https://doi.org/10.1037/0000362-004
The Cultural Betrayal of Black Women and Girls: A Black Feminist Approach to Healing From Sexual Abuse, by J. M. Gómez
Copyright © 2023 by the American Psychological Association. All rights reserved.

Sexual abuse against Black women and girls is a complex problem, with contextual and cultural dynamics, such as racial loyalty (e.g., Bent-Goodley, 2001), affecting its meaning and impact. A way to systematically investigate complex psychological phenomena is theory-driven research (e.g., Snowden & Yamada, 2005). In the context of Black male–perpetrated sexual abuse against Black women and girls, a Black feminist, critical race, scientific theory can provide value in and of itself, while offering new avenues for both healing and scientific discovery.

The current chapter begins with my critical visioning for cultural betrayal trauma theory (CBTT) as a method for healing and not harm. I then briefly define betrayal trauma theory (e.g., Freyd, 1996). Next, I detail CBTT—the theory itself, its postulates, and the empirical evidence—with a focus on the work with Black populations. Then, I provide a real-life example of what sexual abuse in the context of CBTT can actually look like for a young Black woman. Finally, I close with future theoretical and methodological directions for CBTT research, followed by a summary of bullet points with takeaway messages from the current chapter.

CRITICAL VISIONING: CBTT FOR HEALING, NOT HARM

U.S. society violently, structurally, and insidiously oppresses Black people (e.g., Beliso-De Jesús, 2022; Gómez, 2014, 2015d, 2022b; Hicken et al., 2018; Obasogie, 2021; V. Ray, 2019). Moreover, Black women and girls— and our experiences of sexual abuse—are elided within a void between racist White feminism and sexist antiracist activism (Crenshaw, 1991). Begun over a decade ago (Gómez, 2012), CBTT is directly situated within these intersectional oppressions while simultaneously indicting the same. As such, there is a consistent parallel process (e.g., Tracey et al., 2012) of what the theory is describing, alongside what the CBTT research and myself as the researcher, are contending with. One such example is my fear that the CBTT research will expose Black people to increased discriminatory harm by virtue of its highlighting violence, abuse, and trauma within the Black community.

Cultural Betrayal Trauma Theory Lens

Eerily enough, my aforementioned fear of CBTT causing harm is classically explained in CBTT itself. Here is a brief autoethnographic example: Because of anti-Black racism, I have developed (intra)cultural trust with Black people. I am aware of cultural betrayal trauma in the form of sexist sexual abuse that is perpetrated by Black men against Black women and girls. My knowledge resides within the context of (intra)cultural pressure—I am driven to keep problems in-house to protect the whole of the Black community. Oppressively, however, through representational intersectionality (Crenshaw, 1991), Black women and girls are often not included in the category of the "Black community" (Cole, 2009; Gómez & Gobin, 2020b).

Therefore, the issue of sexual abuse is additionally not prioritized within the Black community. With metatheoretical engagement with CBTT, I feel (intra)cultural pressure as a researcher to protect the Black community from an unjust, unequal, and violently oppressive society. That (intra)cultural pressure may be also experienced by those of us who have endured cultural betrayal sexual trauma.

The Tension and My Critical Visioning

> When we speak we are afraid our words will not be heard nor welcomed, but when we are silent, we are still afraid. So it is better to speak, remembering we were never meant to survive. (Audre Lorde, 1978, p. 32)

Stemming from White supremacy, the tension is between using CBTT to research the depth of experiencing abuse within the context of inequality versus suppressing such work for the ostensible protection of the entire Black community. On the one side, is it ethical and responsible to create and test a theory that highlights abuse within the Black community, given the context of the structurally oppressive society? On the other side, wouldn't casting aside all the psychological, empirical, clinical, and Black feminist tools at our disposal simply serve to promote silencing and erasure of Black women and girls' experiences of sexual abuse? Complicating matters is that CBTT and its body of work have only just begun. Isn't that nascence further cause to abandon, or at least hide, CBTT research to protect us from further stereotyping and oppression?

My critical visioning begins with acknowledging my fears explicitly, while naming the realities of our racist society that breathe life into those fears. Knowing that White supremacy as a unified political system (Mills, 1997) is as strong as it is harmful, I, as the creator and lead researcher of CBTT, cannot allow that reality to silence me. Moreover, both CBTT and myself are perched atop the Black feminist scholarship and activism over more than 150 years that have identified much of the same harms, albeit without the "cultural betrayal" language and framework (e.g., Combahee River Collective, 1977, as cited in K. Taylor, 2017; Anna Julia Cooper and Sojourner Truth in the 1850s, as cited in Crenshaw, 1989). There is strength and solidarity to be gained by knowing our courageous history (e.g., Mosley et al., 2020).

Finally, as with any good scientific research program, no one study, or even one book, should be appraised as the Definitive Work. Should I live so long, when I retire in approximately 25 years, the CBTT work will be far from done. I will simply pass the baton on to the next generation of researchers, clinicians, and activists (Gómez, 2014). Furthermore, my expansive critical visioning reminds me that the pressure to Be Right with CBTT is an instantiation of the toxic narrative that complex phenomena can be understood through simplistic, White supremacist work that is cloaked as rigorous science (for a discussion, see Gómez, 2022b). I remind myself that I created CBTT to first and foremost provide a framework for asking better questions that can be systematically tested. My goal is to get closer to the veracious lived experiences of Black women and girl (and other marginalized) survivors of cultural betrayal trauma to identify more effective avenues of healing within and outside of therapy, while working to create a world in which such healing is unnecessary because oppression and abuse have been abolished.

That said, it is possible that the dominant society ultimately is "too racist" for CBTT. However, my continued critical visioning reminds me that waiting for the oppressors' morality to engender change has never served the oppressed (Shakur, 2020). Moreover, to the extent that Black women are indeed the foremost stewards of Black women (Combahee River Collective, 1977, as cited in K. Taylor, 2017), then we must do the work with courage and humility, remembering that "perfection is neither required nor possible. Ongoing correction and improvement are possible, expected, necessary, *and* our responsibility as researchers who do work related to the impact of trauma and inequality on human beings" (Gómez, 2020a, p. 2).

BETRAYAL TRAUMA THEORY

Identifying a nonpathologizing way for defining and understanding trauma and outcomes, betrayal trauma theory (e.g., Freyd, 1996) incorporates attachment theory (Bowlby, 1969) and the interpersonal context as important mechanisms in understanding trauma. As such, betrayal trauma theory (e.g., Freyd, 1996) focuses on the social relationships in which the trauma occurs to understand posttraumatic outcomes (e.g., Freyd, 1997; Gómez, Kaehler, et al., 2014). Specifically, a parent's sexual abuse of their child includes a high betrayal, as it violates the trust and/or dependence that the child has on their parent. During the abusive relationship, the child can engage in *betrayal blindness*, or knowledge isolation, for the high betrayal trauma to preserve the needed relationship with the parent (e.g., Freyd, 1996). Facets of this knowledge isolation can include *rotating betrayal blindness* (Noll & Gómez,

2013), in which awareness of the trauma is inconsistent and context-specific across time (Gómez et al., 2022). In the 25 years of empirical research, the work has included and expanded beyond child sexual abuse, showing that high betrayal is a contributing factor in costly outcomes (e.g., Adams-Clark et al., 2022; Adams-Clark et al., 2020; Gómez, 2019d, 2019i, 2020c, 2021e; Gómez & Freyd, 2019; Gómez, Noll, et al., 2021; Gómez, Smith, et al., 2014).

CULTURAL BETRAYAL TRAUMA THEORY: THE FRAMEWORK

> The antiracist agenda will not be furthered by suppressing the reality of intraracial violence against women of color. (Kimberlé Crenshaw, 1991, p. 1282)

Building from the intersectionality (e.g., Crenshaw, 1991), sexual abuse against Black women and girls (e.g., Bent-Goodley, 2001), and betrayal (e.g., Freyd, 1996) literature, CBTT (e.g., Gómez, 2012, 2019i) is a critical race, Black feminist, scientific theory of trauma that, within its theoretical abstraction, is situated in the sociocultural context. As such, it is contrasted with dominant, race-less trauma theories that divorce themselves from structural aspects of sociohistorical and present life (Mills, 1997) that create the impetus for the abuse itself and trauma sequelae, as well as the meaning derived from each. Thus, in CBTT, I continue the tradition of Black psychology in which self-definition creates relevant frameworks for Black people that deliberately disinhabit White, Eurocentric notions of both harm and healing (White, 1970). With CBTT, my goal is not to reify the racial hierarchy (Mills, 1997) but to instead subvert it by understanding and investigating the prevalence and impact of sexual abuse within the context of anti-Black racism and intersectional oppression. Though CBTT can apply to various marginalized populations and instantiations of structural inequality, its foundation is within Black feminist and critical race work, with specific cultural applicability to Black women and girls who have been sexually abused by Black boys and men (e.g., Gómez & Gobin, 2020a).

Trauma in Context

The majority of mainstream trauma research has been conducted with White American samples, using theoretical paradigms within segments of the dominant culture (Gómez, 2015b, 2015e). Those theoretical paradigms then produce work that is limited in its application and utility in marginalized populations (Gómez, 2014, 2015h). Adapted for CBTT, the Bronfenbrenner socio-ecological systems model provides relevant contextual information for Black women and girl survivors (see Figure 4.1). In the Black woman's microsystem are the Black male perpetrator; health care; and the Black community, including

FIGURE 4.1. Bronfenbrenner Ecological Systems Model

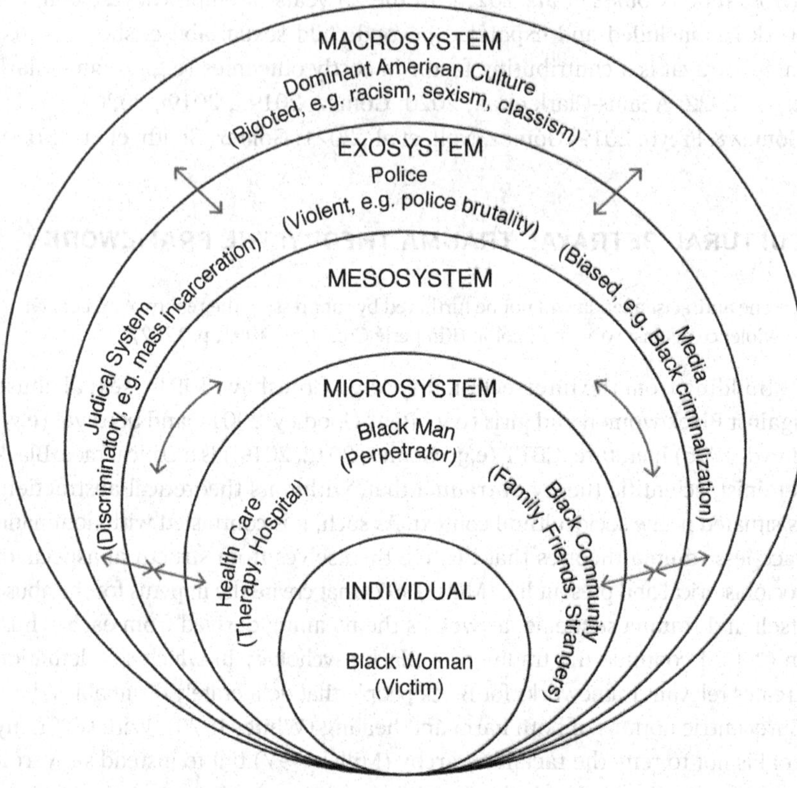

MACROSYSTEM
Dominant American Culture
(Bigoted, e.g. racism, sexism, classism)

EXOSYSTEM
Police
(Violent, e.g. police brutality)

Judicial System
(Discriminatory, e.g. mass incarceration)

Media
(Biased, e.g. Black criminalization)

MESOSYSTEM

MICROSYSTEM
Black Man
(Perpetrator)

Health Care
(Therapy, Hospital)

Black Community
(Family, Friends, Strangers)

INDIVIDUAL
Black Woman
(Victim)

© Jennifer M. Gómez, Sasha Johnson-Freyd, and Robyn L. Gobin, 2018

Note. Data from Bronfenbrenner (1979). Copyright 2018 by J. M. Gómez, S. Johnson-Freyd, and R. L. Gobin. Reprinted with permission.

family, friends, and strangers. Cross-talking across the mesosystem, the exosystem includes police who engage in racialized police brutality (e.g., Obasogie, 2021); the judicial system, which contributes to racialized mass incarceration (e.g., Alexander, 2010); and the media, which is racially biased in its portrayal of Black men as criminal (e.g., Dukes & Gaither, 2017). With the whole model occurring across time, the macrosystem is the dominant American culture of racism, sexism, intersectional oppression, and more. The Black woman not only endures the perpetrator(s)' abuse but also is exposed to this oppressive macrosystem, exosystem, and microsystem. In kind, the Black male perpetrator(s) additionally endures these oppressive systems and contexts. In addition to the unique aspects of oppression by genders, there is also a shared anti-Black racist oppression due to unified White supremacy and the racial contract (Mills, 1997).

Whereas the adapted Bronfenbrenner socioecological systems model places the trauma within the sociocultural context, CBTT is further situated within the betrayal literature (e.g., Freyd, 1996; see Figure 4.2). As in Item a of Figure 4.2, traditional models of trauma are predicated on the fear paradigm (for a discussion, see DePrince & Freyd, 2002), in which diverse traumas—from hurricane exposure to incest—are conceptualized as harmful due to the fear they cause. Within this paradigm, individuals are appraised as having defenses against such harm, with a subset developing so-called pathology, such as posttraumatic stress disorder (PTSD). As discussed earlier in this chapter and in Item b, the interpersonal context of abuse (e.g., parent and child) creates a vulnerability that makes such high betrayal traumas uniquely toxic (e.g., Freyd, 1996; Freyd & Birrell, 2013). In CBTT, the first trauma is societal trauma (Item c in Figure 4.2), such as anti-Black racism, in which Black people develop a bond with each other, known as (intra)cultural trust, that serves as a buffer against this societal trauma. In Item d in Figure 4.2, akin to the vulnerability found in abusive families, (intra)cultural trust makes the harm of within-group violence in marginalized communities—known as cultural betrayal trauma—particularly costly.

Figure 4.3 further fleshes out CBTT. As mentioned from Figure 4.2, societal trauma (e.g., anti-Black racism) engenders (intra)cultural trust among some members of the Black community. Within-group violence breaks that (intra) cultural trust and, as such, is a cultural betrayal. As seen in Figure 4.3, CBTT predicts that cultural betrayal traumas are associated with abuse outcomes, such as mental, behavioral, and physical health, as well as cultural outcomes, such as internalized prejudice. Moreover, (intra)cultural pressure is a within-group cultural mandate to "keep problems in-house" in order to protect the Black community from the dominant culture's and systems' further stigmatization, oppression, and abuse. Building from this brief snapshot of CBTT, I fully detail the tenets of the theory next.

(Intra)Cultural Trust

The collective sense of sweet solidarity in Blackness. (bell hooks, 1994, p. 67)

In the context of the Black community, (intra)cultural trust "is defined as connection, attachment, dependency, love, loyalty, and responsibility" (Gómez & Gobin, 2020a, p. 3) to other Black people and the Black community. While fundamentally a cultural collective sense of being (Alexander et al., 2004; Nobles, 1972), perceived group victimization can also increase trust and connection with the ingroup (Rotella et al., 2013). Within that connection through shared struggle, (intra)cultural trust also serves a protective function

FIGURE 4.2. Trauma Psychology and CBTT

a) **Traditional Model of Trauma:** Traditional models of trauma expect that individuals have defenses (represented by circle) to trauma. Arrow = all forms of trauma

b) **Betrayal Trauma Theory:** Betrayal trauma theory[a] contextualizes trauma in interpersonal relationships with trust and/or dependency, which creates unique vulnerability (perforated defenses) to traumatic betrayal. Arrow = betrayal trauma

c) **(Intra)Cultural Trust:** Cultural betrayal trauma theory[b] contextualizes betrayal trauma within larger socio-cultural dynamics. Cultural minorities pool defense resources (represented by ellipse) to buffer against societal trauma. Arrow = societal trauma

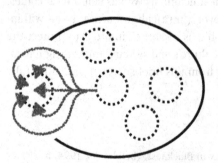

d) **Cultural Betrayal Trauma:** A member of a cultural minority has uniquely vulnerable defenses to betrayal of (intra)cultural trust. When a victim is violated by a perceived in-group perpetrator, the victim's (intra)cultural trust is also betrayed. Arrow = cultural betrayal trauma

© 2015, Sasha Johnson-Freyd and Jennifer M. Gómez
[a]Freyd, 1996; [b]Gómez, 2012

Note. Copyright 2015 by S. Johnson-Freyd and J. M. Gómez. Reprinted with permission. [a]*Betrayal Trauma: The Logic of Forgetting Childhood Abuse*, by J. J. Freyd, 1996, Harvard University Press. [b]"Cultural Betrayal Trauma Theory: The Impact of Culture on the Effects of Trauma," by J. M. Gómez, in *Blind to Betrayal*, 2012, https://web.archive.org/web/20221006011353/https://sites.google.com/site/betrayalbook/betrayal-research-news/cultural-betrayal

FIGURE 4.3. Cultural Betrayal Trauma Theory

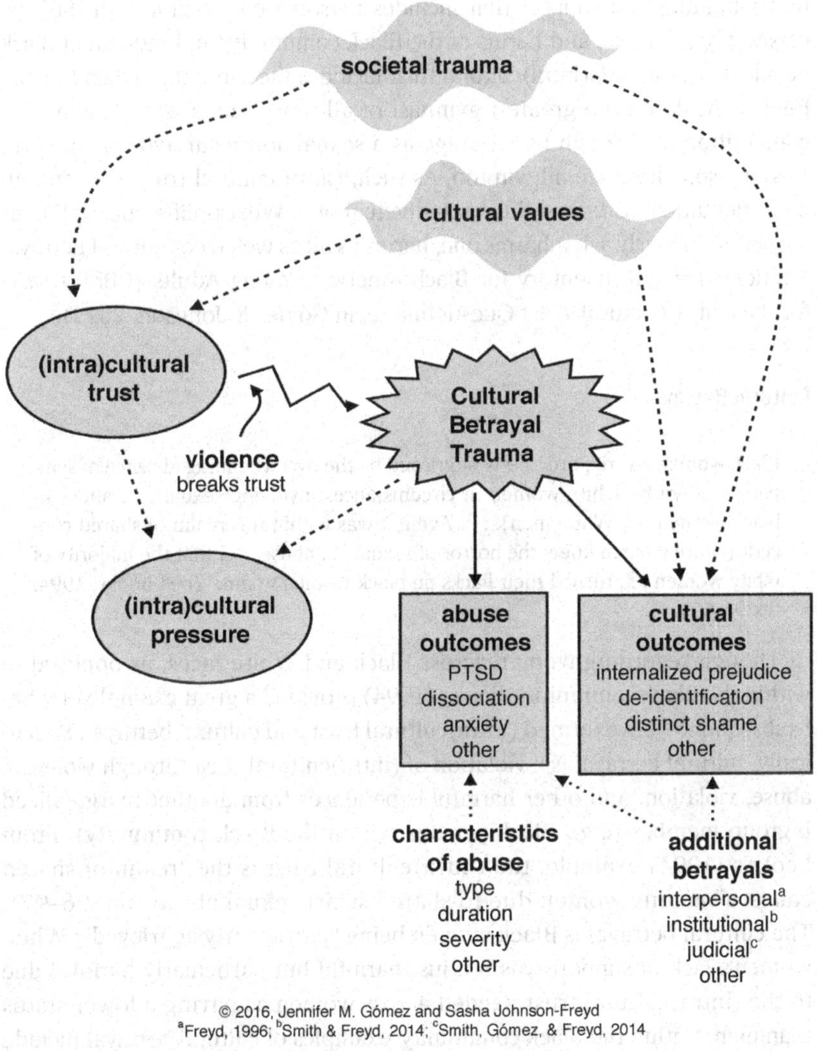

[Diagram showing: "societal trauma" and "cultural values" as cloud shapes at top feeding into the model. "(intra)cultural trust" oval connects via "violence breaks trust" to "Cultural Betrayal Trauma" (starburst shape), which leads to "(intra)cultural pressure" oval. Cultural Betrayal Trauma leads to "abuse outcomes" (PTSD, dissociation, anxiety, other) and "cultural outcomes" (internalized prejudice, de-identification, distinct shame, other). Inputs from "characteristics of abuse" (type, duration, severity, other) and "additional betrayals" (interpersonal[a], institutional[b], judicial[c], other).]

© 2016, Jennifer M. Gómez and Sasha Johnson-Freyd
[a]Freyd, 1996; [b]Smith & Freyd, 2014; [c]Smith, Gómez, & Freyd, 2014

Note. Copyright 2016 by J. M. Gómez and S. Johnson-Freyd. Reprinted with permission. [a]*Betrayal Trauma: The Logic of Forgetting Childhood Abuse*, by J. J. Freyd, 1996, Harvard University Press. [b]"Institutional Betrayal," by C. P. Smith and J. J. Freyd, 2014, *American Psychologist*, 69(6), 575–587 (https://doi.org/10.1037/a0037564). [c]"The Psychology of Judicial Betrayal," by C. P. Smith, J. M. Gómez, and J. J. Freyd, 2014, *Roger Williams University Law Review*, 19(0), 451–475.

against structural racism. Namely, the bond and connection within Blackness can be a buffer that provides protection and emotional safety from racial discrimination. Within (intra)cultural trust, there is a need and expectation of understanding and support that includes personal connection with the successes, joys, failures, and harms of the Black community and individual Black people. For example, (intra)cultural trust includes the sense that when Simone Biles, considered the greatest gymnast of all time (Ennis, 2021), wins—in competition or through her courage as a sexual abuse survivor of Dr. Larry Nassar—somehow, we all win too. As such, (intra)cultural trust is a community orientation, as opposed to an individual one: What uplifts one, uplifts us all; simultaneously, what harms one, harms us all as well (see Cultural Betrayal Multidimensional Inventory for Black American Young Adults [CBMI-BAYA] for the (Intra)Cultural Trust Questionnaire, in Gómez & Johnson, 2022).

Cultural Betrayal

> Black women "were particularly aggrieved by the overwhelming absence of sympathy shown by white women in circumstances involving sexual . . . abuse of black women [by White men]. . . . Again it was within this realm of shared concern (white women knew the horror of sexual . . . abuse . . .) that the majority of white women . . . turned their backs on black women's pain." (bell hooks, 1994, pp. 96–97)

Though regarding women across Black and White races, as opposed to within the Black community, hooks (1994) provided a great example of what I subsequently have termed (intra)cultural trust and cultural betrayal. Specifically, cultural betrayal is a violation of (intra)cultural trust through violence, abuse, violation, and other harmful experiences from another marginalized ingroup member (e.g., Black persons within the Black community). From hooks's (1994) example, the (intra)cultural trust is the "realm of shared concern" among women due to shared sexist sexual abuse (pp. 96–97). The cultural betrayal is Black women being "particularly aggrieved": White women's lack of support was not just harmful but particularly harmful due to the (intra)cultural trust needed across women as having a lower status than men. Within the Black community, examples of cultural betrayal include being rejected by other Black people, being the target of secondary marginalization (C. J. Cohen, 2009), being accused of "acting White" (e.g., Durkee & Gómez, 2022), and experiencing threats to social identity. Evidence suggests that such harms are more costly when perpetrated by ingroup members (e.g., other Black people; Branscombe et al., 1999; Durkee & Gómez, 2022; see CBMI-BAYA for the Cultural Betrayal Questionnaire, in Gómez & Johnson, 2022).

Cultural Betrayal Trauma

Cultural betrayal trauma is violence, abuse, or trauma (e.g., physical, sexual, psychological abuse) in which the victim and the perpetrator(s) share at least one marginalized identity. In reference to Black people, cultural betrayal trauma is within-group violence in the Black community. In this way, the cultural betrayal is implicit in the abuse; even if the perpetrator did not intend to betray and/or the survivor did not feel betrayed, the abuse would still be considered a cultural betrayal trauma. The implicit nature of cultural betrayal in trauma is based on the same in betrayal trauma theory (e.g., Freyd, 1996). The CBMI-BAYA (Gómez & Johnson, 2022) has a Violence and Discrimination Questionnaire in which witnessing or experiencing physical, sexual, and psychological abuse; racial discrimination; and police violence are assessed. Sexual abuse items include child sexual abuse through grooming, sexual abuse through force, sexual abuse through incapacitation (e.g., drugging), sexual harassment, and sex trafficking. Further, the Violence and Discrimination Questionnaire inquires about the closeness of the perpetrator (betrayal trauma theory; Freyd, 1996; close or unclose other[s]), the racial identity of the perpetrator(s) (CBTT; another Black person[s], another person[s] of color, or a White person[s]), and the developmental period of victimization (before age 13, ages 13 to 17, or 18 years and older) by item. These same identity questions for the perpetrator(s) are additionally asked regarding whom the survivor disclosed to, if anyone. With Items 1 to 15 being behavioral, the questionnaire closes with a question on whether the person has ever been abused. This difference in language (behavioral vs. direct) can be used to examine moderating factors for when a victimized person will endorse an abusive history or not (see CBMI-BAYA for the Violence and Discrimination Questionnaire, in Gómez & Johnson, 2022).

(Intra)Cultural Pressure

> The real work of marginalization . . . happens systematically through the daily actions of individuals, many of whom seem to be nice people who are simply doing their jobs and have no obvious plan to actively participate in exclusion. (Cathy Cohen, 2009, pp. 47–48)

(Intra)cultural pressure is similar to racial loyalty (e.g., Bent-Goodley, 2001) and involves promoting silence in the name of protecting the Black community (e.g., Zounlome et al., 2019). Specifically, (intra)cultural pressure is a negative transformation of the largely positive (intra)cultural trust, with the needs of the victim being overshadowed by the perceived needs of the perpetrator(s)and/or the entire marginalized group. That is, the Black community as a marginalized whole is privileged over the needs of the individual(s) victimized. With the Black community being diverse, whose needs are determined to be those of the "Black community" is subjected to representational intersectionality (Crenshaw, 1991), in which Black women and girls are elided within the Black community. (Intra)cultural pressure includes Black people telling the victimized woman or girl to keep problems in-house, thereby not disclosing to law enforcement, clinicians, and other professionals because doing so would reflect poorly on and/or harm the Black perpetrator(s), other Black people, and the Black community generally. Moreover, violent silencing is perhaps the most obvious and extreme form of (intra)cultural pressure. Violent silencing includes Black men's death threats against Tarana Burke (founder of the #MeToo movement; Burke, 2021; Gómez, 2019k).

Black Men Protected From Exclusion

Women of color who dare to discuss male predation/violence in minority communities often meet with violent backlash—rape and death threats, etc. (Anonymous commenter from Gómez, 2019a)

The theory of marginalization (C. J. Cohen, 2009) discusses how within-group management and policing of others' objectionable behavior can occur. Importantly, what is considered "objectionable" is based on internalizing the White supremacy and discrimination enacted on the group from the outside, with management and policing within the Black community serving to "reconstruct themselves for the white gaze" (C. J. Cohen, 2009, p. 4). For instance, the dominant White supremacy culture perceiving Black sexuality as deviant is related to internal policing of sexuality by Black leaders (C. J. Cohen, 2009).

Given that sexual violations of all kinds can be erroneously conceptualized as "sex" and "sexuality," predictions from the theory of marginalization (C. J. Cohen, 2009) could be that those engaged in perpetrating sexually violent behavior—for example, some Black men and boys—would be excised from the Black community to protect the group's current precarious standing and potential for elevated societal status. Instead, what happens is the rejection—sometimes, violent rejection—of Black women and girls who are subjected to this behavior but who, by definition, are not the cause of it. How can we explain this?

Black Women Subjected to Secondary Marginalization

Abuse aside, within secondary marginalization (C. J. Cohen, 2009), Black women and girls' behavior is managed and policed. Within a framework of gender interdependence, sexism—including instantiations like sexist sexual abuse—operates differently than other oppressions (Pateman, 1988). Within this "sexual contract" (Pateman, 1988), Black women and girls not only are made responsible for abusive Black men's abhorrent behavior but also are actually required to take ownership of the behavior itself. In the case of a Black man raping a Black girl, the rape is not conceptualized as belonging to him; instead, the rape is hers (e.g., Dick & Ziering, 2020). Since the rape is perceived as hers, and since the behavior remains abhorrent, (intra)cultural pressure through secondary marginalization (C. J. Cohen, 2009) and other cultural dynamics are hers to bear as well. This inverse of responsibility serves to preserve the power dynamics and hierarchy within the Black community: Black men are protected, while Black women and girls are structurally and interpersonally crushed, disposable, and disregarded. This differential protection and degradation contribute to multiplicity (Hames-García, 2000, 2011): What it means to be Black is different for Black women and girls because of what it means to also be female.

(Intra)Cultural Support

(Intra)cultural support is an extension of (intra)cultural trust. Among Black people, (intra)cultural support functions with the needs of the victim being as important as the needs of the entire Black community. As such, Black people support the victim in the aftermath of cultural betrayal sexual trauma, including in the tensions created by inequality, such as the need to protect the Black community from discriminatory systems like the police and the criminal (in)justice system (e.g., Muller, 2021; Page & Soss, 2021; Rucker & Richeson, 2021). For Black women and girl survivors of cultural betrayal sexual trauma, examples of (intra)cultural support include another Black person telling them they are not responsible for protecting those who victimized them. Furthermore, within the context of (intra)cultural support, there can be a discussion about the pros and cons of disclosing the abuse to formal sources, including those, such as police and clinicians, who have been and currently are discriminatory against Black people (e.g., Gómez, 2019b). The CBMI-BAYA (Gómez & Johnson, 2022) combines (intra)cultural pressure and (intra)cultural support into one questionnaire for participants (see CBMI-BAYA for the (Intra)Cultural Pressure and Support Questionnaire, in Gómez & Johnson, 2022).

Outcomes

CBTT predicts two classes of cultural betrayal trauma sequelae: abuse outcomes and cultural outcomes. Abuse outcomes are so named because they are typically studied in trauma research; they include mental, physical, and behavioral health outcomes, such as dissociation, physical illness, and suicidality, respectively. Stemming from the contextual nature of CBTT, cultural outcomes are identity based, cultural, and/or sociocultural in nature, and include internalized prejudice, (intra)cultural pressure, (intra)cultural mistrust (mistrust within the Black community and interpersonal mistrust of other Black people; Gómez & Gobin, 2022), and changes to (intra)cultural trust and/or racial identity.

As a new, unofficial staple in CBTT research, posttraumatic growth is emerging as a regularly measured outcome for Black women and girl survivors of cultural betrayal sexual trauma. Posttraumatic growth is intra- and interpersonal processes and behaviors that reflect wisdom, strength, and positivity that survivors engage in after victimization. Assessing healthy behaviors, interpersonal connection, supportiveness, activism, emotions, and spirituality, the inclusion of a measure of posttraumatic growth in CBTT research reflects a shift in scope (see CBMI-BAYA for the Posttraumatic Growth Questionnaire, in Gómez & Johnson, 2022). Namely, the majority of trauma research, including my own with CBTT, documents the harm of trauma by measuring deleterious and costly outcomes. This work is vital, as both the prevalence and impact of trauma remain high. However, these negative outcomes are only part of the aftermath of trauma and can inadvertently pathologize survivors by solely highlighting negatives.

Therefore, posttraumatic growth is necessary to examine in research with survivors for at least two reasons. The first is that posttraumatic growth exists (e.g., Gómez & Johnson, 2022), so its absence in research findings communicates an erroneous and inaccurate picture of lives following trauma. That erroneous state is at odds with goals for research to be approximations of the capital T "Truth," with those approximations reaching closer to the reality of lived experiences as the evidence base builds (Gómez, 2014). Second, understanding posttraumatic growth—and strengths in general (Hope & Spencer, 2017; Spencer et al., 1997)—can be used to develop and incorporate, in this case, Black women and girl survivors' strengths into the healing process—both within and outside of therapy. Put simply, when we are aware of them, we can leverage survivors' strengths for healing and growth.

CULTURAL BETRAYAL TRAUMA THEORY: THE EMPIRICAL EVIDENCE

In addition to providing a critical race, Black feminist understanding of the impact of abuse, CBTT makes 10 postulates, or predictions, that can guide scientific empirical research through identifying testable hypotheses (see Exhibit 4.1). These postulates are organized as follows: *premises* (inequality and marginalization, (intra)cultural trust, and within-group variation), *prevalence* (common cultural betrayal), *counterhypotheses* (cultural betrayal vs.

EXHIBIT 4.1. CBTT Postulates

Premises

1. Inequality and marginalization: Cultural betrayal can exist only within marginalized populations due to inequality, with increased structural and/or interpersonal discrimination exacerbating the impact of cultural betrayal.
2. (Intra)cultural trust: (Intra)cultural trust creates a vulnerability that exacerbates the harm of cultural betrayal trauma.
3. Within-group variation: Within-group variation in prevalence, sequelae, and healing exists and should be examined.

Prevalence

4. Common cultural betrayal: Perpetrators of trauma are more likely to be within-group.

Counterhypotheses

5. Cultural betrayal versus between-group trauma: With trauma and other harms, within-group victimization explains additional variance in outcomes—above and beyond that of between-group victimization.
6. Cultural betrayal versus high betrayal[a]: With trauma and other harms, within-group victimization explains additional variance in outcomes—above and beyond that of high betrayal trauma victimization.
7. Cultural betrayal and high betrayal[a]: With trauma and other harms, within-group victimization together with high betrayal victimization explains additional variance in outcomes—above and beyond that of between-group and medium betrayal[a] victimization.

Outcomes

8. Abuse outcomes: Cultural betrayal trauma predicts mental, behavioral, and physical health outcomes, including dissociation, suicidality, and cardiovascular disease indicators.
9. Cultural outcomes: Cultural betrayal trauma predicts cultural outcomes, including internalized prejudice, (intra)cultural pressure, (intra)cultural mistrust, and changes to marginalized identification (e.g., changes to centrality of racial identity).
10. Abuse outcomes and cultural outcomes: Abuse outcomes are related to cultural outcomes, such as dissociation being related to (intra)cultural pressure.

[a]*Betrayal Trauma: The Logic of Forgetting Childhood Abuse*, by J. J. Freyd, 1996, Harvard University Press.

between-group trauma, cultural betrayal vs. high betrayal, and cultural betrayal and high betrayal), and *outcomes* (abuse outcomes, cultural outcomes, and abuse and cultural outcomes).

The postulates related to *premises* state that cultural betrayal occurs within the context of marginalization—and thus is relevant for only marginalized groups—with (intra)cultural trust being important and within-group variation being expected. As such, CBTT should not be used to understand dominant or majority populations regarding within-group violence; put plainly, within-group violence between White people—with Whiteness as the shared group status—should not be examined through the lens of CBTT. However, CBTT can be researched among White persons with shared marginalized status (e.g., lesbians), with the cultural betrayal related to sexual minority status and not race. The postulate for *common cultural betrayal* indicates that cultural betrayal trauma will be more common than between-group trauma. The *counterhypotheses* of the postulates probe research questions that attempt to falsify the theory: *Instead of cultural betrayal, could the findings be explained by X?* These counterhypotheses examine the unique and conjunctive impact of cultural betrayal compared with between-group, high betrayal, and medium betrayal trauma (e.g., Freyd, 1996). Finally, the postulates related to *outcomes* include abuse and cultural classes of outcomes, as well as their relations with one another.

Through the research generated by these postulates, CBTT can be appraised based on the state of the evidence within and across populations as relates to supporting or failing to support each postulate. Even though the postulates are framed around behavioral and psychological phenomena, it is important to remember that people are at the center of the theory. This means CBTT research can be undertaken with different marginalized populations, provided such research is culturally responsible, with findings generalized only as appropriate within and across groups. Therefore, in the next two subsections, I review the literature first across diverse marginalized populations that provide general evidence for CBTT and then that specifically within Black populations in the United States.

General Evidence for CBTT Across Diverse Marginalized Populations

Organized by the categories of the postulates in the previous subsection, there is promising research in support of CBTT across diverse marginalized young adult populations (see Table 4.1). Regarding the first postulate, *inequality and marginalization* under *premises*, Gómez and Freyd (2018) found that the association between within-group sexual violence and mental health outcomes—total trauma symptoms, depression, sexual abuse sequelae, sleep disturbance, and sexual problems—was stronger for young adults with minority status based on ethnicity, sexual orientation, religion, and nationality compared with their majority counterparts. These findings suggest that the increased harm of cultural betrayal is specific to marginalized populations. There is not yet research on the exacerbating nature of increased structural and/or interpersonal discrimination on the impact of cultural betrayal.

Additionally, under *premises*, there is evidence for the second and third postulates regarding *(intra)cultural trust* and *within-group variation*. In the same marginalized young adult sample from Gómez and Freyd (2018), Gómez

TABLE 4.1. Postulates of Cultural Betrayal Trauma Theory

Postulates	Evidence	Type of Harm	For Whom
Premises			
1. Inequality and marginalization	Yes, ?	Sexual trauma	Black young women; diverse marginalized YA
2. (Intra)cultural trust	Yes	Sexual trauma	Black young women; diverse marginalized YA
3. Within-group variation	Yes, in progress	Sexual trauma; witness/experience physical, sexual, verbal trauma, sexual harassment, sex trafficking, police violence, discrimination	Black young women (yes); Black American YA (in progress); diverse marginalized YA (yes); Desi American YA (in progress)
Prevalence			
4. Common cultural betrayal	Yes, no	Campus sexual violence	Black young women (yes); YA of color (no)
Counterhypotheses			
5. Cultural betrayal versus between-group betrayal	Yes, no	Physical, sexual, verbal trauma (yes); internal discrimination (yes); sexual harassment (no)	Black young women (yes, no); diverse marginalized YA (yes); YA of color (yes); AAPI YA (yes); Black and Latino/a/x YA (yes)
6. Cultural betrayal versus high betrayal[a]	Yes	Sexual trauma; physical, sexual, verbal trauma	YA of color; diverse marginalized YA
7. Cultural betrayal and high betrayal[a]	Yes, no	Physical, sexual, verbal trauma (yes, no); witness/experience physical, sexual, verbal trauma, sexual harassment, sex trafficking, police violence, discrimination (no)	YA of color (yes, no); Latina/o/x YA (no)

(continues)

TABLE 4.1. Postulates of Cultural Betrayal Trauma Theory (*Continued*)

Postulates	Evidence	Type of Harm	For Whom
Outcomes			
8. Abuse outcomes	Yes, no	Physical, sexual, verbal trauma (yes, no); witness/experience physical, sexual, verbal trauma (yes), sexual harassment (no), sex trafficking (yes), police violence (yes), discrimination (yes)	Diverse marginalized YA (yes); YA of color (yes); AAPI YA (yes); Black and Latino/a/x YA (yes); Black young women (yes, no)
9. Cultural outcomes	Yes	Physical, sexual, verbal trauma	Black young women; YA of color; young women of color
10. Abuse outcomes and cultural outcomes	Yes	Physical, sexual, verbal trauma	Black YA; young women of color

Note. YA = young adults; AAPI = Asian American/Pacific Islander. [a]*Betrayal Trauma: The Logic of Forgetting Childhood Abuse*, by J. J. Freyd, 1996, Harvard University Press.

(2021f) found that cultural betrayal sexual trauma was associated with clinically significant levels of PTSD symptoms for only those survivors who endorsed (intra)cultural trust. The results provide evidence for the importance of (intra) trust on the impact of cultural betrayal sexual trauma, while introducing (intra) cultural trust as a factor that can contribute to within-group differences in outcomes. More direct ways to examine within-group differences come from the CBMI-BAYA (Gómez & Johnson, 2022), as well as the CBMI for Desi/South Asian Young Adults (CBMI-DSAYA; Jilani et al., 2022).

For *common cultural betrayal*, Gómez (2022e) found that there was a higher percentage of campus sexual violence perpetrated by between-group perpetrators (12.2%) compared with within-group perpetrators (7.2%) for college men and women of color. These findings are contrasted with the literature that shows that perpetrators of sexual abuse are more likely to be of the same racial group as the victims (e.g., Bryant-Davis et al., 2009). It is possible that this finding relates to the differential context of a predominantly White university compared with violence occurring within the community (Gómez, 2022e).

There is a relatively large amount of research providing evidence for CBTT when testing *counterhypotheses*. This includes support for the fifth postulate, showing that cultural betrayal in trauma predicts outcomes above and beyond that of between-group trauma for mental health outcomes (Gómez, 2017, 2019e, 2019i, 2021c, 2021d, 2021f) and cultural outcomes, such as internalized prejudice (Gómez, 2019j) and (intra)cultural pressure (Gómez, 2019e), across Asian/Asian American/Pacific Islander (Gómez, 2017), Latina/o (Gómez, 2021d; Howard Valdivia et al., 2022), and of color (Gómez, 2019e, 2019i, 2021c) young adults. Additionally, among Black and Latina/o/x college students, Durkee and Gómez (2022) found that cultural betrayal in internal discrimination—specifically, being accused of acting White—was associated with depression and anxiety symptoms when controlling for White-perpetrated accusations of acting White. This work suggests that cultural betrayal is an additional traumatic dimension of harm.

Similar support from fewer studies has been found for Postulate 6 regarding high betrayal trauma (e.g., Freyd, 1996). Specifically, when controlling for both between-group trauma and high betrayal trauma (e.g., Freyd, 1996), cultural betrayal trauma predicts mental health outcomes, such as dissociation, hallucinations, and symptoms of PTSD, among young adults of color (Gómez, 2019i, 2021c) and diverse marginalized young adults (Gómez, 2021f). This research suggests that cultural betrayal in trauma is a harm distinct from that of the perpetrator being someone close, trusted, and/or depended upon.

There is mixed evidence for CBTT's last *counterhypothesis*, Postulate 7. In a sample of young adults of color, Gómez (2021c) found that cultural betrayal trauma with high betrayal predicted symptoms of PTSD while controlling for between-group trauma and cultural betrayal trauma with medium betrayal. However, in this same model, cultural betrayal trauma with medium betrayal also predicted this mental health outcome. Moreover, Howard Valdivia and colleagues (2022) found that cultural betrayal trauma predicted mental health when incidents of high betrayal trauma were low among Latina/o/x young adults. These findings do provide support for the impact of cultural betrayal in trauma on mental health, though are mixed regarding the conjunctive impact of both cultural betrayal and high betrayal in trauma.

The last set of postulates for CBTT relates to *outcomes*. There is much evidence showing that cultural betrayal trauma is associated with *abuse outcomes* (Postulate 8) in various marginalized young adult populations (Gómez, 2017, 2019e, 2019i, 2021c, 2021d, 2021f; Gómez & Freyd, 2018; Howard Valdivia et al., 2022). Additionally, research shows that cultural betrayal trauma is associated with *cultural outcomes* (Postulate 9) in young women of color (Gómez, 2019e) and young adults of color (Gómez, 2019j). Finally, one study with young women of color shows the link between *abuse and cultural outcomes* (Postulate 10)—specifically the association between (intra)cultural pressure and dissociation and symptoms of PTSD (Gómez, 2019e). Taken together, the general evidence across diverse young adult populations is largely in support of CBTT.

Quantitative Evidence Within Black Populations

With the theoretical work coming from a Black feminist perspective (Gómez & Gobin, 2020a), the CBTT research across diverse marginalized young adults complements that done within Black populations. As previously mentioned, the CBMI-BAYA (Gómez & Johnson, 2022) provides a methodological avenue for not only testing CBTT but also furthering postulate three under *premises* through examining within-group variation. Currently, evidence within Black populations is mixed for CBTT. Specifically for Postulate 5, cultural betrayal sexual harassment did not predict any mental health outcomes when controlling for between-group harassment among Black college women (Gómez, 2022a). This may be due to racialized sexual harassment (Buchanan & Ormerod, 2002; Woods et al., 2009) and the co-occurrence of racial and sexual harassment (Buchanan & Fitzgerald, 2008) of White male–perpetrated between-group harassment. Conversely, there is evidence for *outcomes* among Black young adults. Specifically, Gómez (2019c) shows that cultural betrayal trauma is associated with symptoms of PTSD (Postulate 8), while (intra) cultural pressure is linked with dissociation (Postulate 10) among Black college students at a predominantly White university. Finally, I have two studies in preparation where I examine the roles of (intra)cultural trust, (intra)cultural pressure, and (intra)cultural support on Black young women survivors' healing (Gómez, n.d.-a, n.d.-b).

Given its contextual nature related to inequality, understanding CBTT necessarily requires understanding White people's perceptions of cultural betrayal sexual trauma. Using an experimental design, we found evidence of White young people's prejudice against Black young men and women within an acquaintance rape vignette (McDaniel et al., 2022). These findings suggest that (intra)cultural pressure to protect the Black community may result from this veracious prejudice. Thus, structural implications include intervening both on White people's prejudice and their ability to activate their prejudice into discrimination (e.g., police, judges).

Quantitative work in progress that can further examine all postulates (for more details, see Gómez, n.d.-b) includes the following: (a) ENRICH, the Experimental Study of Violence and Race in High School (principal investigator: Jennifer M. Gómez; experimental vignette design: Breanne Helmers and Jennifer M. Gómez); (b) SUID Heal, the Study on Suicidality, Disclosure, and Healing (principal investigator: Jennifer M. Gómez); and (c) CARA, the Cardiovascular Disease and Cultural Betrayal Trauma in Black Middle Age and Older Adults Study (principal investigators: Jennifer M. Gómez and Samuele Zilioli).

Qualitative Evidence Within Black Populations

> As sick as it sounds, it will always feel worse than the trauma I've faced from non-black people because it comes with that added "betrayal" component. (Black young woman survivor of cultural betrayal sexual trauma, as described in Gómez & Gobin, 2022, p. 11)

The first qualitative investigation of CBTT comes from SUID Heal. In this study (Gómez & Gobin, 2022), we asked Black young women survivors of cultural betrayal sexual trauma for their thoughts on the theory itself. Following completing the quantitative portion of the study, participants ($N = 37$) read the following:

> The current research study uses cultural betrayal trauma theory (CBTT) by Principal Investigator Jennifer M. Gómez to better understand Black young adults' experiences in the world. According to CBTT, inequality, such as racism, means that violence that happens within our communities has a *cultural betrayal* that can further impact survivors' mental health. What are your thoughts on cultural betrayal potentially being a harmful part of violence within our communities?

Just under 75% of Black young women survivors expressed agreement with CBTT in some form or fashion, with themes related to cultural betrayal trauma's harms, outcomes, community, and healing. In line with cultural betrayal trauma being a community-oriented harm, over 50% of Black young women survivors spontaneously demonstrated a community orientation in their responses. Taken together, this study provides support for all *premises* and *prevalence* postulates, as well as the *counterhypothesis* of *cultural betrayal versus between-group betrayal* (Postulate 5) and *outcomes* postulates of *abuse outcomes* (Postulate 8) and *cultural outcomes* (Postulate 9).

WHAT THIS CAN ACTUALLY LOOK LIKE

> This sense of isolation compounds efforts to politicize sexual violence within communities of color and permits the deadly silence surrounding these issues. (Kimberlé Crenshaw, 1991, p. 1282)

Examples of cultural betrayal sexual trauma as detailed in this chapter are numerous (e.g., Feminist Campus Team, 2017; Gómez, 2016)—with a notable example being to-be-confirmed Supreme Court Justice Clarence Thomas's (cultural betrayal) sexual harassment of Anita Hill (Gómez & Gobin, 2020a; A. Hill, 1997, 2021). In the hypothetical vignette that follows (Gómez, 2015b), I describe a cultural betrayal sexual trauma endured by a Black female college student. The context of racism and (intra)cultural trust is implied as the cultural betrayal sexual trauma takes place during a Black fraternity party at a predominantly White university. Outcomes are both abuse and cultural in nature. In this brief vignette, I highlight the inherent complexity in such sexual abuse: a complexity that CBTT readily incorporates.

> A Black American woman attends a party hosted by a Black American fraternity that has been a source of emotional support for her at the predominantly White university she attends. At this party, she is raped by a presumed Black American male party-goer. Following the cultural betrayal trauma, this woman experiences symptoms of PTSD—hypervigilance around Black American men of the same build and complexion as the perpetrator. This heightened fear also contributes to internalized racism, as she thinks, "Maybe Black people really are violent and criminal." (Jennifer M. Gómez, 2015b, p. 41)

The above example illustrates the conundrum central to cultural betrayal trauma. This Black female college student is stuck in an isolating void between a university via oppression and the Black community via cultural betrayal trauma (for illustration through dance, see Gómez & Johnson-Freyd, 2015). Chapters 5 and 6 detail how clinicians and members of the Black community can support, uplift, and cocreate healing with Black women and girl survivors of cultural betrayal sexual trauma. Moreover, Chapter 7 focuses on large-scale structural change through institutional courage (e.g., Freyd, 2014b). Therefore, cultural betrayal sexual trauma does not have to be the end for Black women and girls. Instead, we together can heal through formal and informal strategies, while working to disrupt the world that allows such oppression and abuse in the first place.

FUTURE DIRECTIONS

> A critique of any theoretical system is not an examination of its flaws and imperfections. It is not a set of criticisms designed to make the system better. It is an analysis that focuses on the grounds of the system's possibility. The critique reads backwards from what seems natural, obvious, self-evident, or universal in order to show that these things have their history, their reasons for being the way they are, their effects on what follows from them and that the starting point is not a (natural) given but a (cultural) construct, usually blind to itself. (Joan Wallach Scott, 2005, p. xv)

As a single theoretical framework, CBTT is predicated on my assumptions, worldview, and understanding, which incorporates those of prior research, scholarship, and activism. That is not to say that CBTT is an academic object that serves as an extension of me. However, it is to alert that, as is true of all work, CBTT—the theory and related research—is both expanded and restricted based on my own standpoint (e.g., Collins, 1991/2000). As such, a starting place for identifying future directions is to examine those assumptions that have guided my research questions and my interpretation of findings. First, in line with recommendations for racial inequalities research (Hicken et al., 2018), CBTT is situated within the reality that structural racism and intersectional oppression exist, with research questions stemming from that reality. Moreover, underlying assumptions include a nonpathologizing frame in which "pathology is in the violence and the society/culture, not the person victimized; discrimination is real and impacts people; strong minority identity + ingroup solidarity is important, positive, and meaningful" (Gómez, 2020a, p. 2). Ways that CBTT theoretical and empirical research moves the needle toward equality include "speaking truth to power; centralizing inequality and its myriad impacts; legitimizing trauma and inequality as real & impactful; contextually . . . and culturally . . . congruent framework for independent researchers to test and hone culturally specific constructs" (Gómez, 2020a, p. 1). There are additionally ways that CBTT can re-instantiate the status quo of inequality, including engaging in "essentialism; homogenizing diverse marginalized groups and individuals; promoting a singular perspective of inequality & trauma" (Gómez, 2020a, p. 1).

With the above in mind, I detail some future directions that can build on the current state of the evidence regarding antiracist, Black feminist, and intersectional approaches and theoretical and methodological next steps. As such, I contribute CBTT with the desire for others to expand what we know about the impact of abuse in the context of inequality through theoretical and/or empirical uptake of CBTT and/or CBTT sparking additional disparate directions for understanding and healing from such oppression and abuse. In doing so, my hope is that the below recommendations serve as a humble guide by which independent researchers can incorporate their own standpoints, worldviews, and methodological leanings in ways that benefit the diverse marginalized populations we come from, collaborate with, and are responsible to.

Antiracist Approaches

> I talked to Derrick Bell. . . . He told me, "Write a lot. Whatever you write will be highly objectionable to a lot of people, but if you write enough of it, they probably can't derail your career." (Imani Perry, 2019, as cited in Arjini, 2019)

It took 5 years of rejections before the first peer-reviewed manuscript in CBTT was published (Gómez, 2017). This delayed trajectory serves as a single case study of the vast systemic biases and epistemic oppression (e.g., Buchanan et al., 2021; Dotson, 2012, 2014; Teo, 2008) in the peer review process (e.g., Gómez, 2022d; Greco et al., 2016; D. D. King et al., 2022) and a general devaluation of research by and with marginalized people (e.g., Buchanan et al., 2021; Buchanan & Wiklund, 2021; Guthrie, 2004). In that time and since, I wrote a lot for both peer-reviewed and non-peer-reviewed outlets, which has resulted in a relatively prolific body of research.

With that basis under my belt, clear and deliberate antiracist future CBTT research is warranted. From Buchanan and colleagues (2021), some antiracist steps to implement in CBTT research are as follows: conducting research in diverse marginalized populations (e.g., within Black urban and rural communities, community colleges, historically Black colleges or universities (HBCUs), Black teens and elders through bidirectionally beneficial community partnerships, and middle-aged Black women); using strength-based approaches (e.g., examining posttraumatic growth using the CBMI-BAYA; Gómez & Johnson, 2022); using Black feminist positionality and reflexivity (e.g., Collins, 1991/2000; Hamilton, 2020; Milner, 2007) throughout the research process, including within research teams, during research design, and in shared publications and presentations as comfortable and safe for the authors; and further using system-centered language that centralizes racism as a system of oppression. Moreover, racial equity should be explicitly omnipresent in all stages of the research process—from the composition of the research team to the early stages of research design and to the dissemination of the findings (Chatterjee et al., 2022; Hattery et al., 2022).

Intersectional Approaches

> Attention to power helps us see how systems of domination are operating even in the absence of obvious disparities. (Patrick Grzanka, 2020a, p. 255)

Cole (2009) and Grzanka (2020a) provided six questions for grounding psychological research within intersectional frameworks (for additional examples, see MOSAIC framework, in Hall et al., 2019; and Matsuzaka et al., 2022). Cole's (2009) questions are as follows: Who is included in this category? What role does inequality play? And where are there similarities? These questions necessitate truly interrogating who the population of interest is, as well as the systems of oppression that serve to exclude prospective members of that population. This means that in a study with Black women and girls, we should deliberately define who those people are (e.g., cisgender), while interrogating the system of transphobia that has erased Black trans*women and girls. Next steps would be to define and redefine the populations, including designing research under critical stances of various interlocking oppressions for Black women and girls beyond racism and sexism. This process can serve to place participants and their experiences within historical and cultural contexts (e.g., transphobia within and outside of the Black community), while better understanding within-group variation (e.g., Leath, Quiles, et al., 2022; Volpe et al., 2022) in the prevalence, meaning making, and outcomes of cultural betrayal sexual trauma. By responsibly comparing findings across nested groups (e.g., diverse women of color; Black and Indigenous peoples), sites of potential coalition building can occur (Cole, 2009; Moradi & Grzanka, 2017).

Grzanka (2020a) built on Cole's (2009) questions with three additional ones: How can I address constructs and systems, not just identities? How is social power operating in this situation? And what role can psychologists play in addressing this social problem? For CBTT, systems are noticeably absent in the extant research. While there is some work that labels systemic oppression (e.g., Gómez & Gobin, 2020a), the vast majority of the work has used identities as proxies for oppression (e.g., race as a proxy for racism; e.g., McDaniel et al., 2022) while amalgamating diverse populations under a single paradigm of inequality (e.g., racism across diverse people of color; e.g., Gómez, 2021c). This omission has resulted in a lack of clarity of whom the research should be generalized to as well as an absence of interrogating how social power is operating in relationships of trauma, abuse, and violence.

For instance, how cultural betrayal is operating within sexual abuse depends on whom the victim and perpetrator are in relation to each other and society. An adult male perpetrator may have power over a female child due to the age difference, unidirectional relational dependency from child to adult, sexism, sexualization, and more. Different in important ways would be a sexually violent adolescent romantic relationship between a first-year boy perpetrator and a fourth-year girl survivor. Further important is work with middle-aged adults and elders who spent their formative years in different instantiations of inequality and cultural understanding of sexual abuse. These absences of diversity in the research fundamentally limit what is currently known about cultural betrayal. Therefore, deliberate attention should be given to identifying and examining these differential contexts in which cultural betrayal sexual trauma occurs.

Importantly, the research must serve our vision of ultimately dismantling inequalities (e.g., Cole, 2009; Crenshaw, 1991; Grzanka, 2020a; current book). While I will continue to engage in public scholarship (e.g., Gómez, 2019i), all work—from myself and independent researchers—should be systematically shared with Black communities (e.g., Gómez & Partridge, 2022). This can transform CBTT into a critical theory that is dedicated to the praxis of social justice, by definition (Collins, 1991/2000). As such, this work can be evaluated based on its community engagement and social impact, in addition to its scholarly reach (Eaton et al., 2021; Grzanka & Cole, 2021; Moradi & Grzanka, 2017; Neville et al., 2021).

Black Feminist Critical Praxis

> One key role for Black women intellectuals is to ask the right questions and investigate all dimensions of a Black women's standpoint with and for African-American women. . . . The . . . taken-for-granted knowledge shared by African-American women . . . constitutes a first and most fundamental knowledge. . . . Experts or specialists who participate in and emerge from a group produce a second, more specialized type of knowledge. (Patricia Hill Collins, 1991/2000, p. 30)

Black feminist critical praxis includes identifying where the foundation for the study comes from: scholarly literature versus marginalized community (DeBlaere et al., 2010; Lewis & Grzanka, 2016; Moradi & Grzanka, 2017). For CBTT research, other marginalized scholars, and myself, the distinction between *literature* and *marginalized community* is not always a clear one. Namely, as the creator of CBTT, I am part of multiple marginalized communities, as are many of the scholars on whom my work is built. Complicating matters is that I have been educated and currently work within a White supremacist educational system. Additionally, of course, neither I nor other marginalized scholars can be representative of all the diverse constituents within intersecting marginalized communities.

A noticeable example of my own lack of representativeness is the exclusion of class oppression and capitalism (Rucks-Ahidiana, 2021) within CBTT theoretical and empirical research. Furthermore, in 10 years, no one has ever inquired about the impact of classism in reference to CBTT, which can likely be explained by the hegemonic, upper-class systems within which CBTT and I predominantly operate. This absence is particularly glaring given the importance of classism and racial capitalism (e.g., Leroy & Jenkins, 2021) as a systemic oppression that interlocks with other oppressions against Black and other women of color (e.g., Anzaldúa & Moraga, 1981; Bozarth et al., 2020; Collins, 1991/2000; Combahee River Collective, 1977, as cited in K. Taylor, 2017). Therefore, for us, the interrogation of precisely where the work is building from perhaps needs to be deeper and more nuanced than that of a White researcher who wants to work with Black populations.

Moreover, this social justice frame happens within the research design itself, in which engaging intersectionality as "a comprehensive methodological framework for conceptualizing and evaluating all stages of the research process—including the shape, content, goals, and imagined outcomes of the project" (Moradi & Grzanka, 2017, p. 508). As such, there is a symbiotic and recursive process and relationship between social justice research with CBTT and activism (Moradi & Grzanka, 2017). With oppression and resistance being coconstitutive—known as the *dialectical relationship of Black feminist thought* (Collins, 1991/2000)—any research that documents intersectional oppression and its instantiations is making meaning out of the resistance that battles against such oppression. In CBTT, this dialectic has only newly emerged with the addition of posttraumatic growth into research (e.g., Gómez & Johnson, 2022). Even still, that dialectic is currently underrealized and underappreciated in this work, thus providing open space for future work to meaningfully engage within this dialectic for Black women and girls.

For future researchers of CBTT, including myself, this symbiotic relationship between social justice research and activism can better align with our sustained and desperate need for change (Bryant-Davis & Moore-Lobban, 2020; Campbell, 2009; Cho et al., 2013; Fine & Torre, 2019; Neville et al., 2021). As outsiders-within (Collins, 1991/2000), the aforementioned future directions engage with the multifaceted responsibility placed on Black feminist scholars: (a) connection with and approval of the self, one's lived experiences, and ordinary people; (b) acceptance by the community of Black women scholars; and (c) preparation to confront (and resist) White male, Eurocentric epistemological requirements (Collins, 1991/2000). Thus, our challenge is to embark on CBTT research through the lenses of paradigm shifts in theory, methodology, and epistemology.

Theoretical and Methodological Next Steps

> The criteria for the methodological adequacy of positivism illustrate the epistemological standards that Black women scholars have to satisfy in legitimating Black feminist thought using a Eurocentric masculinist epistemology. (Patricia Hill Collins, 1991/2000, p. 205)

Though scientific in nature, CBTT is fundamentally a critical race and Black feminist theory. That dialectical landscape provides a conundrum for its methodology. To date, my collaborators and I have scientifically tested CBTT using empirical quantitative methods, which have resulted in finding support for the theory. More recent work (Gómez & Gobin, 2022) has deliberately used Black feminist tenets of dialogue and connectedness and the ethic of caring (Collins, 1991/2000) to feature the wisdom of young Black women survivors in this work. Therefore, while the methodological directions I delineate follow naturally from the current theoretical puzzles within CBTT, the epistemological underpinnings of such methodologies should be chosen based on if and how they match with CBTT's cultural assumptions and underlying premises.

That said, two conceptualizations of cultural betrayal sexual trauma as detailed in the current book need further theorizing. As currently conceptualized, cultural betrayal sexual trauma includes cultural betrayal as its focal point of harm. However, I theorize additional harm stems from the instantiated oppression of sexism within this male-perpetrated sexual abuse. Therefore, the harms that exist above and beyond that of the trauma itself, the perpetrator potentially being someone close, developmental period, and more are due to both cultural betrayal and sexist oppression. Examined this way differentially contextualizes this cultural betrayal sexual trauma from other cultural betrayal traumas within the Black community, including Black woman–perpetrated cultural betrayal sexual trauma against Black boys (see Gómez, cited in Anca, 2022). Through incorporating the matrix of domination—simultaneous interlocking oppressions (Collins, 1990)—and cultural betrayal, this differentiation can serve to better inform healing efforts within and outside of the therapy room.

Next, there is the need to incorporate structural intersectionality (e.g., Crenshaw, 1991) within our understanding of the oppressions on which cultural betrayal is predicated. Crenshaw (1991) proposed three potential permutations of discrimination against Black women: that which is similar to Black men and White women, that which has additive or multiplicative effects (e.g., double jeopardy), and that which is specific to Black women. In line with Cole (2009), CBTT research can examine similarities across groups (e.g., Black women and men), while interrogating unique oppression against Black women and girls. Here, such examination should not be limited by the psychological, theoretical need for parsimony, as parsimony's value expires when the truth of complexity is absent. Incorporating structural intersectionality (Crenshaw, 1991) further, multiple cultural betrayals within cultural betrayal sexual trauma need to be theorized and examined. These include cultural betrayals due to marginalization that is shared across several domains, such as between individuals who endure both racism and homophobia.

In addition to the CBMI-BAYA (Gómez & Johnson, 2022), methodological next steps need to be culturally relevant and appropriate, while engaging in antiracist and intersectional approaches (e.g., Buchanan et al., 2021; Moradi & Grzanka, 2017) that do not use White methods (Zuberi & Bonilla-Silva, 2021). This includes the abandonment of White comparison groups, as well as the underlying premise for which such work proliferates: that Black people have no inherent value and are only worth learning about as they relate to White people as the paragon of the human experience (Bowleg, 2021; Buchanan et al., 2021; Cole, 2009; Crenshaw, 1989; Guthrie, 2004; Henrich et al., 2010; Roberts & Mortenson, 2022). Useful approaches include those stemming from community-based participatory principles (e.g., Buchanan et al., 2021), latent profile/class analyses that examine systems (e.g., Moradi & Grzanka, 2017), and mixed methods and qualitative work that depend on dialogue and connectedness (e.g., Bowleg, 2008; Collins, 1991/2000; Grzanka & Moradi, 2021; Lyons et al., 2011; Watson-Singleton et al., 2021). Additionally, research should be applied to therapeutic settings, including examining the necessary parameters to responsibly implement screening of trauma exposure and costly outcomes akin to that used for substance use (Gómez & Partridge, 2022; see Ondersma et al., 2015, for a model of electronic screening and brief intervention regarding substance use).

Moreover, future research should address the exclusion of diverse populations of Black women and girls (see Chapter 3) by specifically grounding theoretical and empirical work with Black Latinas, Black trans*women, Black Muslim women and girls, Black immigrant women and girls, Black women and girls who are incarcerated (e.g., Quina et al., 2008), and other underrepresented Black female populations. In line with the first CBTT research (Gómez, 2017, 2019c, 2021d), there is value in including exploratory hypothesis testing in this new research (e.g., Rubin & Donkin, 2022). Within-group research is in line with calls that heterogeneity should be a starting point in research, not an afterthought or confounding variable to control for (Stronks et al., 2013; R. J. Taylor et al., 2021).

Finally, given the compounding nature of high betrayal (e.g., Freyd, 1996), family betrayal (Delker et al., 2018), institutional betrayal (Smith & Freyd, 2014), and cultural betrayal (current chapter/book; e.g., Gómez & Gobin, 2020a) within sexual trauma in the home, longitudinal work should examine both costly outcomes and healing for individuals through their childhood, adolescence, young adulthood, middle ages, and elder years. With CBTT being in relationship with social justice activism (e.g., Moradi & Grzanka, 2017), such research should be conducted in tandem with prevention efforts that ultimately eradicate child sexual abuse everywhere, including in the home.

SUMMARY BULLET POINTS

1. Theoretical and empirical research with cultural betrayal trauma theory (CBTT) occurs within the context of societal inequality and as such is vulnerable to being weaponized against the oppressed.

2. Through leveraging (intra)cultural trust and support, CBTT's vulnerability for weaponization occurs alongside its potential to (a) document racism, intersectional oppression, additional inequalities, cultural betrayal, abuse, and outcomes and (b) identify trauma-informed, culturally competent, and liberating avenues of healing within and outside of therapy while advocating for an equal and peaceful society.

3. Betrayal trauma theory and its empirical support suggest that abuse perpetrated by a person who is trusted and/or depended on includes a high betrayal that negatively affects outcomes.

4. Building from the intersectionality, sexual abuse against Black women and girls, and betrayal literatures, CBTT is a critical race, Black feminist, scientific theory that identifies cultural betrayal as a contributing factor to the harm of abuse within marginalized communities due to societal inequalities.

5. The tenets of CBTT include (intra)cultural trust, cultural betrayal, cultural betrayal trauma, (intra)cultural pressure, (intra)cultural support, abuse and cultural outcomes, and newly minted construct of (intra)cultural mistrust, while highlighting the importance of incorporating posttraumatic growth into CBTT research.

6. CBTT's 10 postulates fall under four categories: (a) premises: inequality and marginalization, (intra)cultural trust, and within-group variation; (b) prevalence: common cultural betrayal; (c) counterhypotheses: cultural betrayal versus between-group betrayal, cultural betrayal versus high betrayal, and cultural betrayal and high betrayal; and (d) outcomes: abuse outcomes, cultural outcomes, and abuse and cultural outcomes.

7. Across diverse marginalized populations and within Black populations, the burgeoning, foundational evidence for CBTT is strong.

8. CBTT can contribute to what is known about the impact of abuse in the context of inequality through theoretical or empirical uptake of CBTT and/or CBTT sparking additional directions for understanding and healing from such oppression and abuse.

9. Independent researchers should incorporate their own standpoints, worldviews, and methodological leanings in ways that benefit the diverse marginalized populations we come from, collaborate with, and are responsible to.

10. Humble guides for antiracist and intersectional theoretical/methodological approaches for CBTT research include multiple cultural betrayals; positionality; reflexivity; systems of oppression; community-based participatory principles; latent profile/class analyses; mixed methods, qualitative, and ethnographic work; and longitudinal research that incorporates multiple types of betrayal (e.g., high betrayal, family betrayal, institutional betrayal, cultural betrayal).

5

CULTURALLY COMPETENT TRAUMA THERAPY

Holistic Healing

CHAPTER AT A GLANCE

In this chapter, I focus on clinicians' therapeutic role in promoting holistic healing with Black women and girl survivors of cultural betrayal sexual trauma through (a) critically interrogating the veracity, function, and utility of the medical model; (b) detailing diverse outcomes of sexual abuse; (c) describing components of individual and structural cultural competency; (d) highlighting processes and practices for trauma therapy; (e) reviewing relational cultural theory and the liberation health framework as models for culturally competent trauma therapy; and (f) providing clinical case examples that personify clinicians' roles in accompanying clients on their healing journeys in culturally competent and trauma-informed ways that promote individual, interpersonal, and structural healing.

https://doi.org/10.1037/0000362-005
The Cultural Betrayal of Black Women and Girls: A Black Feminist Approach to Healing From Sexual Abuse, by J. M. Gómez
Copyright © 2023 by the American Psychological Association. All rights reserved.

Practitioners accompany POCI [people of Color and indigenous individuals] and bear witness to their pain, working with them to recognize systemic racial oppression and colonization thereby embracing resistance over maintaining the status quo.

—Bryana H. French et al., 2020, p. 22

Cultural betrayal trauma theory (CBTT; e.g., Gómez & Gobin, 2020a) starts from uncomfortable realities of racism (e.g., Mills, 1997), intersectionality (e.g., Crenshaw, 1989), and sexual abuse existing and affecting the lived experiences of Black women and girls. As such, CBTT implicitly interrogates the very systems that allow such violence and oppression to thrive—including in mental health care (Gómez, 2015d). That complexity means that in this chapter I am not responding to implicit questions, such as this: What do I do when a Black woman or girl survivor of cultural betrayal sexual trauma comes into my therapy room? Instead, I use this chapter to engender trauma-informed and culturally competent worldviews that lead to humble, critical thinking, reflected in questions such as these: How do I think, feel, and engage with a Black woman or girl client who lives in the context of intersectional oppression, cultural betrayal sexual trauma, and (intra)cultural pressure? Further, how do I decide what to do? How do I understand the context of inequality and abuse while not pathologizing my client through searching for only struggles and not strengths? How do I monitor myself continuously so that I do not intrapersonally, interpersonally, and/or structurally engage in violent silencing? How do I work with the cultural similarities I have with this client—as a Black woman versus a Black man versus a White person versus other people of color and Indigenous individuals from the same neighborhood, and so on? How do I not overreach in perceived similarity—or conversely, in attempting to bridge the cultural gap created by difference—thus tripping into stereotyping? What differential meaning could such an error have if I am also Black? Also a woman? Diametrically privileged?

In the current chapter, I open with critical visioning on problematizing the medical model and eliminating the White Read. Then, I provide a brief primer on understanding the role of the self as the clinician in working with Black women and girls as clients. Next, I interrogate the medical model, offer alternative conceptualizations of mental health, and detail diverse outcomes of trauma. I then explain individual and structural cultural competency and highlight processes and practices of trauma therapy. I review relational cultural theory (e.g., Miller, 1976) and the liberation health framework (e.g., Belkin Martinez, 2014) as therapeutic models for culturally competent trauma therapy. Finally, I detail what therapy can actually look like with clinical case examples from clients I have worked with as a student clinician. I close with a summary of the current chapter with takeaway messages.

CRITICAL VISIONING: REPLACING THE MEDICAL MODEL WHILE ABOLISHING THE WHITE READ

As is further discussed in this chapter, dominant clinical practice is framed around the medical model, including human distress conceptualized within discrete disorders (e.g., Burstow, 2005). Moreover, evidence-based treatments situate themselves within this medical model framework, as there are no evidence-based treatments for trauma or people themselves; there are simply evidence-based treatments for disorders (e.g., Gómez, Lewis, et al., 2016). Mainstream cultural adaptations promote attendance to culture and context within evidence-based treatments. However, other arguments criticize the premise of individual pathology entirely, while reconceptualizing human distress within the context of oppression and abuse.

Cultural Betrayal Trauma Theory Lens

> Healing means the creation of a whole being: with hurts, pains, wrongs, strengths, helplessness, vigor, fight, retreat, connection, and integrative and iterative reconnection to the self and others . . . healing is not only possible in the abstract sense, but is in fact a continuous ever-evolving lived experience that survivors . . . can give themselves. (Jennifer M. Gómez, Lewis, et al., 2016, p. 177; winner of the Richard P. Kluft Award for *Journal of Trauma & Dissociation* 2016 Best Article)

In addition to its critical race and Black feminist foundation, I created CBTT in the tradition of Freyd's (e.g., 1996) betrayal trauma theory, which is a nonpathologizing framework for understanding trauma-related memory, dissociation, and mental and physical health. In framing CBTT as nonpathologizing, by definition, the theory itself rejects any construction of mental health, including but not limited to that which is trauma related, which conceptualizes pathology within the victimized individual. Given that the medical model, and by extension, the fifth edition of the *Diagnostic and Statistical Manual of Mental Disorders* (*DSM-5*; American Psychiatric Association, 2013), carries an individualistic pathological stance, it does not fit with CBTT as a nonpathologizing framework. Furthermore, the medical model is at odds with CBTT as an explanatory framework that can aid in understanding cultural outcomes, such as internalized prejudice, in addition to mental, physical, and behavioral health. In doing so, CBTT centralizes the individual and their experiences within the larger context of inequality. As such, evidence-informed therapies, such as relational cultural therapy (e.g., Miller, 1976; Miller & Stiver, 1997; as discussed in Gómez, 2020e, and Gómez, Lewis, et al., 2016) and the liberation health framework (Belkin Martinez & Fleck-Henderson, 2014), that prioritize the collaborative therapeutic relationship while centralizing the client's context are much better equipped to effectively promote healing and wellness with Black women and girl survivors.

An example can help make the mismatch between the medical model and CBTT clearer. Several years ago, a senior clinical psychologist who is a White man met with me following a talk I gave on CBTT. He told me that CBTT made him feel as if he perhaps was missing something in his clinical work. He told me (paraphrased):

> Through CBTT, you are saying that even times when I thought the evidence-based treatment was effective for a Black child, let's say the PTSD was reduced, maybe treatment wasn't effective to the client or in reality. Because I was not assessing, incorporating, or tracking the harm of cultural betrayal or other outcomes like internalized prejudice. So, what CBTT provides me, as a practicing psychologist, are additional ways to understand potential harm of abuse while incorporating cultural competency into therapy.

His appraisal of CBTT augmenting understanding that is currently absent in dominant evidence-based treatments is an important one. I would say further that CBTT contributes to questioning the medical model foundation that those evidence-based treatments are built on in the first place.

The Tension and My Critical Visioning

> But I am not tragically colored. (Zora Neale Hurston, 1928/2015, p. 6)

The tension for Chapter 5 is that I am being interrupted by the White Read. The White Read is essentially an infiltrated appraisal of my thoughts when I am writing: What will They think? You can't say that. If you write that, they will disregard your whole book! As such, the White Read is an internalized bigot who rudely interrupts my train of thought while planting insecurity and promoting self-censorship. The White Read ultimately tells me, first, that I do not belong here and, second, if I am to exist, I can do so only if playing by Their rules.

A common White Read internal contribution for me is this: You can't be so radical in your approach because They won't understand it. With those words echoing in my head, I begin my critical visioning. I think, Who is the *They* who won't understand this? I remember that the White Read tells lies, as it presumes all the readers of this book are not just White but also defensive, ignorant racists—some of whom may be additionally well meaning but oppressively rejecting nonetheless. As such, the White Read provides an image of a homogenous White community while simultaneously promoting an acceptance of White person–perpetrated prejudice and discrimination as inherent, unchangeable by-products of Whiteness. It seems to me that our need for systemic change necessitates that we demand more from those at the top of the racial hierarchy (Mills, 1997).

Most important, I am fundamentally and deliberately not writing for a White Read audience. In fact, I instead choose to emancipate myself from "the business of keeping White people comfortable" (Bowleg, 2021, p. 244). Within the Black feminist tradition, in this book, I unapologetically center Black women and girls and our experiences, as well as approaches that can best understand and serve our diverse population. As a Black woman myself who grew up as a Black girl, I follow the Combahee River Collective's (as cited in K. Taylor, 2017) sentiment that we must privilege ourselves because our perspectives, our words, and our actions are worthy and valuable. Therefore, in not centering the *They*, I have instead designated primary space for our *Us*.

I, THE CLINICIAN, WITH BLACK WOMEN AND GIRLS AS CLIENTS

> Intersectional subordination need not be intentionally produced; in fact, it is frequently the consequence of the imposition of one burden that interacts with preexisting vulnerabilities to create yet another dimension of disempowerment. (Kimberlé Crenshaw, 1991, p. 1249)

I have chosen to devote a section to explicitly naming the humanity of clients and the fallibility of clinicians because I have witnessed and experienced how Black women and girls are discriminatorily treated both within and outside of therapy. Black women and girl clients who have experienced cultural betrayal sexual trauma are not abstract entities, but are human beings. As humans, we are not pathological, crazy, broken, damaged, dirty, disgusting, dumb, in need of repair, or beyond repair. As clinicians who are also human, it is therefore not our job to fix Black women and girls. Instead, these clients are providing us with the opportunity to be with them on this part of their life journey and share our skills and amplify theirs, while they rediscover and/or re-create their true selves: souls, spirits, psyches, personalities, wants, needs, hopes, and desires. In this cocreation, we as clinicians hold hope for these humans, while truly knowing their wisdom, their beauty, their strength, their courage, and their vulnerability—particularly in those times when all they can know of themselves are their own mistakes, their shame, their fear, their pain, and their toxic secrets. We, as clinicians, hold that they are already worthy. We further internalize that our work with them occurs alongside their own self-determination of their lives.

For Black clinicians who have learned to separate the Good Blacks (themselves) from the Black community as a whole, as well as for clinicians of other ethnicities in which anti-Blackness is a cultural feature (e.g., Hernández, 2022), the following is foundational: As a class of professionals, clinicians are no more superior than any other human beings living and learning in societies predicated on inequality. Though clinicians do have a responsibility in the context of therapy given the power differential, that responsibility is not synonymous with inherent goodness. Therefore, it would be a mistake to presume there is a world in which people can be easily separated into good and bad categories (Gómez, 2020d), with clinicians automatically landing in the good people box.

Moreover, unintentional intersectional oppression does not preclude clinicians from responsibility. Instead, it means that continuous, intentional identification of and opposition against intersectional oppression is a required part of the clinical enterprise. Such intersectional oppression can occur interpersonally within the therapeutic context, as well as structurally within the clinical setting. Moreover, such oppression affects Black women and girl clients outside of the therapy room. Therefore, therapeutic approaches must include attendance to how such forces are affecting our clients—and what we individually and in collaboration with our clients can do to combat such oppression.

THE MEDICAL MODEL: TIME TO ASK A DIFFERENT QUESTION

> The master's tools will never dismantle the master's house. They may allow us to temporarily beat him at his own game, but they will never enable us to bring about genuine change. (Audre Lorde, 1984, p. 112)

The fields of psychology and psychiatry have long histories of harm—including oppression, violence, and other human rights violations—against Black and other marginalized people (e.g., American Psychological Association Council of Representatives, 2021a; Carter et al., 2022; Gómez, Smith, et al., 2016; Guthrie, 1976; Hilliard, 1978; Hoffman et al., 2015; Sue, 1978). The medical model for psychological distress flourishes within the racism of these fields, while providing the argument for individualized mental health treatment. However, from the field of philosophy, the conclusion of an argument cannot be accepted based on false premises (M. Tshivhase & K. Vavova, personal communication, December 2, 2021). The medical model's relevant premises are as follows: (a) The medical model is a factual, acultural explanation of humans' psychological distress; (b) psychological distress is pathological; and (c) such pathology, like a broken bone (Gómez, Lewis et al., 2016), resides medically within the individual. Based on those premises, the conclusion is that individualized treatment in the forms of medication and therapy is warranted to correct the pathology—akin to fixing a broken bone—thus returning the individual to a prepathological baseline, if possible. Consequently, there are dominant treatment approaches that aim to fix the "broken bones" of posttraumatic stress disorder (PTSD), schizophrenia, depression, and other so-called disorders.

Challenges to the Medical Model's Premises

> Reclaiming the Black feminist intellectual tradition involves much more than developing Black feminist analyses using standard epistemological criteria. It also involves challenging the very definitions of intellectual discourse. (Patricia Hill Collins, 1991/2000, p. 15)

The medical model's premises are not beyond reproach. First, the medical model is a dominant White American conceptualization of humans' psychological distress (e.g., Burstow, 2005). Given that the medical model is its foundation, the *DSM-5* is necessarily a *cultural* document. Second, psychological distress is not by definition inappropriate or otherwise pathological. Plainly, people's natural responses, such as hypervigilance and depression to painful events like rape, make sense. Finally, psychological distress is distinct from a broken bone, as

> to have a broken bone means that previously there was a fully formed bone that was then broken, only to be healed in such a way that it functions as if previously unbroken. Yet with . . . trauma, what was broken was not a static entity but rather a dynamically evolving sense of self. As growth occurs relationally from birth, there are no fully formed, psychologically, and traumatically untouched selves to which people can return. (Gómez, Lewis, et al., 2016, pp. 176–177)

This does not mean healing is impossible. On the contrary, healing is a lifelong, multifaceted process that is not to be conceptualized as getting back what was lost or never had (Gómez, Lewis, et al., 2016). Importantly, a stance against the medical model is not a wanton disregard for human suffering (e.g., Szasz, 2011). Nor is it a mechanism to withhold aid, knowledge, relational connection, or resources. Instead, abandoning the medical model can be a liberating way of understanding the human condition that results in nonpathologizing approaches to working with people, including Black women and girl survivors.

Epistemic Injustice, Violence, and Oppression

> Because elite white men and their representatives control structures of knowledge validation, white male interests pervade the thematic content of traditional

scholarship. As a result, Black women's experiences . . . have been routinely distorted in or excluded from traditional academic discourse. . . . Black women have had to struggle against white male interpretations of the world in order to express a self-defined standpoint. (Patricia Hill Collins, 1991/2000, p. 201)

Knowledge validation processes (Collins, 1991/2000) in psychology are based on Eurocentric, White male epistemologies that include cultural assumptions often not shared in Black feminist circles. Consequently, epistemic injustice (e.g., Fricker, 2007), epistemic violence (e.g., Dotson, 2011), epistemic oppression (e.g., Collins, 2022; Dotson, 2014; Hoang, 2022), and the resulting discrimination against the subject as the "knower" have occluded many concerns of the medical model and related treatment from the dominant discourse. Epistemic injustice is a "distinctive class of wrongs, namely those in which someone is ingenuously downgraded and/or disadvantaged in respect to their status as an epistemic subject" (Fricker, 2017, p. 53). As such, epistemic injustice is similar to epistemic violence (Dotson, 2011) in which information from those already marginalized is degraded, disbelieved, or otherwise ignored, as such information is deemed unworthy. Finally, epistemic oppression excludes germane scholarship on a given topic due to the marginalization of the scholar producing the knowledge and/or the marginalized topic of inquiry, such as critical theories on systems of power and oppression (Dotson, 2014; for examples, see Gómez, 2022d, and Grollman, 2018).

Evidence Against the Medical Model

The fact that minority women suffer from the effects of multiple subordination, coupled with institutional expectations based on inappropriate nonintersectional contexts, shares and ultimately limits the opportunities for meaningful intervention on their behalf. Recognizing the failure to consider intersectional dynamics may go far toward explaining the high levels of failure, frustration, and burn-out experienced by counselors who attempt to meet the needs of minority women victims. (Kimberlé Crenshaw, 1991, p. 1251)

Many have argued that the premises and treatment conclusions of the medical model (e.g., Szasz, 1960, 1961, 2011), including reliance on pharmaceutical drugs (e.g., Mackler, 2008; Whitaker, 2010), are at best not relevant for all persons and at worst harmful, damaging, and oppressive to many individuals (e.g., Read & Moncrieff, 2022). These include, but are not limited to, long-standing arguments against individualized coping strategies for rape survivors (e.g., Fine, 1984) and marginalized peoples generally (e.g., Carpenter-Song et al., 2010); decontextualized understanding of psychological distress (e.g., Belkin Martinez, 2014); biological and organic explanations of trauma-related distress in lieu of environmental ones, such as conceptualizing trauma-related hallucinations as necessarily psychotic as opposed to dissociative in nature (e.g., Moskowitz, 2011); psychiatric intervention as useful for marginalized persons at all (e.g., Burstow, 2003, 2005); and the ableist underpinnings of the medical model in the United States, including the invocation of the perceived defective Black body (e.g., Ralph, 2012).

Additional work has discussed how profound psychological distress can be useful, not pathological, as it can provide insight into the structurally oppressive forces that harm disenfranchised Black women (Ralph, 2015; P. Williams, 1991). Moreover, there is a remarkable lack of evidence for so-called chemical imbalances in the brain existing and causing mental health difficulties (e.g., Lane, 2022; Mackler, 2008; Moncrieff et al., 2022; Whitaker, 2010). Last, we cannot forget the long history of how White people's medical pathologization of Black people has been used to promote systemic racist murder, such as the contemporary, pseudoscientific diagnosis of excited delirium syndrome that blames Black people who die from police killing them (Beliso-De Jesús, 2022; Obasogie, 2021).

According to the American Psychological Association (APA) Guideline Development Panel for the Treatment of PTSD in Adults (2017), the evidence for certain PTSD psychotherapies and pharmacological treatments is said to be "strong" (p. 83). Simultaneously, however, they find that evidence for effectiveness across racial, ethnic, and cultural groups; types of trauma; and clinical presentation (severity, acute vs. chronic, comorbidity—e.g., co-occurring substance use, suicidality) is all lacking, with remission (e.g., absence of symptoms) and client treatment preferences often unmeasured and unreported. Furthermore, such PTSD treatments have high dropout rates (e.g., 50%, Schnurr et al., 2022; see, for a review, American Psychological Association Guideline Development Panel for the Treatment of PTSD in Adults, 2017), indicating they are intolerable to many people for whom the treatment was ostensibly designed. Moreover, PTSD as conceptualized is far from the only potentially costly outcome of trauma (e.g., Gómez & Gobin, 2020a; Herman, 1997). Therefore, from false, or at least contested, premises of the medical model to underwhelming evidence for treatments under this model, as well as APA's stated commitment to antiracism (American Psychological Association Council of Representatives, 2021a, 2021b), it may be time to ask a question different than "What is so very wrong with these people?"

Asking a Different Question, Getting a Different Answer

With its aforementioned fallacies and limitations, it is pertinent to question whether the medical model is leading us to ask the wrong question. The medical model has a predetermined premise that the pathology sprouts from within the individual. That foregone conclusion then leads us to ask questions about what is wrong with the person, with our proposed solutions beginning and ending solely within the individual. In pioneering culturally relevant pedagogy, Gloria Ladson-Billings (2021) shifted the query from "What is wrong with those Black kids?" to "What is right with Black students? And what is happening in successful classrooms with Black students?" We can ask parallel questions in therapy: For Black women and girls who have experienced cultural betrayal sexual trauma, where is the origin and locus of the problem? When we ask that question, we find answers associated with sexist violence, racism, sexism, intersectional oppression, White supremacy, and more. We further align ourselves with strength-based, holistic, and social justice–oriented approaches to therapeutic healing with Black women and girls (e.g., Belkin Martinez & Fleck-Henderson, 2014; Bryant-Davis, 2005; Bryant-Davis & Comas-Díaz, 2016; Gómez, Lewis, et al., 2016; Miller, 1976).

However, we should not stop there. We must further suppose that there are so many things right with Black women and girls. It is up to us to find that rightness within ourselves and within them through deliberate rejection of a pathological, damage narrative (Tuck, 2009) that permeates dominant, and often internalized, conceptualizations of Black women and girls. As such, asking different questions not only facilitates different lines of inquiry but also leads to different solutions for holistic healing.

DIMENSIONS OF HARM AND HEALING

The medical model purports discreet outcomes for trauma, like PTSD. However, foundational feminist trauma work understands the potential downstream harm of interpersonal trauma—including cultural betrayal sexual trauma—being multifaceted. Herman (1997) referred to this multidimensional harm as the *disguised presentation of trauma*. Simply, the disguised presentation of trauma is the myriad of outcomes that have been empirically associated with trauma (e.g., Bryant, 2022; Herman, 1997; Gómez & Gobin, 2020a), such as dissociation, anxiety, depression, suicidality, and relationship difficulties, which can be present among survivors who are seeking therapy generally and not for trauma work specifically.

CBTT also delineates diverse outcomes, including cultural outcomes like internalized prejudice (e.g., Gómez, 2019j; Gómez & Gobin, 2022). Additionally, the Six Dimensions of Wellness model (Hettler, 1976) is a holistic framework in which the interconnectedness of disparate aspects of one's life becomes apparent. The dimensions are occupational, physical, social, intellectual, spiritual, and emotional. According to Hettler (1976), the Six Dimensions of Wellness model explains: how a person contributes to [their] environment and community, and how to build better living spaces and social networks; the enrichment of life through work, and its interconnectedness to living and playing; the development of belief systems, values, and creating a world-view; the benefits of regular physical activity, healthy eating habits, strength and vitality, as well as personal responsibility, self-care and when to seek medical attention; self-esteem, self-control, and determination as a sense of direction; creative and stimulating mental activities, and sharing your gifts with others. (p. 2)

Including art as special in influencing both feelings and knowledge (Davis, 1989), Bryant-Davis (2005) identified the following strategies for healing: arts and crafts, journaling/poetry, movement, drama/theater, music, nature, spirituality, social support, and activism. By design, these overlap with the posttraumatic growth questionnaire of the Cultural Betrayal Multidimensional Inventory for Black American Young Adults (CBMI-BAYA; Gómez & Johnson, 2022), which has subscales for healthy behaviors/activities, interpersonal connection, relational connection, activism, cognitions/emotions, and spirituality. Through using holistic and contextualized understandings of life and trauma, the opportunities for growth through multiple dimensions of healing are more relevant and impactful for Black women and girl survivors of cultural betrayal sexual trauma.

CULTURAL COMPETENCY

The internal locus of control and responsibility world view is most characteristic of western counseling approaches and assumptions. Cultural oppression occurs when this world view is blindly imposed upon the culturally different client. (Derald W. Sue, 1978, p. 419)

Cultural competency's value is in its omnipresence of therapy (for an example, see Tummala-Narra, 2016). Cultural competency in working with Black women and girl survivors of cultural betrayal sexual trauma includes cultural humility (see Bent-Goodley & Gómez, in press; Tervalon & Murray-García, 1998), cultural congruency (Bryant-Davis & Comas-Díaz, 2016), and liberation (J. C. Harris et al., 2021). Cultural competency is manifested throughout the current chapter, including in the dismantling of the medical model and the multifaceted dimensions of harm and healing, as well as in the below sections on processes in trauma therapy, cultural competency and trauma-informed theoretical orientations, and the clinical case examples toward the end of the chapter. Therefore, in the current section, I present a framework for individual cultural competency (Sue et al., 1992) followed by detailing structural cultural competency (American Psychological Association, 2017b; Grzanka, 2020a; Metzl & Hansen, 2014).

Individual Cultural Competency

In 1992, Sue and colleagues provided a conceptual framework for cross-cultural counseling competencies. Painfully, my own formal clinical training from 2011 to 2017 was not grounded within this or similar frameworks, though I attempted to teach myself and practice these concepts nonetheless (e.g., Gómez, 2020g). Sue and colleagues' (1992) full article, including Appendix A with proposed cultural competencies and objectives, is worth reviewing in depth. Here, I provide a snapshot of this important work. Sue et al. (1992) identified the following three competencies, with related attitudes and beliefs, knowledge, and skills: counselor awareness of own cultural values and biases, counselor awareness of client's worldview, and culturally appropriate intervention strategies.

I. Counselor awareness of own cultural values and biases

   A. Attitudes and beliefs: awareness "of how their own cultural backgrounds and experiences and attitudes, values, and biases influence psychological processes" (p. 485).

   B. Knowledge: possession of "knowledge about their social impact on others. They are knowledgeable about communication style differences, how their style may clash or foster the counseling process with . . . clients, and how to anticipate the impact it may have on others" (p. 485).

   C. Skills: continued engagement in "educational, consultative, and training experiences . . . seeking to understand themselves as racial and cultural beings and are actively seeking a nonracist identity" (p. 484).

II. Counselor awareness of client's worldview

   A. Attitudes and beliefs: willingness to "contrast their own beliefs and attitudes with those of . . . clients in a nonjudgmental fashion" (p. 485).

   B. Knowledge: understanding "about sociopolitical influences that impinge upon the life of racial and ethnic minorities" (p. 485).

   C. Skills: familiarity "with relevant research and latest findings regarding mental health of various racial and ethnic groups . . . and educational experiences that foster their knowledge, understanding, and . . . skills" (p. 485).

III. Culturally appropriate intervention strategies

   A. Attitudes and beliefs: respecting "clients' religious and/or spiritual beliefs and values, including attributions and taboos . . . that affect worldview, psychosocial functioning, and expressions of distress" (p. 485).

B. Knowledge: knowledge of "bias in assessment instruments . . . relevant discriminatory practices at the social and community level that may be affecting the psychological welfare of the population being served" (pp. 485–486).

C. Skills: ability to "exercise institutional intervention skills on behalf of their clients. They can help clients determine whether a 'problem' stems from racism or bias in others (the concept of healthy paranoia) so that clients do not inappropriately personalize problems" (p. 486).

Though these competencies are framed in terms of cross-cultural counseling—implicitly White clinicians with clients of color—I have found them useful in my own work with both culturally different and similar clients, as evidenced in the Power-Over Approach With Disrespect of Cultural Difference clinical case example in the What This Can Actually Look Like section of the current chapter. Importantly, these competencies are relevant for me in navigating my own power, privilege, oppression, and culture, as well as those of my clients. Finally, though client-perpetrated discrimination is rarely discussed in clinical training for cultural competency (for a discussion, see Moon & Sandage, 2019), I include a clinical case example of such in the What This Can Actually Look Like section of the current chapter.

Structural Cultural Competency

The APA (2017b) Multicultural Guidelines provide guidance on the understanding of the self as a cultural being, awareness of biases, the importance of context, and culturally congruent and strength-based approaches (e.g., Therapy for Black Girls, https://therapyforblackgirls.com/about/) in working with individuals. Guideline 5 speaks specifically to structural cultural competency, stating that

> psychologists aspire to recognize and understand historical and contemporary experiences with power, privilege, and oppression. As such, they seek to address institutional barriers and related inequities, disproportionalities, and disparities of law enforcement, administration of criminal justice, educational, mental health, and other systems as they seek to promote justice, human rights, and access to quality and equitable mental and behavioral health services. (p. 4)

As applied by Grzanka (2020a) to therapy, Metzl and Hansen (2014) proposed five principles of structural competency: (a) recognizing how structural and social forces shape clinical interactions and clinicians' perceptions and treatment of clients; (b) using literature across disciplines to understand how mental health and inequality are socially constructed (in line with recommendations by Gómez, 2022c); (c) reconceptualizing so-called cultural presentations in structural terms through understanding how both cultural dynamics and systemic cultural formations are predictors of health outcomes; (d) envisioning structural intervention that uses scientific expertise and institutional resources for systems-level change; and (e) developing structural humility: understanding the limitations of a single discipline (e.g., psychology) and one's own interpretation of a client's presenting problem in order to engage in more accurate and comprehensive perspectives on the client's lives. Through centralizing and expanding the question of what role inequality plays (Cole, 2009), structural cultural competency serves as a prime avenue for eliminating oppression in therapy (Sue, 1978).

PROCESSES AND PRACTICES IN TRAUMA THERAPY

> It is . . . easy to train the mind, more difficult to train the heart . . . the training . . . include[s] self-knowledge, thoughts, and sensory awareness . . . to witness [their] own process, noticing how interactions with the client impact body, mind, and emotions. That expanded awareness helps attune the therapist's responses to the client—either through what is said in the moment or as part of an ongoing consciousness about the client. (Lynette S. Danylchuk, 2015, p. 1)

With cultural competency as a necessary foundation (Brown, 2008), practicing trauma therapy as the clinician requires both the mind and the heart, meaning that questions such as "How do I work with a person who has been traumatized?" miss the mark in their simplicity. As with all responsible work with people, there is no therapy-by-numbers. Nevertheless, that does not mean there is no plan or guidance. Instead, engaging in a trauma-informed approach is akin to adopting a worldview in which thoughts, feelings, and behavior follow naturally from that worldview. So, if I believe in the inherent worth of Black women and girls, their right to self-determination, and my role as a collaborator and not a dictator, then my therapeutic actions would be nonpathologizing in case conceptualization and treatment planning, respectful of the agency and the autonomy of my clients, and collaborative with my clients in determining the course of therapeutic healing. That worldview would further bar me from behaviors that decontextualized my client and her experiences, while powering over her through strict adherence to manualized treatment (for discussion, see Cloitre, 2015).

Based on the ethical premise of "do no harm" (APA, 2017a), there are six principles of trauma-informed care: safety; trustworthiness and transparency; peer support; collaboration and mutuality; empowerment, voice, and choice; and cultural, historical, and gender issues (Bent-Goodley, 2017). These principles are personified in the Culturally Competent and Trauma-Informed

Theoretical Orientations section of the current chapter, which highlights relational cultural theory (e.g., Miller, 1976) and the liberation health framework (e.g., Belkin Martinez, 2014). Therefore, in this section, I focus on processes for clinicians working with Black women and girl survivors in trauma therapy in the following subsections:

1. Ambiguity, Emotional Intensity, and Coexistence of Good and Evil. Working with and through the emotional intensity and complexity of trauma, oppression, and human beings

2. Clinician: Know Thyself. Engaging with continuous critical self-reflection related to your own trauma history, experiences with oppression and discrimination, worldview, prejudice, and more

3. Power-With Collaboration. Working alongside clients in growth-fostering ways that respect clients' self-determination, autonomy, and wisdom

4. Bearing Witness. Co-creating space in therapy where you bear witness to clients' traumas, oppression, and pain

5. Holding Hope Even When Hopeless. Continually finding and rediscovering hope for your clients and their lives, and sharing that hope with them when clinically indicated

6. Cultural Competency in Trauma Therapy. Centralizing individual and structural cultural competency throughout all facets of therapy

7. Self-Care. Engaging in individual and structural self-care that includes multiple emotional, psychological, and behavioral strategies for dealing with being intimately familiar with the depraved violence and oppression people do to one another

Ambiguity, Emotional Intensity, and Coexistence of Good and Evil

Danylchuk (2015) detailed the many qualities necessary for effectiveness and longevity as a trauma clinician. The first three qualities are tolerance of ambiguity, tolerance for emotional intensity, and tolerance for holding the reality of good and evil coexisting within the world and within one person. The first two—tolerance of ambiguity and emotional intensity—are antithetical to clinical training that promotes so-called mastery of skills within objective and emotionally disconnected therapeutic orientations. Working with Black women and girl survivors of cultural betrayal sexual trauma necessarily includes grappling with uncertainty; feelings and the reality of inadequacy; and a willingness to continue to learn about trauma, the client, and oneself both personally and professionally. This ocean of complexity further includes knowing emotionally and intellectually that within the world, including many of our clients and ourselves, exists a dialectic of infinite brilliance and deep depravity (Freyd, 1996). Such a dialectic calls for not only cognitive flexibility but also emotional intelligence.

Clinician: Know Thyself

Danylchuk (2015) further discussed the importance of the clinician knowing themselves, including their inner emotional and cultural landscape, their history, their emotional triggers and reactions, and their unconscious and automatic responses to trauma. This knowledge comes from not external resources but rather a deep and loving curiosity of the self. As a student clinician and beyond, I have found processing journals in the form of freewriting extremely useful in uncovering both hidden and obvious aspects of myself—particularly how I move within myself and with my clients when under extreme vicarious traumatic distress. Such a processing journal additionally furthers self-reflection and ongoing correction and reconnection with the self and the client (see Miller & Stiver, 1997), as well as identifying one's own sociocultural context (e.g., Tummala-Narra, 2016), including racist, sexist, classist, and other bigoted aspects of ourselves that we prefer to believe do not exist. Rewarding yourself when you discover your own bigotry can help make the process of self-discovery less scary. Because everyone has prejudice, finding and refinding bigotry within yourself should be unsurprising. Moreover, doing so enables you to do less and less harm in the world.

Power-With Collaboration

Mutuality and power-with collaborative approaches (e.g., Bryant-Davis & Comas-Díaz, 2016) between client and clinician are further discussed in the Relational Cultural Theory (Miller, 1976) and Liberation Health Framework (Belkin Martinez, 2014) sections in this chapter. However, I highlight collaboration in the current section specifically due to its importance, as well as its deviation from, some dominant frameworks for therapy and clinical training that place the clinician as expert and the client as the pathological other. Specifically, Black women and girl survivors of cultural betrayal sexual trauma have already been subjected to power-over, oppressive relational approaches within the abusive context—and potentially in other aspects of their lives as well. Therefore, a trauma-informed approach that is culturally congruent and relationally healthy requires a rejection of clinician domination over clients (e.g., Gómez, 2020e). This includes an abandonment of strict adherence to manualized protocols that force or coerce clients to engage in therapeutic endeavors without their autonomy, agency, and self-knowledge being respected (Cloitre, 2015). In the current chapter, I provide clinical case examples relevant to power-with versus power-over approaches in the What This Can Actually Look Like subsections Respecting Autonomy and Power-Over Approach With Disrespect of Cultural Difference.

Bearing Witness

Another fundamental process in trauma therapy is bearing witness to the client's trauma (Bryant-Davis & Comas-Díaz, 2016). Black women and girl survivors often experience cultural betrayal sexual trauma in isolation—that is, in spaces where only they and the perpetrator(s) were present. In these times, as well as those where others directly witnessed the violence, the internal experience is a solitary one. For instance, the perpetrator(s) may have been overtly physically violent, dissociative, hateful, or faux-loving. The survivor exists both in relation to the perpetrator(s) and disconnected from them. They are inside of themselves, yet also far away. Whether after a single event, years of complex trauma (Herman, 1997), or anywhere in between, what is left from the cultural betrayal sexual trauma lives within the survivor. The pain, confusion, shame, anger, frustration, sadness, mourning, fear, love, hate, and many other emotions and reactions can exist in varying degrees across time within this one person. Under the principles of respecting agency and autonomy, what the survivor shares and when it is shared is determined by the survivor, with support and validation from the clinician. Throughout the therapeutic process, the clinician being able to sit with, hold, and emotionally connect with the survivor and their experience is vital. As will be detailed in the Relational Cultural Theory (e.g., Miller & Stiver, 1997) section of the current chapter, it is that relational connection that engenders healing, including the survivor's reconnection with themselves.

Holding Hope Even When Hopeless

An additional role of the clinician is proactively holding hope for the client while identifying and highlighting the client's strengths and wisdom. As a student clinician, I was consistently surprised by the distance between how amazing I knew my clients to be compared with how awfully they felt about themselves. For example, there would be times when clients would have shared details and insight into the cultural betrayal sexual trauma they had endured in ways they had never done before with anyone, including themselves. All I knew and felt was their strength and hope for their future.

Simultaneously, however, they were overcome with feelings of weakness, shame, and a future-oriented process of endless pain. It was in those times I would gently tell them how I perceived them, while demonstrating curiosity about the reasons they understood themselves so differently.

There were, of course, other times when I myself would be emotionally, psychologically, and spiritually overwhelmed because I had witnessed so much of a client's pain and suffering while being vicariously exposed to the degradation, intersectional oppression, and cultural betrayal sexual trauma they had endured. In these times, neither the client nor myself could easily detect a light at the end of the tunnel. In those moments, I would remind myself that there is always a light, no matter how faint. I would find that light by truly being with the client. Their work, their vulnerability, their courage, their strength, and so much more would shine clear as day if only I would orient myself to them. In sharing that reorientation, the client could either join me in this hope or simply be aware that such hope existed at least enough for me as their clinician to believe in it.

Cultural Competency in Trauma Therapy

As cannot be overstated, trauma therapy must be culturally competent (e.g., Bent-Goodley & Gómez, in press; Brown, 2008), which necessarily includes direct and indirect attunement to the macrolevel context (Belkin Martinez, 2014; Miller & Stiver, 1997). That is, the client and their experiences must be conceptualized within the broader context of intersectional oppression (e.g., Crenshaw, 1991), (intra)cultural trust, cultural betrayal, (intra)cultural pressure and support, and more. This conceptualization is neither abstract nor withheld from the client. Instead, it is directly incorporated into healing mechanisms, such as critical consciousness (see the Liberation Health Framework section of the current chapter), that promote radical healing (Adames et al., 2022).

Self-Care

> What Self-Care Isn't: accepting and adjusting to the injustices of the world ... internalizing the messages of self- and others' worth dictated by trauma and inequality (e.g., "minorities"; "hysterical woman"; "dirty") ... never feeling negative emotions (sad, overwhelmed, helpless). (Jennifer M. Gómez, 2019g, p. 1)

Perhaps in a parallel process (e.g., Tracey et al., 2012) with cultural betrayal sexual trauma itself, being a trauma clinician can make you disconnected and isolated, as we each go home alone every day carrying with us our therapeutic relationships with our clients and their traumatic experiences.

Thus, systematically incorporating connection with the self and others is vital. The aforementioned processing journal can serve as a primer for self-connection. Additionally, regular (e.g., monthly) peer supervision with other culturally competent trauma clinicians can result in shared wisdom and solidarity.

Discussed further in the current chapter within the What This Can Actually Look Like subsection Self-Care, my working definition of self-care is as follows:

- Identifying and attending to your own needs
- Sitting with (and sometimes soothing yourself through) intense distress about the interpersonal, cultural, and societal travesties that are out of your control—self-caring engagement with the existential dimension of bearing witness to trauma (Delker, 2019)
- Emotionally and intellectually externalizing the pathology onto the trauma, inequality, dominant culture . . . , and off of yourself
- Using your emotions as potential cues for appraising situations, systems . . . (e.g., as problematic; healthy . . .)
- Connecting with others
- Engaging in protective behaviors, including defending yourself, promoting equality (Gómez, 2019g, p. 1)

Delker (2019) further described institutionalized self-caring that becomes structured into the therapeutic process, such as in peer supervision and on a clinical team. Such institutionalization can include a structured reflection that asks not "What are you doing for self-care?" but instead "How are you making sense of the violence and suffering you witnessed today?" Importantly, self-caring happens in both our professional and our personal lives (Delker, 2019).

CULTURALLY COMPETENT AND TRAUMA-INFORMED THEORETICAL ORIENTATIONS

Clinically working with Black women and girl survivors of cultural betrayal sexual trauma requires emotional, psychological, and intellectual dexterity. Specifically, the proliferation of harms related to racism (e.g., Mills, 1997), intersectional oppression (e.g., Crenshaw, 1989), secondary marginalization (Cohen, 2009), cultural betrayal (e.g., Gómez, 2019c), violent silencing (current book), and more operate alongside the diversity, pain, wisdom, and strength of Black women and girls. Theoretical orientations that promote the depth of human connection and the importance of theoretical and actionable alignment against systems of oppression may be best suited for clinical work with Black women and girl survivors. Therefore, in this section, I review two complementary theoretical orientations, relational cultural theory (e.g., Miller & Stiver, 1997) and the liberation health framework (e.g., Belkin Martinez, 2014) that clinicians can incorporate into their practice.

Relational Cultural Theory

Perhaps the gifts that treatment providers could offer, as coparticipants in survivors' healing processes, would be (a) placing . . . trauma firmly within the relational and sociocultural contexts in which it occurred; (b) actively combating the supposition that pathology lies within those who have experienced . . . trauma; (c) cocreating growth-fostering relationships with clients in which they can experience connection and mutual empathy; and (d) encouraging clients to explore developing growth-fostering relationships with others outside of the context of therapy through mutuality, respect, and bearing witness to the deepest harms. In doing so, healing from . . . trauma means truly living. (Jennifer M. Gómez, Lewis, et al., 2016, p. 177)

Within the context of feminist therapy (L. S. Brown, 2008), Miller's (1976) relational cultural theory (RCT) challenged the masculine-normed individualistic nature of therapy. Conceptualizing this stance as necessarily harmful to women, Miller (1976) emphasized the interconnectedness of women (e.g., Collins, 1991/2000), specifically how growth occurs through relationships. In centering relationships, an additional premise of RCT is that the primary cause of suffering is relational disconnection from the self, others, cultures, and society (Miller & Stiver, 1997), which is also compatible with Black experiential understanding of harm (e.g., Bent-Goodley, 2009; Martin & Martin, 1995). Instead of employing power-over relational dynamics that are oppressive, abusive (Gómez, Lewis, et al., 2016), or otherwise remove agency from the individual, RCT emphasizes that power-with, collaborative relational dynamics centered on mutuality result in an interconnected, cocreated path for healing (Brans & Trimble, 2001; Miller, 1988). This collaborative orientation may be particularly beneficial for Black and other marginalized individuals (e.g., Gómez, Lewis, et al., 2016; Rose & Brown, 2022) because it rejects oppressive power-over dynamics. M. Walker (2010) beautifully detailed RCT within the clinician–client dyad:

(1) The goal of therapy is not separation or autonomous power. Rather, the goal is increased initiative and response capability within relationship. (2) Chronic disconnection . . . is the primary source of human suffering. Such suffering gives rise to the relational paradox, a deep-seated yearning for connection along with a near-primal terror of the vulnerabilities inherent in connection. . . . Together the client and therapist develop practices for engaging the dialectic of power

and vulnerability. (3) The treatment process requires direct engagement with operative power dynamics. . . . The schemata held by the therapist and the clients are interrogated through the treatment process. Movement towards healing represents a transformation of the power dynamics that shape the client–therapist relationship. (p. 42)

Akin to combatting the individualizing nature of the medical model, RCT further argues against individualized outcomes, such as symptom reduction, which is often sought after in therapy under that premise (Birrell & Freyd, 2006). Moreover, RCT is in direct contrast with decision-making processes that are decontextualized and disconnected (Birrell, 2011). Specifically and importantly, wellness, healing, and maturity are not synonymous with isolation or staunch self-reliance. As such, reaching out for help, leaning on others for support, and being community oriented are not conceptualized as indicators of defect or pathology. Instead, it is understood that it is growth-fostering relational connections that bring solace and joy.

Within the therapeutic dyad, a true relational ethic includes the power, compassion, willingness, and ability to be with uncertainty within the relational space (Birrell, 2011). Authentic presence and curiosity of the client's internal and external experiences engender a grounded authenticity and curiosity within the client herself. Such authenticity (Miller et al., 1999) allows clients to show up to relationships more fully as their true selves, thus creating deeper, sustaining connections with relationally healthy others.

As discussed by M. Walker (2010) in the second tenet above, the relational paradox provides a trap for the client. The strong need to be in connection with others is matched by the fear of such closeness. Understood within the context of CBTT (e.g., Gómez & Gobin, 2020a), this relational dialectic can act as a push-and-pull mechanism that drives survivors to vacillate between connection and disconnection with others—particularly as needed and trusted others have violated them. The therapeutic relationship, then, serves as a practice ground in which clients, in their own time, learn to trust and connect with the clinician. Importantly, as in any relationship, the therapeutic one includes relational breaches and other mistakes. Therefore, healthily repairing relational connections through validation, apology, and reconnection can be a relearning process for many clients who have learned that conflict or hurt within a relationship precedes rejection and abandonment.

Cultural betrayal sexual trauma (e.g., Gómez & Gobin, 2020a), which at times includes high betrayal (perpetrator is trusted and/or depended on; e.g., Freyd, 1997), can disrupt connection with the self, community, and others. Therefore, culturally competent RCT (Gómez, Lewis, et al., 2016) paves the way for multifaceted reconnection and healing. As I (Gómez, 2020e) have discussed elsewhere regarding RCT's effectiveness in working with a female client of color leaving an abusive relationship,

> psychotherapy had helped her realize that she was someone worthy of love and could therefore choose to find non-toxic love and connection in other relationships. This result was the personification of RCT (Miller & Stiver, 1997): through power-with approaches, [she] was able to develop relational connections with herself and me as her clinician, which led her to seek out other healthy relationships outside of psychotherapy. (p. 63)

With its focus on social justice (Comstock et al., 2008), RCT can be incorporated into other therapeutic modalities, including the liberation health framework (e.g., Belkin Martinez, 2014).

Liberation Health Framework

> Think of analyses of power as ways to imagine how clients may not need "equality" in their lives, but to feel empowered to name inequality and demand genuine equity in work, school, family life, church. (Patrick Grzanka, 2020a, p. 256)

Historically and presently, the field of psychology as a whole has problems with inequality being embedded within its foundational practices (Buchanan & Wiklund, 2020; Buchanan et al., 2021; Gómez, Smith, et al., 2016); therefore, influence from other practice fields can further psychology along faster than it could do by itself. From the field of social work, the liberation health (LH) framework (Belkin Martinez & Fleck-Henderson, 2014), as a justice-focused mental health practice (D. Belkin Martinez, personal communication, March 14, 2022), tangibly combines a sociopolitical analysis of ideological and institutional factors with microlevel clinical practice. This leads to a holistic assessment and intervention plan that target all of the factors influencing the identified problem. In line with the radical healing framework for therapy (Adames et al., 2022) and within the community (French et al., 2020), the foundation of the LH framework stems from Paolo Freire and popular education, liberation psychology, and the tradition of radical social work (Belkin Martinez & Fleck-Henderson, 2014). As this foundation aids in fully grasping the LH framework, I describe each briefly here.

As detailed by Belkin Martinez (2014), the practice of Freire's (1974) popular education includes the following: (1) the starting place of transformative education being at the individual's experience within the collective experience of the group (e.g., a Black teen girl's lived experience within the collective experience of Black women and girls); (2) three basic steps for educational processes: (a) identifying a problem as experienced by the individual, (b) examining the root causes of the problem, and (c) creating an action plan to address the problem; and (3) engaging in a critical consciousness, which is perceiving "social, political, and economic contradictions and to take action against the oppressive elements of society" (Freire, 1970, p. 35). Thus, Freire's (1974) understanding of education as the practice of freedom laid important groundwork for liberation in mental health care.

Liberation psychology is based on the premise that systemic oppression exists and causes harm to those it oppresses. In line with work on structural racism (e.g., V. Ray, 2019), liberation psychology argues that systemic oppression upholds oppressive social conditions, which are then internalized by the oppressed; moreover, individuals often interpret oppression and its outcomes (e.g., violence, poverty) as proof of the correctness of the unequal and oppressive societal order (Martín-Baró, 1994; for application to theory, method, practice, and social justice, see Comas-Díaz & Torres Rivera, 2020). As an example of applied liberation psychology, the cultural context framework uses clinical strategies for relational healing and liberation from oppression (Almeida et al., 2008). As such, liberation psychology links the individual and society with the goals of radically transforming both through clearly identifying and dismantling the personal and societal oppressions that bind (Martín-Baró, 1994).

Finally, the tradition of radical social work serves to reconcile the individualism of microlevel practice with the field's imperative of systemic change (Belkin Martinez, 2014). With society, and not the client, understood as pathological (McQuaide, 1987), organizing for social change is directly essential to clinical practice. Within the radical social work tradition, Fook (1993) identified five necessary aspects of clinical work:

> 1) a structural analyses of which person problems can be traced to causes in the socio-political-economic structure; 2) an ongoing analysis of the social control functions of the social work profession and the social welfare system; 3) an ongoing critique of the existing social, political, and economic arrangements; 4) a commitment to protecting individuals against oppression by more powerful individuals, groups, and structures; and 5) goals of personal liberation and social change. (p. 7)

Therefore, the radical social work tradition further underscores the interconnectedness of the individual and broader societal context, along with clinicians' responsibility to mitigate and ultimately eradicate oppression on individual and societal levels.

The Framework

Built upon this transdisciplinary foundation, the LH framework has five general principles (Belkin Martinez, 2014):

1. Situating clients' problems within a social context: Deliberately connect the clients' social conditions with their problems.

2. Reaffirming that practice must be both individual and social: Solutions must be both individual and social/societal in nature.

3. Recognizing the importance of worldview: How clients understand their problems, their relationship with their problems, and make meaning of the world around them is essential to the healing process.

4. Engendering client critical consciousness and engagement: Help clients achieve agency and ownership over their own lives, including gaining a critical understanding of how oppression shapes their lives and can be fought against.

5. Engaging in clinician's collaborative role with clients: Similar to relational cultural therapy (Miller, 1976), clinicians are allies that work collaboratively with clients.

In this process for clinicians, a parallel dynamic occurs where clinicians grapple with their own worldview—and that of the mental health care profession—related to the existence, breadth, depth, and impact of various solitary and intersectional instantiations of oppression on themselves, their clients, their field, and society writ large.

Clinical Application
Similar to how I have constructed the current chapter without proscriptive therapy-by-numbers strategies, the LH framework is also uneasy with such static recommendations. With that in mind, Belkin Martinez (2014) provided guidance on two overarching processes within LH clinical work: conceptualizing a problem in its totality (Freire, 1996; Martín-Baró, 1994) and developing and implementing an action plan. The first process—conceptualizing a problem in its totality—is not as simple as putting the presenting problem into context, such as solely linking sexism to the male-perpetrated rape a woman experienced. First, the conceptualizing happens in open collaboration with the client. Clinicians can engender this collaboration by being genuinely curious about the client's experience and thus motivating such curiosity in the client themselves (RCT; e.g., Miller & Stiver, 1997). Together, the conceptualizing broadens the depth and scope of the problem while also interrogating the underlying assumptions guiding the client's view of the problem and themselves (Belkin Martinez, 2014). Namely, this collaborative work continues with "thickening" the problem statement, thus going beyond a narrow, superficial understanding of the problem using internalized scripts from dominant and oppressive worldviews. In "thickening" the

problem statement, the client—with the clinician as partner and ally—fills in gaps of misunderstanding oneself and the problem, while making the hidden thoughts, feelings, and assumptions psychologically visible.

"Triangulating the problem" furthers this conceptualizing. Triangulating the problem is a recursive process that analyzes the thickened problem statement through purposefully incorporating the three triangular points of personal, institutional, and cultural contributors. In this way, a Black teen girl survivor of cultural betrayal sexual trauma—Toni, for instance—can understand her "I am so ashamed of myself" problem statement as stemming from personal factors (3-year abusive relationship, history with and estrangement from a sexually abusive father), institutional factors (gendered racism within high school curriculum and teacher–student interactions), and cultural factors (intersectional oppression, [intra]cultural pressure).

The client's fleshed-out problem statement shifts blame and responsibility from the victimized client onto the oppressive and violent society. Such transformative deconstruction of the client's worldview (Belkin Martinez, 2014; Martín-Baró, 1994) lays the foundation for developing and implementing an action plan. The form of the action plan can vary, and the content will ultimately change and grow along with the client. A starting format for the action plan, however, may be a four-column chart: "column #1: the various aspects of the problem; column #2: what needs to change in relation to each; column #3: the long range vision or goal in relation to each; and column #4: specific activities and initiatives for week" (Belkin Martinez, 2014, p. 24). Given that the LH framework deliberately incorporates institutional and cultural factors in addition to personal factors, the specific healing mechanisms, or takeaway therapy, also include these three classes of factors. As I have used it in my work with clients as a student clinician, the phrase *takeaway therapy* can be used in lieu of *homework* in order to avoid eliciting stereotype threat (e.g., Steele, 1998) for clients who have negative associations with formal education due to racism, sexism, classism, and other instantiations of oppression. The framework of takeaway therapy also provides a meta-message that healing continues in daily life, not just during therapy sessions with the clinician. For Toni, takeaway therapy can include monitoring the antecedents of feelings of shame (personal factors), with foci on institutional precipitators, such as toxic teacher–student interactions. Together in session, the clinician could further introduce public scholarship on relevant research, such as "The Unique Harm of Sexual Abuse in the Black Community" published in *The Conversation* (Gómez, 2019h), and discuss with Toni the ways CBTT does and does not provide insight into her experience (see Gómez & Gobin, 2022).

Summary
With its cross-disciplinary foundation from popular education (e.g., Freire, 1974), liberation psychology (e.g., Martín-Baró, 1994), and the radical social work tradition (e.g., Fook, 1993), the LH framework (Belkin Martinez & Fleck-Henderson, 2014) tangibly combines macrolevel cultural and institutional factors with microlevel clinical practice. In the LH framework, the individual is societally contextualized, thus providing a nonpathologizing method of understanding human distress—particularly that related to oppression and violence (Gómez, Lewis, et al., 2016). As such, the LH framework can provide a road map for case conceptualization and treatment planning in clinical work that is culturally competent, radical, and transformative on both individual and societal levels. Relevant within the LH framework and stemming from psychologists' (and psychologists-in-training) roles in social justice advocacy (e.g., Grzanka, 2020a), I provide the Advocating for Social Justice clinical case example in the following section.

WHAT THIS CAN ACTUALLY LOOK LIKE

So far in this book, I provided information for therapeutically working with Black women and girl survivors in trauma-informed and culturally competent manners. As such, I have used the foundational chapters (2–4) to relay basic knowledge on structural racism, intersectional oppression, sexual abuse, and cultural betrayal, whereas the current chapter has information directly relevant for clinical work. In this section, I aim for that background to come to fruition through detailing mostly disguised and/or amalgamated clinical cases and situations from my clinical and clinically related work as a student. Consequently, this section has clinical case examples, with lessons for trauma therapy (Respecting Autonomy; Self-Care); trauma therapy and cultural competency (Power-Over Approach With Disrespect of Cultural Difference); cultural competency (Discrimination in Therapy); and liberation health (Advocating for Social Justice). My hope is these examples will be useful in primary education for students (e.g., Gómez, Noll, et al., 2021) and continuing education for professionals, while being insightful for Black women and girl survivors of cultural betrayal sexual trauma, including but not limited to those who are clients.

Trauma Therapy: Respecting Autonomy—The Power of Power-With

> Intervention strategies based solely on the experiences of women who do not share the same class or race backgrounds will be of limited help to women who because of race [racism] and class [classism/capitalism] face different obstacles. (Kimberlé Crenshaw, 1991, p. 1246)

An important aspect of being both culturally responsive and trauma informed is that clinicians work collaboratively with clients, engaging in power-with approaches that promote mutual empowerment (e.g., Gómez, Lewis, et al., 2016). This is in direct contrast with manualized evidence-based treatments for PTSD that require rigid adherence to predetermined structure and rules. For instance, I used cognitive processing therapy (CPT; e.g., Resick & Schnicke, 1992) when working with Lisa (pseudonym), a Black woman client in her late 20s who experienced cultural betrayal sexual trauma a few years prior from a family friend she had known all her life. When she brought in her trauma narrative that she had written for takeaway therapy, she apologetically confessed two things: (a) she was not going to be able to read the narrative out loud, as was required in CPT; and (b) she was not able to put the perpetrator's real name in the narrative and instead chose the name of a Black male celebrity. I trusted my education with relational cultural therapy (e.g., Miller & Stiver, 1997) to not push either issue. After empathically saying that it was interesting—and good!—that using the Black male celebrity's name helped her complete the takeaway therapy, I asked if it would be okay if I instead read the narrative out loud. She agreed. In sessions that followed, we always referred to the perpetrator by the name of the celebrity.

In coming to session with her second trauma narrative completed weeks later, Lisa shared a revelation. She told me that as she sat down to rewrite the trauma narrative, she was curious as to why it was so difficult for her to say the perpetrator's actual name; she didn't really understand why she could not say his name, given how much work we were doing in discussing what he had done and how it had affected her. Therefore, she tried to write his name and found out that she could. In doing so, she described that he had much less power over her than he had in the past. This person—not the celebrity but the actual person—was a rapist who betrayed her. He was no longer a larger-than-life, all-powerful demon who did to her only what she herself deserved. After we cheered this revelation, I asked her if she would like me to read the trauma narrative out loud like last time. She told me that wouldn't be necessary because now she could do it herself. And she did.

From this situation, I learned several things. The first is that power-with approaches, like the ones used here, are beneficial in both process and outcome. In other words, a primary goal of the narratives in CPT is to healthily reinterpret the trauma in ways that correct cognitive distortions and shift blame from the client to the perpetrator. An intermediate goal is for the client to read the narrative aloud in session. This client achieved both goals with flying colors, but not from me forcing her. Instead of pressuring or coercing her to do things she was not ready for, I affirmed her choices, thus engendering both curiosity and trust in herself. As such, I engaged in what Steven J. Ondersma terms "the capsule inside," in which the skills-based work is but a capsule within therapy that is supportive, empathic, collaborative, mutually empowering, and client approved (personal communication, January 20, 2022). In that process, Lisa succeeded in healing that broke through the shackles of shame that had bound her for years. Last, I learned there is simply no replacement for thinking, feeling, and being with a client while privileging their humanity over therapy rules that were never made with this particular human being in mind.

Trauma Therapy: Self-Care—What to Do When All I Feel Is Pain

> If Antonia is murdered by her boyfriend, what would you want her psychotherapy sessions to have been like for her before she died? (clinical supervisor, in Jennifer M. Gómez, 2020e, p. 63)

There is a spectre of death hanging over trauma clinicians' heads. The violence our clients actively experience is, at times, just a stone's throw away from death through murder or suicide. Sometimes that spectre turns into a suffocating cloud where death is potentially imminent and one's own helplessness as the clinician has never felt so palpable. In this case, Antonia (pseudonym) was a client of mine who was in the long, arduous process of leaving her abusive boyfriend, whom she still lived with. There was a period when I worried week to week whether she would survive his desperate violence. In supervision, I talked with my phenomenal supervisor, Julie (pseudonym), about my desire to dictate Antonia's actions so she would be safe. In reminding me of the importance of client agency and autonomy, Julie also stayed with me as we entertained my biggest fear: Antonia's murder. In facing that potential reality, Julie helped me explore what I would want Antonia's experiences in therapy with me to be like if her boyfriend ultimately did kill her. I knew I wouldn't want her to be judged, isolated, or otherwise emotionally unsafe with me in therapy. As I have written previously, "I would want to cocreate a space with Antonia in which she could safely explore her feelings, her worries, and her pain while being supported in her agency, autonomy, and sense of self" (Gómez, 2020e, p. 63). I worked my hardest to be emotionally, psychologically, and spiritually there, alongside Antonia, during that time.

Gratefully, this was not the end of her life. She safely left her boyfriend, telling me that our therapy together taught her that she was worthy of loving relationships in which abuse was absent (Gómez, 2020e). I still exhale deep sighs of relief whenever I think of her years later. Not only did she survive physically, but also she transformed psychologically and spiritually. She reminds me that there is perhaps no greater privilege than being able to be with our clients during such transformation.

The obvious lesson here is the importance of power-with, collaborative approaches with clients (e.g., Belkin Martinez, 2014; Miller & Stiver, 1997). Even when wanting to power-over a client "for their own good," we must remember we are not the judge, jury, probation officer, or life boss of our clients. Engaging in such authority is the opposite of trauma-informed care (Cloitre, 2015) and, in my case, would have indulged my own anxiety, while not actually being what was best for Antonia anyway. As the focus of therapy is on the client and not yourself, it can be easy to project and then translate your own issues as stemming from the client (à la "I am just worried about my client") as opposed to yourself (à la "I cannot tolerate my own anxiety and sense of helplessness; therefore, I will regain some semblance of control through powering-over my client").

While the above lesson is paramount in therapy, I discovered a deeper, more uncomfortable truth in working with Antonia. Through this therapy, I found myself struggling with self-care. I then realized that my premises of self-care were inaccurate. I had understood self-care as activities and rituals that serve as balms that protect you from ever feeling pain: No matter the horrors of the world, have a good cry inside a warm bath and all will be right as rain. Right? Wrong. I realized that self-care isn't a happiness pill that results in never feeling negative emotions, such as sadness (Gómez, 2019g).

In working with Antonia, I struggled with what self-care could look like when I was worried that her abusive boyfriend would kill her. I found no easy solutions. I suffered, I cried, I felt anxious, I faced my own helplessness, I cared, I hoped, I dreamed, I prepared, I mourned, and I lived and breathed as I connected with her each and every week. I have reconceptualized that my emotions and my pain are okay, as I am human. I would much prefer my agonizing experience than to be a clinician who is emotionally, psychologically, physically, and spiritually unaffected by my clients. Therefore, perhaps one of my biggest lessons from Antonia is that passive disconnection in the face of fear is not ideal. I instead choose to live, which means feeling all the emotions that come with such connected living.

Trauma Therapy and Cultural Competency: Power-Over Approach With Disrespect of Cultural Difference—I Am Not Always Right

As an undergraduate, I had the honor of being a group discussion coleader regarding teen relationship violence for a group of Black and Brown adolescent girls. With this as one of my first clinically adjacent roles, I was honored to spend a couple hours each week for 2 months with these kids, who were intelligent, thoughtful, sensitive, funny, and so very wise. Framed as primary prevention against violent romantic relationships, our curricula could be more accurately understood as secondary prevention, given many of the girls had already experienced violence by the time they were in the program. As is so often the case in working with people, particularly youth, these girls taught me a tremendous amount.

In speaking one-on-one during a group session, Mya (pseudonym), a Black 15-year-old girl, asked me about rape in the context of "blue balls." She told me that when guys are sexually excited, they cannot stop sexual activity because, if they do, they will experience the unbearable physical pain of so-called blue balls. I told her that boys can always stop continuing with sex; there's nothing physical or physiological that keeps them from stopping. She told me that's not true; they can't stop. I told her, yes, they can. We went back and forth with this a few times until she finally asked me how old I was. In telling her I was 26, she said that maybe things have changed since way back when I was in high school because, now, boys can't stop. In that moment, I realized that to her, I was very old, pretty uncool, and way out of touch.

However, I knew I was right—boys always do have the choice to not rape—but I also knew I was not going to convince her of that in this interaction. So, I shifted gears. I said,

> Okay, let's say that's true. Boys can't stop once they have started. So, just because a boy can't control himself, that means you have to do something you don't want to do? You have to be hurt? He gets what he wants, but you get hurt. Why? Just because you're a girl? That doesn't seem fair.

As tears sprung to her eyes, I knew an emotional light bulb had gone off. I knew we had gotten somewhere deep. Without explicitly naming sexism, we named sexism: the racist sexism that tells us as Black girls that our feelings, our wants, and our needs do not matter at all, and certainly not when compared to that of boys and men. In that moment, I got to be alongside her as she reclaimed herself. Valued herself. Because I still held on to my role as psychoeducator, the last thing I told her, with a playful smile on my face was, "And they can control themselves." Mya nodded and briefly chuckled.

On reflection, I learned two things from this courageous girl. The first was the wisdom in my choice to pivot. To ask a different question. I moved away from telling her that boys could in fact sexually control themselves and shifted into pulling in the societally unequal context by exposing the intersectionally oppressive, racist–sexist unstated assumptions that she had internalized: By virtue of being a Black girl, she didn't matter. That lesson—to shift—has stayed with me.

However, in this interaction, I also made a profound mistake. My strong investment in being right prevented me from learning about Mya's experiences. Factually, sexual frustration is not an unstoppable vehicle to rape. Period. That is true. However, I held on to that truth at the expense of hers. I didn't ask myself or her, "What is the truth in what she is saying?" and "What is she saying that I am missing?" Instead, I clung to my rightness at the expense of learning from her. Maybe the truth in her statement is that a boy had raped her before, and she made sense of his rape by thinking that he couldn't help it because of his male physiology. Maybe that explanation was a way in which she did not blame herself or him. Maybe that understanding helped her to preserve the (intra)cultural trust and relationship with both the Black community and with him, thus depowering the cultural betrayal. Or maybe it was simply a high school myth she had no direct experience with but was trying to understand. Or maybe it was something else entirely. However, I will never know. The reason I will never know is that I was so obsessed with my perceived rightness that not only did I fail to ask but also I did not even consider that she had a perspective different from mine that mattered. In that way, I reenacted the same oppression that we subsequently called out: She, her perspective, and her feelings didn't matter at that moment because I—like those sexually frustrated boys who rape—knew better than she and used my power to get my way anyways.

This lesson struck me hard with the understanding that none of us, including myself, is immune from enacting oppression against others, including in situations where our role is to help and share our knowledge. Furthermore, our precious good intentions are not blankets we can hide under to abdicate our responsibility to equitably do better. Each of us must hold a mirror up to our own behavior, shining a light on the oppressions we have internalized because it is those unchecked bigotries and biases that perpetuate our therapeutic oppression of other people. More than 10 years later, this remains a lesson I hope I never forget.

Cultural Competency: Discrimination in Therapy—Client to Clinician Discrimination Is Real and Not Okay

Throughout my clinical training in graduate school, the education in cultural competency was profoundly rudimentary, inadequate, and at times ridiculous, including such recommendations as "Do not call your Black client the n-word" regarding implicitly White clinicians working with Black clients. This education also did not prepare me for White clients' discrimination against me as the clinician. Over time, I experienced microaggressive (for a review, see Gómez, 2015d) and seemingly unintentional discrimination from White clients, which was simultaneously painful while offering opportunities for therapeutic resolution following these relational breaches (for an example, see Gómez, 2020e).

However, I also had instances of White male clients' discrimination that appeared intentional, while being very hurtful and intolerable. One such instance was a client who, in rapid succession, made anti-Black, anti-Mexican, and anti-woman comments to me in our therapy session. I interpreted his choice to say these things to me as attempts to shift the power dynamic in a way that was sure to encapsulate my marginalized statuses as a Black female Gómez. Another White male client described missing his former career as a police officer, in which he was able to beat Black people in the street at the end of a frustrating day. He expressed longing for the freedom granted to him as a police officer to be violent against multiple individuals with no repercussions.

I learned several things from these and other instances of clients' overt, extreme, and direct discriminatory comments. The first was that the therapeutic relationship is an actual relationship in which I can get hurt. Second, power in therapy is not one dimensional, with me as the powerful clinician with a depowered client. Those dynamics become complicated by societal dynamics in which clients' privileged identities can interface with my marginalized ones. Last, I learned that I do not have to be a love-filled, sacrificial lamb for my clients in the face of such discrimination. As such, orienting this discrimination as stemming from societal problems can pave the way for structural solutions within clinical settings. Instead, in my experience, there were times I shared my discomfort with this discrimination with a White woman clinical supervisor, who told me it was my job to work with clients, including difficult clients. That was the end of the discussion.

Structural solutions would look quite different. If in line with the clinician's desires, avenues could be undertaken to use the therapeutic relationship to work with the client on their biases, which would require expertise on the part of the clinician and structural support within the institutional clinical setting. For instance, a clinical team that minimizes the harm of discrimination and/or a clinic that imposes a 10-session maximum would not be equipped to support such work with a client. Another option would be to transfer the client to another clinician who matched the majority identities of the client. Protocols would need to be in place to facilitate such transfers, in line with clinician preferences. That is, clinicians should have a choice in determining what is best for the client—including assessing their own ability to provide effective care—as well as what they want for themselves. An expectation that clinicians of color must be subjected to discrimination at their workplace while providing optimum care for this and all their clients is not only unreasonable but also inescapably oppressive.

Liberation Health: Advocating for Social Justice—The Uniting Force of Institutional Courage

> I plead to your humanity that . . . you cease to continue to betray the UO [University of Oregon] community and its members with these public statements of

mindless defense of a system that is clearly broken. Instead of watching a Ducks sporting event (as you suggested in an email you sent . . .), I will instead mourn for all the students on this campus who continue to be punished into silence following being sexually assaulted. (Jennifer M. Gómez, 2015a, an open letter to UO interim president Scott Coltrane)

As a graduate student, I existed within this odd space of power and disempowerment. I was earning an advanced degree while being a supervised clinician in the therapy room and a teacher in the classroom—all of which gave me power. Simultaneously, I was also just a student, a new and insecure supervised clinician, and a teacher who at times was sexually harassed by White male students (Gómez, 2015a). And of course, in all spaces, I was a light-skinned, middle-class Black woman, which meant that within my personhood I held the dialectic of privilege and oppression (Gómez, 2019f). Within myself, I vacillated between needing to fight for change and being overwhelmed by my smallness amid the larger systems I was part of. Yet one experience emboldened me to take part in a big fight for justice.

At my university at the time, the University of Oregon, an undergraduate student, Jane Doe, was in the midst of a Title IX lawsuit against the institution following student athletes allegedly gang raping her (Read, 2015b). The sexual violence included cultural betrayal. As I understood, university employees, including Shelly Kerr, were licensed clinical psychologists, who accessed the student's therapy records from the university counseling and testing center and gave them to the general counsel (Kingkade, 2015). They did this without the knowledge or consent of Jane Doe or her clinician, with the university's ostensible goal of using the content of the therapy records against the student in the lawsuit. Their devastating actions took place within the context of the University of Oregon's capitalist corruption, including within athletics (e.g., Hunt, 2018).

Karen Stokes and Jennifer Morlok courageously reported this ethics violation, resulting in the case going to the state ethics board for ruling. At the time, I was a clinical psychology doctoral student who was unlicensed. I felt helpless. I knew I was not high powered, but I also knew that the seizing of therapy records without consent to be used in a lawsuit was deeply wrong. So, in leaning into my vantage point as a student, I wrote to the Oregon Board of Psychologist Examiners, citing the ethical principles and codes of conduct that I perceived the psychologists in question violated, as well as the following:

Given the violations of confidentiality against a fellow student that occurred by psychologists employed by my university . . . I worry that students who are in need are fearful to utilize therapy services because of these psychologists' behavior. I further worry that if the psychologists who engaged in these behaviors are not held strongly accountable for their actions that many more students will elect not to seek help when they need it, thus being further harmed, suffering in silence, or even taking their own lives as a result of their pain.

I further am concerned that if these psychologists are not held accountable for these ethical violations, then perceived standards for the profession will be lower amongst students like myself who soon will decide on whether they will continue the practice of psychology after graduation. I worry about highly intelligent and ethical students with Master's degrees and doctorates in psychology opting out of the profession to pursue endeavors in which ethical standards are both written and adhered to, with violations being given the appropriate consequences. These consequences serve to protect the integrity of the profession, protect the professionals who are doing quality work, and ultimately protect those people who the profession seeks to serve. Without an expectation of adherence to professional ethics codes, the practice of psychology may become an increasingly less viable option for both outstanding professionals and for the communities they serve. (Jennifer M. Gómez, 2015c [written when I was a graduate student])

In the end, the state ethics board sanctioned Shelly Kerr for her conduct (Read, 2015b), Jane Doe settled her lawsuit against the university (Read, 2015a), and courageous truth-tellers Karen Stokes and Jennifer Morlok also settled their own Title IX and Oregon's Whistleblower lawsuit against the university regarding retaliation (Correia & Puth, 2016). The State of Oregon enacted tighter laws to protect student therapy records (Gray, 2016). Yet, sadly, this immoral and unethical violation of seizing student therapy records during lawsuits is still occurring at universities across the country years later (Pryal, 2022).

I learned innumerable lessons from this situation—far too many to name. One lesson I share with my students when using this situation to teach about ethics is that the flip side of retaliation and ostracization is respect and community. So often we are afraid of who will harm us if we do what is right. In that fear, we often overlook whose company we get to be alongside in the fight. While I do not know if my correspondence to the state ethics board had any bearing on the outcome, I did learn it was worth it to be courageous even when overwhelmed and frightened (Gómez, in press): The cost of silence would have been far greater.

Finally, I can only imagine how much pain, fear, and harm the university and its institutionally betraying (Smith & Freyd, 2014) members did first to Jane Doe and next to Karen Stokes and Jennifer Morlok. However, from afar, these women will always be heroes to me. Maybe that is a lesson in and of itself: Even in the isolated darkness, your courage brightly inspires people you have never even met.

Culturally Competent Trauma Therapy • 111

SUMMARY BULLET POINTS

1. The White Read is an internalized bigot who provides an image of a homogenous White people while promoting an acceptance of White person–perpetrated prejudice and discrimination as inherent, unchangeable by-products of Whiteness.

2. Within the Black feminist tradition, in this book, I unapologetically center Black women and girls, thus designating a primary space for our *Us*.

3. Black women and girls have inherent value as human beings, with survivors not being pathological, crazy, broken, damaged, dirty, disgusting, dumb, in need of repair, or beyond repair.

4. Clinicians collaborate with Black women and girl survivors as clients in their healing journey while engaging in continuous and intentional identification of and opposition against intersectional oppression.

5. The medical model is a White Western cultural conceptualization of human distress based on at least three premises: (a) It is factual and acultural, (b) psychological distress is pathological, and (c) such pathology resides medically within the individual akin to a broken bone. Individualized treatment stems from these faulty premises, despite contestations of their veracity and weak evidence for such treatments.

6. The origin and locus of harm related to cultural betrayal sexual trauma include sexist violence, racism, intersectional oppression, White supremacy, and more. Therefore, strength-based, holistic, and social justice–oriented approaches to therapeutic healing with Black women and girl survivors are warranted.

7. Cultural betrayal sexual trauma can affect Black women and girl survivors' mental, relational, physical, and cultural health. The Six Dimensions of Wellness model and Bryant-Davis's (2005) book *Thriving in the Wake of Trauma* provide domains and avenues of healing, respectively.

8. Individual cultural competency includes clinician awareness of one's own cultural values and biases, clinician awareness of client worldview, and culturally appropriate intervention strategies.

9. Within understanding historical experiences of power, privilege, and oppression, five principles of structural cultural competency include recognizing the role of structural and social forces on clinical work; basing conceptualization on relevant, cross-disciplinary literature; reconceptualizing cultural presentations structurally and systemically; promoting

systems-level change based on scientific expertise and institutional resources; and engaging in structural humility.

10. Processes and practices of trauma therapy include (a) working with and through emotional intensity and complexity; (b) engaging in critical self-reflection; (c) collaborating with clients throughout the therapeutic process; (d) bearing witness to clients' traumatic experiences, oppression, and pain; (e) holding hope for clients and their futures; (f) centralizing individual and structural cultural competency in therapy; and (g) engaging in self-care.

11. Based on the interconnectedness of women, relational cultural theory (RCT) posits that the primary cause of suffering is relational disconnection from the self, others, cultures, and society, with the mechanism of healing being reconnection with the above.

12. As a justice-focused mental health practice, the Liberation Health (LH) framework tangibly combines a sociopolitical analysis of ideological and institutional factors with microlevel clinical practice. This leads to a holistic assessment and intervention plan that targets all of the factors influencing the identified problem. Therefore, the LH framework can provide a road map for case conceptualization and treatment planning in clinical work that is culturally competent, radical, and transformative on both individual and societal levels.

13. Providing application and summaries of lessons learned for trauma-informed and cultural competent therapy, my clinical case examples review aspects related to respecting autonomy, self-care, problematizing power-over approaches and disrespect of cultural difference, client-perpetrated discrimination in therapy, and advocacy for social justice.

14. Being a clinician who works with Black women and girl survivors of cultural betrayal sexual trauma requires continuous critical thinking, reflexivity, and a worldview that is oriented toward (a) the inherent worth, value, self-determination, and autonomy of Black women and girls; (b) incorporation of cultural factors and micro- and macrolevel racism, intersectional oppression, and other inequalities into all facets of clinical work (e.g., case conceptualization, session content); and (c) institutional courage through micro- and macrolevel engagement in social justice.

6 RADICAL HEALING IN THE BLACK COMMUNITY

CHAPTER AT A GLANCE

In this chapter, I detail the psychological framework of radical healing in communities of color, followed by describing concrete strategies for radical healing for Black women and girl survivors, the Black community, and the Black family.

Women need to know they can reject the powerful's definition of their reality. . . . They need to know that this exercise of their basic personal power is an act of resistance and strength.

—bell hooks, 1984/2015, p. 92

Despite its pitfalls and complexity, culturally competent trauma therapy can be beneficial for some Black women and girls who have experienced cultural betrayal sexual trauma within the broader context of intersectional oppression

https://doi.org/10.1037/0000362-006
The Cultural Betrayal of Black Women and Girls: A Black Feminist Approach to Healing From Sexual Abuse, by J. M. Gómez
Copyright © 2023 by the American Psychological Association. All rights reserved.

(Crenshaw, 1991). Nevertheless, lifelong growth and healing cannot be confined within therapy walls (e.g., Bryant-Davis, 2005; French et al., 2020; Moore-Lobban & Gobin, 2022; Mosley et al., 2020), as advocacy and activism are constitutive elements of intersectional praxis (Collins, 1991/2000; Grzanka, 2018; May, 2015). Therefore, in this chapter, I speak directly with Black women and girl survivors of intersectional oppression (e.g., Crenshaw, 1989, 1991) and cultural betrayal sexual trauma (e.g., Gómez, 2019c; Gómez & Gobin, 2020a, 2022). Given that some Black women are both survivors and professionals, clinicians and researchers can use the current chapter in their own healing and growth. Clinicians can also share this information with their clients, as macrolevel change is a necessary part of the healing process (Belkin Martinez, 2014). Finally, both researchers and clinicians can share the chapter's contents with their lab members and clinical staff, respectively, to (a) engender personal growth, healing, and wellness of team members; (b) implement institutional support in self-knowledge (Danylchuk, 2015), self-care (Gómez, 2019g), and structured reflection (Delker, 2019); and (c) collaborate with community stakeholders to design and evaluate programming that promotes radical healing in the Black community.

I begin this chapter with my critical visioning of tackling violent silencing. Next, I review French and colleagues' (2020) psychological framework for radical healing in communities of color. I then provide concrete strategies for engaging in radical healing on the individual level. Next, I discuss radical healing in reference to the Black community and the Black family. I follow this with a brief exposition on what is subjectively considered "free," with direct examples of what radical healing processes can actually look like for a Black woman. Finally, I close with summary bullet points of the takeaway messages of the chapter.

CRITICAL VISIONING: PEACEFUL AMPLIFYING AND COURAGEOUS VULNERABILITY

> Following a quarter of a century—from the testimonies of Anita Hill, J.D., to Dr. Christine Blasey Ford—the U.S. is still struggling: with both how not to violate women, as well as how not to silence them. (Jennifer M. Gómez, 2018, para. 6)

In 1991, Anita Hill exposed to-be-confirmed Supreme Court justice Clarence Thomas's (cultural betrayal) sexual harassment (A. Hill, 1997, 2021). In 2018, history repeated itself when Brett Kavanaugh became a Supreme Court justice after Christine Blasey Ford testified about his prior sexually abusive behavior (Stolberg, 2018). Though occurring decades apart, these situations highlight society's silencing and disregard of women and their experiences, even across races. However, Black women and girls endure additional pressures and harms following similar sexual abuse because of the intersectional oppressions that degrade them while simultaneously privileging the perspectives and needs of Black men (e.g., Crenshaw, 1991). Therefore, it is true that society does engage in silencing all women. Simultaneously, however, there is another aspect of this silencing—what I term *violent silencing*—that Black women and girls additionally endure within the Black community.

Cultural Betrayal Trauma Theory Lens

> The sad irony is of course that black women are often most victimized by the very sexism we refuse to collectively identify as an oppressive force. (bell hooks, 1981/2015, p. 81)

From a CBTT perspective, violent silencing emerges from (intra)cultural pressure, which is the need to protect Black men who perpetrate, Black men who do not, and all of the Black community at the expense of the health, well-being, and safety of Black women and girls who are sexually victimized (e.g., current book; Gómez & Gobin, 2020a; Zounlome et al., 2019). I discussed (intra)cultural pressure at a talk I gave to approximately 100 Black Detroiters at the 2019 Motor City Singers' Space, which is "a themed musical event series designed to remove the stigma from mental health awareness through non-traditional provision of suicide prevention resources to audiences in Southeastern Michigan" (Motor City Singers' Space, n.d.). At this event, I explained how there is a block of protection in the Black community:

> If it's Black, we can't question it. If it's Black, we can't address it. If it's Black, we will stand by it, even if it's drowning us all. Because we can't give Them—the system, the police, the judges, the teachers, the social workers, those well-meaning therapists—we can't give Them another reason to denigrate us. And in that way, in privileging our fear of oppression, we privilege White Supremacy. We let Their beliefs of us and Their societal power over us dictate what is best for us. We let Them decide what we will and will not do to address a problem as big as sexual assault in the Black community. (Gómez, 2019b)

The above context of protection and internalized White supremacy sets the stage for violent silencing through physical, sexual, psychological, and/or discursive violence. I myself live under the spectre of violent silencing even though I have yet to receive it as a professional. For instance, in the comments section of a YouTube video (Gómez, 2019a) I made explaining a research article about cultural betrayal trauma, (intra)cultural pressure, and mental health for young women of color (Gómez, 2019e), a commenter told me I was brave and encouraged me to stay safe. This comment indicates that this spectre of violent silencing hangs over us all.

The Tension and My Critical Visioning

> I will no longer be afraid to write about or voice those thoughts of fear; of "airing our dirty laundry in public." I will be silenced no more! This is a problem that needs to be addressed within the Black community. . . . We must stand united together to expose this ugly monster of patriarchal domination. (Adessina, from the California Black Women's Health Project Info, 1990, as cited in Wiesner, 2022, p. 84)

Coming from White supremacy that is manifested within the Black community, the tension caused by my fear of violent silencing overlays the entire book, as it is an omnipresent thread woven throughout. Specifically, I am afraid for myself of what violent silencing may emerge upon publication of this book. However, I have chosen to discuss this tension in the current chapter because violent silencing is particularly relevant to if and how we can engage in radical healing within ourselves and the Black community as a whole. Furthermore, particularly for women and girls, my fear extends to all of us who subsequently broach these topics in our families, with our loved ones, among our friends, and in our communities.

My critical visioning is a staunch refusal to be silent: I refuse to not write, not research, not teach, and not speak. Instead of succumbing to violent silencing and fear, I will engage in peaceful amplification and courageous vulnerability. I choose to foster radical hope (French et al., 2020; Mosley et al., 2020) in which I tap into our collective history, gaining strength from all the Black women and girls who have spent their lives in this work publicly and privately (for a history, see McGuire, 2010). I will have radical disbelief (hooks, 1984/2015) whereby I reject the racist, sexist, and victim-blaming messages that society imposes upon me. I will engender radical healing (French et al., 2020) within not only myself but also my spheres of influence. Finally, I wish for myself and all of us courage as we create a world in which it is demonstrably safe, peaceful, and healing to discuss cultural betrayal sexual trauma, while we simultaneously work toward designing a world in which such violence and abuse no longer exist.

The Psychological Framework of Radical Healing in Communities of Color

> There are some things which we must always be maladjusted if we are to be people of good will. We must never adjust ourselves to racial discrimination . . . racial segregation . . . religious bigotry . . . economic conditions that take necessities from the

many to give luxuries to the few . . . the self-defeating effects of . . . violence. (Dr. Martin Luther King, Jr., from his Invited Distinguished Address at the 75th Annual Convention of the American Psychological Association, September 1, 1967, in M. L. King, 1968, pp. 10–11)

According to French and colleagues (2020), the psychological framework of radical healing for POCIs (people of color and Indigenous individuals) incorporates liberation psychology (Martín-Baró, 1994), Black psychology (J. L. White, 1970), ethnopolitical psychology (Comas-Díaz, 2007), and intersectionality theory (e.g., Collins, 1990). Going beyond individual and decontextualized approaches to intervention, mental health, wellness, and healing, the psychological framework of radical healing for POCIs has five anchors: *collectivism, critical consciousness, cultural authenticity and self-knowledge, radical hope,* and *strength and resistance*.

Foregrounded within *collectivism* that bridges individual liberation with that of the broader community (French et al., 2020), the psychological process of radical healing "begin[s] with *critical consciousness* as the first step in raising awareness of oppressive systems. Through that *consciousness* . . . [we] can envision a better possibility leading to . . . fostering *hope* . . . [that is sustained through] *strength, resistance, cultural authenticity, and self-knowledge*" (French et al., 2020, p. 25; italics added). With community orientation (e.g., collectivism), critical consciousness includes both critical reflection and action (Watts et al., 2011). Thus, as a form of radical healing, Black women and girl survivors can critically interrogate systems of intersectional oppression, cultural betrayal sexual traumas, and their joint impact on themselves, other Black women and girls, and the Black community.

Collectivism and critical consciousness are nourished by cultural authenticity and self-knowledge, including honoring ancestral wisdom (Moodley & West, 2005). Cultural authenticity and self-knowledge promote self-definition that is distinct from that dictated by oppression and the oppressors (e.g., Collins, 1991/2000). Cultural betrayal trauma theory (CBTT) is an example of such self-definition because it rejects the individualistic perception of abuse and its impact in favor of cultural and contextual understandings centered in an Afrocentric worldview. Further, Black women and girls can engage in radical healing through learning about ourselves, our cultures, and our shared heritage.

Individual to Structural Change

Whenever we envision a world . . . without violence . . . we are engaging in speculative fiction . . . we are dreaming new worlds every time we think about the changes we want to make in the world. (Walidah Imarisha, as cited in a. m. brown & Imarisha, 2015, p. 4)

Without radical hope and strength and resistance, collectivism, critical consciousness, and cultural authenticity and self-knowledge would likely not affect macrolevel community, cultural, institutional, and societal change. From prior scholarship on hope (Freire, 1992; Ginwright, 2010, 2016; Lear, 2008; Miller, 1988), radical hope (Mosley et al., 2020) is the fuel that sustains the psychological, affective/emotional, and behavioral aspects of radical healing (French et al., 2020). With radical hope, strength and resistance, such as engaging in Black activism (Hickson et al., 2022; Leath, Ball, et al., 2022; Neville & Cokley, 2022; Ross et al., 2022; Shaheed et al., 2022; Turner et al., 2022), naturally coexists alongside experiencing the joy and pleasure of life (French et al., 2020). Taken together, Black women and girl survivors can be empowered through radical hope to learn about themselves (cultural authenticity and self-knowledge) and the intersectional oppressions that promote violence against us (critical consciousness) to engage in macrolevel change, such as activism, (strength and resistance) that benefits ourselves and the Black community (collectivism).

RADICAL HEALING IN PRACTICE: WHAT INDIVIDUALS CAN DO

The self has a unique place in collectivist-centered radical healing (French et al., 2020). Specifically, a community connection and collective responsibility do not mean that we as individuals exist solely for the good of others. Because we are part of the Black community, healing the community necessarily includes the lifelong process of healing ourselves as well (Gómez, 2019b). Therefore, we can give ourselves license to remove the shame from intersectional oppression and cultural betrayal sexual trauma. We can allow ourselves to feel anger, sadness, pain, grief, love, and hatred. From a radical healing perspective (French et al., 2020), we can engage in critical consciousness, strength and resistance, and self-knowledge by allowing ourselves to live through and with our traumatic experiences, instead of surviving in spite of them. In doing so, we become wiser, stronger, kinder, more sensitive, and more caring—not just to each other but to ourselves as well.

The Body

> How could a body that holds that kind of pain also hold joy? (Tarana Burke, 2021, p. 74)

Self-knowledge is a primary component of radical healing (French et al., 2020). However, when the body has been the site of violation and abuse, the remnants can stay (van der Kolk, 2015). Therefore, part of healing can be reclaiming your body as yours, knowing that your body is nothing to be ashamed of (S. R. Taylor, 2011). With the self, the spirit, and the soul within it, your body was stolen, but only for a time. Black women and girls who have endured cultural betrayal sexual trauma can reclaim our bodies as our own. As I explained in a panel at Michigan Opera Theatre,

> From a trauma perspective and thinking about sexual violence . . . rape . . . our bodies are taken over, taken away, so the thought about having to be fully in your body . . . is very vulnerable and also has taught us that it's dangerous . . . like "when you're in your body, bad stuff happens." . . . So, re-learning, re-healing . . . at your own pace, your own time, not forcing yourself, not perpetrating against yourself, but trusting that vulnerability and how beautiful it can be to really be in your body, and having the arts as a way to heal . . . mind, body, soul, and spirit. Especially from things that have taken over our bodies and minds and souls and spirits through violence. (Gómez, 2021b)

Therefore, engaging in the arts (e.g., Bryant-Davis, 2005; Gómez, 2021c, 2021d; Gómez & Johnson-Freyd, 2015), self-care (Delker, 2019; Gobin, 2019; Gómez, 2019h), and so much more, can promote self-knowledge, thus serving to reimagine all aspects of ourselves and our relationships with each other and the world (Gómez, 2021c, 2021d).

Things to Do and Know

Bryant-Davis (2005) described specific, multiple artistic expressions and activities to move from surviving to thriving. These include movement, arts and crafts, music, drama/theater, spirituality, social support, nature, activism, and journaling/poetry. Bryant-Davis (2005) described each of the above as relates to key components of the harm-to-healing process: safety, self-care, trust, shame and self-blame, memories, mourning the losses, anger, body image, sexuality, coping strategies, and thriving. Incorporated throughout are self-affirmations that Black women and girls can engage in as they settle into a grounded and connected place within themselves and others (e.g., "I can breathe deeply. I am safe"; Bryant-Davis, 2005, p. 24). From a radical healing perspective (French et al., 2020), these strategies promote collectivism, critical consciousness, strength and resistance, cultural authenticity and self-knowledge, and radical hope.

Infusing these artistic expressions and activities into our lives can take some planning. We can schedule the activities that resonate the most with ourselves into the routines of our everyday lives now (e.g., Gobin, 2019), instead of waiting until we are burnt out, suffering, and struggling. For instance, a schedule could look like this: Saturdays/Sundays: music or drama/theater time where we listen to our favorite songs or watch an act from one of our favorite ballets; Mondays/Wednesdays: walks by the river during lunch breaks; Tuesdays/Thursdays: poetry time where we read and/or write poetry; and Fridays: at least one phone conversation with a trusted loved one, in which we can feel connected and supported. When such a schedule seems untenable, we can begin with 15 minutes a week that we devote to ourselves, our souls, our bodies, and our spirits. Over time, we can add just 15 more minutes per week and so on, as we build up our consistency in behaviorally loving and cherishing ourselves.

RADICAL HEALING IN PRACTICE: WHAT COMMUNITIES CAN DO

> There is a place where violence can meet social justice. Where the self-defeating purposes of violence can be acknowledged and addressed in ways that promote individual and collective healing, as opposed to engendering further harm and even more violence. (Jennifer M. Gómez, personal communication, 2022)

In the prior section, I delineated self-help strategies that can serve the individual, as well as ignite community action (Wiesner, 2022) and grassroots healing (Zounlome et al., 2019). Cultural betrayal trauma is community oriented, by definition, because it is the community—within and beneath societal oppression—where (intra)cultural trust, cultural betrayal, (intra)cultural pressure, and (intra)cultural support all live (Gómez & Gobin, 2022). Therefore, radical healing incorporates collectivism (French et al., 2020) that must include the community directly and indirectly (J. C. Harris et al., 2021). Moreover, reconnection to the self and others are necessary conditions for healing (relational cultural theory; e.g., Miller & Stiver, 1997). Those "others" needed for reconnection can include community, in which communal and cultural sites of abuse—from the self, outward—can be transformed into ones of accountability and healing (Burke, 2021; R. Ray & Rosow, 2012). Within the Black community, it is each person's responsibility to not sexually abuse anyone. This responsibility extends to ensuring that additional harm, through secondary marginalization (C. J. Cohen, 2009), (intra)cultural pressure, and violent silencing is eradicated. In doing so, the same (intra)cultural trust that provided vulnerability to the harm of cultural betrayal can be leveraged for healing as well.

Adapted Principles of Restorative Justice

> Targeted communities and their allies cannot allow conversations to focus on that which does not need to change—an innocent victim's behavior; we must insist that citizens grapple with all that empowers perpetrators. (Koritha Mitchell, 2015, p. 231)

Restorative justice (RJ; e.g., Zehr, 2002, 2005) is a specified process for addressing harm that needs specific training and precautions to implement (Beck et al., 2011). Therefore, in this section, I borrow tenets from RJ as a way of orienting a possible avenue for how healing from cultural betrayal sexual trauma can be conceptualized. With RJ (Leonard, 2011), cultural betrayal sexual trauma is a violation of people and relationships, which creates obligations. As such, justice involves those victimized, those who committed the abuse, and the community (Leonard, 2011). The central focus is the victims' needs, as well as the responsibility that the perpetrator has to repair harm (Leonard, 2011). Three questions personify this focus: "Who was harmed? What are their needs? Whose obligations are these needs?" (Zehr, 2002, p. 21).

In the case of Black male–perpetrated cultural betrayal sexual trauma against Black women and girls, we can answer these questions. The person harmed was a Black woman or girl; her needs may include physical health care, validation and (intra)cultural support, and psycho-education on sexual abuse—including the impact of multiple forms of betrayal in trauma, reconnection with the self and others, creative outlets, and more. As cultural betrayal sexual trauma and (intra)cultural pressure are community-oriented harms, it is the obligation of those in the Black community—including but not limited to the perpetrator(s)—and the broader society that feeds the context of inequality to meet these needs. For a girl whose grown neighbor sexually abused her, for instance, part of the healing process could be the girl's family providing validation and (intra)cultural support, while they together seek out information on sexual abuse from community organizations that specialize in supporting leadership, training, and policy advocacy to benefit Black female survivors (e.g., National Organization of Sisters of Color Ending Sexual Assault, 2017). This collective healing can serve the additional goal of preventing recurring harm (Neeley, 2021) within the Black community.

The Role of Anger

Discussed by Bryant-Davis (2005), the role of anger is vital in identifying and resisting oppression and sexist abuse. Because of intersectional oppression, including Angry Black Woman stereotypes (e.g., hooks, 1984/2015) and Victorian traditions in femininity that calls for docileness (Crenshaw, 1989), Black women and girls can learn to stifle their anger. When expressed, others can misinterpret Black women and girls' anger, weaponizing it against them (e.g., Gómez, 2014; hooks, 1984/2015).

Nevertheless, we must reclaim our emotions, including their validity, in the same way that we reclaim our bodies after cultural betrayal sexual trauma. In other words, others' discomfort with our anger need not be internalized by us. When something infuriating occurs, such as violent silencing, being infuriated makes sense (Hargons, 2020). Those appropriate links between external events and our emotional reactions to them should be protected by us, even when living in a world that would prefer to pathologize them. We can cocreate spaces with others where we can express our range of emotions, including anger. When such spaces don't exist, we can create them within ourselves, by creating art, such as painting and poetry, and by journaling (Bryant-Davis, 2005).

The Conundrum of Hatred
The hatred that Black women and girl survivors can have for the perpetrator(s) can infiltrate their righteous anger. Though such hatred can be toxic for survivors, it can also serve a protective function. Hatred can help abolish the need for the depended-on relationship with the perpetrator(s), which can then lower the likelihood this person continues their abuse. Unilateral hatred can additionally aid in healing in some ways, as it is less complicated to conceptualize the rapist(s) as a demon(s), as opposed to a complicated, harmful, problematic, oppressed, and potentially formerly abused human(s). Nevertheless, the call for Black women and girl survivors to forgive in the name of Black solidarity, faith, convenience, or anything else is both unfair and unhealthy.

Within the RJ framework (e.g., Zehr, 2002), victims do not owe perpetrators anything. It is also true that those responsible for the obligations that stem from the abusive behavior include the perpetrator(s), as well as potentially the family, the Black community (e.g., friends, loved ones, partnerships), and society. Therefore, the obligation to systemically and structurally humanize the perpetrator(s) in ways that allow for paths of redemption—including how the perpetrator(s) can meet the needs of those he has victimized—falls on systems of families, communities, and society. Therefore, while operating within a dehumanizing legal system (e.g., Alexander, 2010), we as a collective can promote social justice by way of reconciliation and primary prevention, thus achieving moral justice for everyone involved (Ralph, 2022).

Radical Healing in Groups

> When sisters take their shoes off and start talking about what's happening, the first thing we cry about is violence. The number one issue for most of our sisters is violence—battering, sexual abuse. Same thing for their daughters, whether they are twelve or four. (Byllye Avery, 1989, p. 15)

> Open discussions (Wiesner, 2022), including the use of storytelling (Chioneso et al., 2020), can occur in radical healing (French et al., 2020). For group-level healing, it is vital to know how to respond well to disclosures of sexual abuse, including cultural betrayal sexual trauma. Fundamentals in healing-promoting

responses to someone who has told you they were abused include (a) respecting the victimized person's autonomy and strengths, including letting adult survivors take the lead on if/when they want to disclose to others (Freyd, 2022; Freyd & Birrell, 2013; Gómez, 2015c; Holland & Bedera, 2019; Holland et al., 2018; Ullman & Peter-Hagene, 2014); (b) placing responsibility on the perpetrator(s); (c) focusing on the victimized person's needs; and (d) sincerely apologizing when appropriate. Further, compassionate listening includes having skills that provide comfort to the person sharing their story: using attentive body language (e.g., consistent eye contact); encouraging the victimized person to continue (e.g., allowing silence, reflecting back what the person has said, not changing the topic); and conveying support (e.g., pointing out the person's strengths, validating their emotions; Foynes & Freyd, 2011).

Emotional Emancipation Circles
> [Emotional emancipation] is the freedom to see ourselves as the beautiful, lovable, intelligent, capable, and worthy human beings we are; the freedom to see ourselves beyond the negative stereotypes that have burdened and limited us for centuries. (Community Healing Network, 2022, "What Is Emotional Emancipation?" section)

From Afrocentric perspectives, connection, care, and accountability are necessary aspects of community (Asante, 1987; Myers, 1988; J. E. Turner, 1984). In collaboration with the Community Healing Network, the Association of Black Psychologists produces Emotional Emancipation Circles within Black communities (Grills, 2013; Myers, 2013). As discussed by Gómez and Gobin (2020a),

> Designing similar circles for Black women and girls who experience cultural betrayal trauma can capitalize on (intra)cultural trust to mitigate the harm of racial trauma and cultural betrayal. Specifically, these EEC-inspired circles can be constructed in collaboration with community partners to create a structure that would meet community members' needs (e.g., Black women only vs. open to all genders). One goal could be to implement EEC-inspired circles that incorporate psycho-education on racial trauma, interpersonal trauma, and cultural betrayal trauma theory, while facilitating individual- and community-level healing through (intra)cultural trust. (p. 8)

Such groups can simultaneously empower Black women and girls while transforming the Black community into sites of support (Collins, 1991/2000) through amplifying collectivism, critical consciousness, strength and resistance, self-knowledge and cultural authenticity, and radical hope (French et al., 2020).

The Role of Black Men
> We feel solidarity with progressive Black men and do not advocate the fractionalization that white women who are separatists demand. Our situation as Black people necessitates that we have solidarity around the fact of race.... We struggle together with Black men against racism, while we also struggle with Black men about sexism. (Combahee River Collective, 1977, as cited in K. Taylor, 2017, p. 19)

As those who benefit from, and at times perpetrate, sexist oppression and abuse, Black men, in particular, have a role to play in radical healing. Instead of domination, Black men can use their power in the Black community to collaborate with and support Black women and girls through acts of resistance (Bush, 1986; Collins, 1991/2000; Terborg-Penn, 1986) that promote strength, community, and radical hope (French et al., 2020; Mosley et al., 2020). In Gómez & Gobin (2020b), we provide eight tips for the many Black men who want to be catalysts for equitable and peaceful advancements in the Black community:

- Listen and support the Black women and girls in your lives when they tell you they've been violated.

- Care—and communicate that you care—about what the other person or people are feeling when you're being sexually intimate with them.

- Understand that sexually abusing Black women and girls happens within the context of a culture—both within and outside of the Black community—that degrades them.

- Recognize power dynamics that exist between you and the Black women you work with. As such, be intentional about not abusing your power.

- Call out all forms of behavior that perpetuate rape culture, such as catcalling, for what they are: Attempts to control Black women and girls by sexualizing them in public.

- Know that your capability of not sexually abusing anyone is the same capability that all Black men have—including those who rape.

- Do not provide excuses for Black men who rape.

- Continue to be part of the solution to end Black male perpetrated sexual violence against Black women and girls.

WHAT OF THE FAMILY?

> What continues to make the Black family so unique is its resilience. (Harriette Pipes McAdoo & Sinead N. Younge, 2009, p. 112)

As is foundational in radical healing (French et al., 2020), a collective sense of being (Nobles, 1972); kinship, communalism, and unity (Komarraju & Cokley, 2008; Nobles, 1972); community orientation (Gómez & Gobin, 2022); and interdependence (Gómez & Gobin, 2020a) are cultural staples of the Black community in the United States. This collective sense of being promotes a collective responsibility in which the whole is often privileged over the individual self; moreover, individual action is appraised on its benefits or consequences for the Black community (Belgrave & Allison, 2018; Komarraju & Cokley, 2008).

It is then unsurprising that the Black family, as a primary institution for many, is often characterized by extended networks of support, including elders, parents, siblings, children, other relatives, loved ones, and friends (McAdoo & Younge, 2009), who provide connection, cultural identity, safety, and protection and solidarity against oppression (Collins, 1991/2000; Crenshaw, 1991; hooks, 1984/2015; Louie & Upenieks, 2022; Pennell & Koss, 2011; R. J. Taylor et al., 2021; Zinzow et al., 2021). As such, the Black family can have richness, depth, and love that amplify the strengths of both individuals and the Black community as a whole.

Cultural Betrayal Sexual Trauma in the Family

> The formation of an oppositional world view is necessary. . . . This means that the world we have most intimately known, the world in which we feel "safe" (even if such feelings are based on illusions), must be radically changed. (bell hooks, 1984/2015, p. 166)

In calling for radical transformation, hooks (1984/2015) was speaking generally and not specifically of the Black family unit. However, I invoke her message here, as the family, unfortunately, can also be the site of human rights violations, including male-perpetrated violence and abuse against women and girls in the home (United Nations General Assembly, 1979, 1993). This intimate terrorism (Herman, 1997) mirrors the disrespect, degradation, abuse, intersectional oppression, and violence that Black women and girls experience in society (hooks, 1984/2015). Thus, it can be tempting for us to simply accept that some forms of harm against the self—from loved ones and strangers—are simply part of life.

While it would be a mistake to characterize the Black family as an institution that is necessarily fraught with sexist oppression and abuse, it would be similarly erroneous to pretend that such harms cannot and do not exist in any of our families. That is, (intra)cultural pressure, including violent silencing, encourages us to not characterize Blackness in a negative light— with the Black family needing specific protection due to Whites' systematic degradation of it (e.g., see Collins, 1989; for a discussion on Whites' pathologization of the Black family, see hooks, 1981/2015). However, deeply needed is the space for truth through shedding the White Read (Bowleg, 2021) and, at least intermittently, eradicating the paralyzing and silencing fear of White supremacy.

There is trauma, abuse, and violence within some Black families. For the purposes of the current book, I will say, specifically, there is Black male–perpetrated sexual violence against Black women and girls within some Black families (e.g., "How Author Created Film Character Precious," Evening Standard, 2012). There are some Black fathers who rape their Black daughters. There are some Black husbands who sexually abuse their Black wives. There are some Black men who sexually molest, abuse, rape, and traffic their Black female relatives. From starting with that truth, we can begin to acknowledge the impact of this violence within the Black family, including cultural betrayal, (intra)cultural pressure, and an omnipresent violent silencing that is compounded by the vulnerability of the harm of abuse within the family (Freyd, 1996). Through those acknowledgments can come solutions and healing.

Choices

> You must choose yourself first. It's not selfish. It is survival. You need to protect yourself. It is your life. (Preston Warren Dugger III, personal communication, 2022)

In the What This Can Actually Look Like section toward the end of this chapter, I discuss healing strategies for Black women and girl survivors of cultural betrayal sexual trauma within the family. Therefore, in this section, I focus directly on the family unit itself. Just as Black solidarity in the community should not be used to accept cultural betrayal trauma (Gómez, 2015b; Gómez & Gobin, 2020b), similarly the strength of the Black family should not be perverted into a house of horrors. Within the family, abuse can be misconstrued as expressions of masculinity and love (hooks, 1981/2015). Though leaving the family would mean abandoning the abuse, it would also result in a loss of connection and safety from other violence and oppressions in society. That cost is high. Yet, there is an argument to be made that remaining within an abusive family can be even more damaging. Though it can seem contradictory, taking care of yourself is a necessary aspect of being part of any whole.

Leaving the Family

> I took a train outta there. . . . I told the engineer I don't think there's no help handy. . . . Heaven help the tie that binds the family. . . . Looks like even God can't save the family. (Nina Simone, 1978)

Importantly, family and Blackness are not synonymous with cultural betrayal and abuse. In other words, when in abusive families, we can create something different. We can make choices to end sexism, thus strengthening the family (hooks, 1981/2015). We can keep the family central while getting rid of abusive dimensions that harm us. Additionally, there may be times when we can leave our family of origin, thus creating new homes, new havens, new loved ones, and even new families without abuse. As Thema Bryant (2022) tells us, "The gift of homecoming is having a positive regard for your presence, your wellness, your life. . . . You can breathe. You can choose sacred stillness. You can rest . . . you . . . give yourself room . . . to come home" (p. 34). In doing so, we disaggregate the toxic notions that love is accompanied by suffering and solidarity lives alongside abuse. We must know—and behave in line with that knowing—that family can be a relational place in which peace, love, equality, and solidarity reign supreme in the absence of degradation and violence.

WHAT IS FREE TO YOU?

> What is free to me? . . . Just a feeling. . . . You know it when it happens. . . . I'll tell you what Freedom is to me: no fear, no fear . . . a new way of seeing. (Nina Simone, 2008)

Radical hope and healing (French et al., 2020; Mosley et al., 2020) exist in the dialectic between you and your community. Creating personal meaning is vital for continuously revitalizing radical hope and healing in beneficial ways for both you and your communities (Mosley et al., 2020). In being asked, "What is freedom?" (Hope, 2021), I find myself being led to even more questions, beyond any narrow, objective definition: If you are free from all the violent and oppressive shackles that bind, what would you feel? What would you do? What would you let go? What would remain the same in your life? What would have to change internally? What would have to change societally? What would have to change within your given family or in creating your made family? Within the space between what the world is and what we need it to be, how can you find freedom within yourself?

Safe Space Within the Self

> This realm of relatively safe discourse . . . is a necessary condition for Black women's resistance. . . . By advancing Black women's empowerment through self-definition, the safe spaces housing this culture of resistance help Black women resist the dominant ideology promulgated not only outside Black communities but within African-American institutions. (Patricia Hill Collins, 1991/2000, p. 95)

Though Collins (1991/2000) above was detailing safe spaces with other Black women, I add that finding such space within yourself to promote self-definition and self-valuation (Collins, 1991/2000) is possible and important through freewriting. Freewriting is simply unfiltered writing, without specified structure or rules. The goals lie in the understanding derived from the process, as opposed to the outcome of the text itself. For our purposes, a timer (e.g., 45 minutes) or external markers, such as having a movie on in the background, can provide the time configuration. You start with a prompt, such as one of the questions listed above (e.g., What is free to you?), and then you write. You do not write for anyone else's mind or comprehension, and you do not write with an external gaze judging your words. Instead, you write just for you. You write just for the process of thinking, feeling, and learning about yourself. In that way, there are answers and healing (Bryant-Davis, 2005) implicit in the act of such writing, distinct from any epiphanies you might uncover. In the next section, I provide two examples of freewriting from a Black woman who endured cultural betrayal sexual trauma.

WHAT THIS CAN ACTUALLY LOOK LIKE

> The voices of these African-American women are not those of victims but of survivors. Their ideas and actions suggest that not only does a self-defined, articulated Black women's standpoint exist, but its presence . . . [is] essential to Black women's survival. (Patricia Hill Collins, 1991/2000, p. 93)

Nikiya: Finding Free

Nikiya is a Black woman in her late 30s who experienced both high betrayal (perpetrator who was trusted and/or depended on; e.g., Freyd, 1997) and cultural betrayal traumas (e.g., Gómez, 2012) throughout her life: Her father sexually abused her in early childhood, her high school boyfriend raped her multiple times, and a coworker and friend at her first job attempted to rape her. All the perpetrators were Black males whom she needed and trusted.

Fast-forward to the summer of 2020. Nikiya watched the video from the previous section in which Nina Simone (2008) grappled with what freedom was to her. Afraid of what the answers might hold for her, Nikiya turned on a scary movie, which strangely comforted her: The fear in the film matched her emotional state while reminding her that she was currently safe from all she was afraid of—the same way she was safe from whatever would happen in the film. With that, Nikiya summoned her courage—and those of all who had come before her, known and unknown—and began to freewrite in her journal. Below is an excerpt of her response to the simple query "What is free to me?" (shared with permission):

> There is COVID wreaking havoc, might there be an insurrection? Are we headed towards civil war? Like never before, I notice the violence of anti-Black racism and sexism against Black women is found within the fabric and in every

corner and aspect of my job. The dehumanization I experience there is the same hate that justifies publicly and privately murdering Black people. I am drowning, I am suffocating. But I am supposed to write about what is freedom to me. . . . I know that I and we are not the first to be confronting a violent, murderous government. Even with that, my life is still my own within every breath I take. I can sit in my home, looking out the window to the trees and knowing that absolutely nothing else exists for me in this moment except for the beauty that is immediately in front of me. I am free deep inside myself. I'm free when I feel loved and when I feel and show love for others. I have within my most grounded self, this No Fear. Whatever happens, I am still me and we are still us until this life ends. There's beauty in that. Beauty in the struggle, beauty in the fight, and beauty in the stillness of being free inside myself. I choose to relish in my beauty of my one life . . . because in my life, there are times when I know that I am free.

Within this excerpt, Nikiya begins with the pain of the weight of the world—societally and individually—on her spirit. She makes links among harms along the spectrum of systemic cruelty, discrimination against herself at work, and murder of other Black people around the country. Through writing, her appraisals evolve into individual and collective strength, solidarity, and sovereignty, including a defiant *No Fear* amid impending physical and cultural death. Through the freewrite, Nikiya's emotions peaked with sadness and anxiety. However, through continued writing, she settled into calmness, wisdom, and peace. Here, Nikiya felt truly free. And from this freewrite, she developed a new strategy for self-soothing: a presence within herself and only her immediate surroundings that provided her with shelter from all the pain she carried from what was happening to her and her community of Black people.

The freewrite also served as an example to herself of her own strength: In facing these destructive, insurmountable harms, she traveled through to the other side. She showed herself that she not only could survive the distress but also was capable of finding peace in and through that pain. In the years that followed, Nikiya returned to this freewrite and all the wisdom that came from it. She repeatedly conceptualized herself within a long line of Black women and girls who are simultaneously fragile, strong, courageous, and afraid. These are real people with real pain who remain really separated from all the shackles that bind the mind, body, soul, and spirit. That day and for many days since, Nikiya has returned to her *free*.

Nikiya: Stillness and Peace Within Unescapable Unknowability

I wrote these words for everyone who struggles in their youth. Who won't accept deception instead of what is truth. (Lauryn Hill, 1998)

While the current chapter has focused on healing with and through community, we know there are times when such connective healing is impossible.

Take, for instance, Nikiya, who is processing her father sexually abusing her for years. A question that keeps echoing in her head is "Why did my daddy rape me all those times?" Like Nikiya, many will never receive an answer at all, from either their father or anyone else. In fact, some fathers may provide a manipulative DARVO (Freyd, 1997) response in which they Deny perpetration: "It didn't happen"; Attack their child: "You're mentally unwell"; and Reverse Victim and Offender: "How could you accuse me of something like this when I love you so much?!" Importantly, perhaps no explanation would suffice even if it were given honestly, insightfully, and truthfully.

This is another example of where freewriting can help. Nikiya chose to freewrite potential reasons for her father abusing her as if it were coming from his voice. An excerpt of Nikiya's freewrite "from her father" is shared with permission:

> Possible reasons why Daddy raped me. . . . "I raped you because: I don't know why; I was selfish; I enjoyed your pain—it increased my sexual gratification; I didn't really notice you were there or that you had feelings; I am narcissistic—in only seeing myself, I just assumed that you liked it to; I hated you and wanted to punish you; I loved you and wanted to be close to you; I hated myself; I needed to dominate you so that I could solidify that I was powerful and would never be abused again myself. . . . But the bottom line is that I, Daddy, should have removed myself from you. Protected you from me by taking myself away. You shouldn't have had to keep this secret, be hurt, be ashamed, and then leave home so young all by yourself. Cos there is no excuse for what I did. I hurt you. I confused you. I am sorry. If I could go back and do it again, I would not do it again. I would make sure you were safe, including making sure you were safe from me. I am sorry. It is all my fault and my responsibility. You did nothing wrong."

Nikiya's above freewrite created a space where her father was imagined to take full responsibility for his abusive actions. In doing so, she internally enacts the restorative justice obligation that her father has to her as a person he has harmed (Leonard, 2011) while explicitly removing responsibility from herself *(I am bad)* and onto him *(he is responsible)*. In that way, such a freewrite can be experienced as relational healing, but one that is safe, is possible, and happens internally within the person.

SUMMARY BULLET POINTS

1. Violent silencing exists due to structural inequality but is not an immutable cultural factor in the Black community. Each of us advocating for equality, guarding against violent silencing within ourselves, and engaging in truth-telling when psychologically, spiritually, and physically reasonably safe to do so can engender positive cultural change.

2. The psychological framework of radical healing for POCI is grounded in five anchors: collectivism, critical consciousness, cultural authenticity and self-knowledge, radical hope, and strength and resistance. These anchors can be found through practical strategies for engaging in radical healing on individual and community levels.

3. Concrete strategies for radical healing on the individual level include dynamic processes of reclaiming your body as your own: journaling/poetry, movement, arts and crafts, music, drama/theater, spirituality, social support, nature, and activism; being attuned to one's emotions; and engaging in the psychological framework for radical healing.

4. Concrete strategies for radical healing on the community level include basing practices of community healing within principles from restorative justice; understanding the roles of anger and hatred, as well as the obligation that the perpetrator(s), family, community, and society have to Black women and girl survivors; responding well to disclosure of cultural betrayal sexual trauma; and engaging in radical healing within groups.

5. As beneficiaries and, at times, perpetrators of sexist oppression and cultural betrayal sexual trauma, Black men have specific roles to play in creating a peaceful and equitable Black community.

6. Sexist oppression and abuse are not innate components of Black families. Black families can work to eradicate such violence where it does exist. Black women and girl survivors have the option to leave their families to create relational spaces without oppression and abuse.

7. The process of freewriting from a general prompt, such as "What is free to me?" can engender individual and even relational healing with others within yourself.

8. Experiencing freedom, liberation, joy, light, and laughter is possible for everyone in the Black community, including Black women and girls who have endured cultural betrayal sexual trauma.

7 INSTITUTIONAL COURAGE TO CHANGE THE WORLD

CHAPTER AT A GLANCE

As a guide for promoting structural healing through systemic change, in this chapter, I (a) discuss institutional betrayal, institutional cowardice, and institutional courage; (b) identify institutionally courageous actions that can benefit Black women and girl survivors; (c) provide three examples of institutional betrayal, institutional courage, and dreamstorming across health care, university, and nonprofit settings; (d) extract institutionally courageous lessons learned from one lawyer-community collaboration; (e) identify how to avoid common barriers to systemic change; and (f) close with hope for creating the peaceful, equity world we dreamstorm about.

One distinguishing feature of Black feminist thought is its insistence that both the changed consciousness of individuals and the social transformation of . . . institutions constitute essential ingredients for social change. New knowledge is important for both dimensions of change.

—Patricia Hill Collins, 1991/2000, p. 221

https://doi.org/10.1037/0000362-007
The Cultural Betrayal of Black Women and Girls: A Black Feminist Approach to Healing From Sexual Abuse, by J. M. Gómez
Copyright © 2023 by the American Psychological Association. All rights reserved.

Perhaps especially in the field of psychology, it can be tempting to misunderstand violence and oppression as individual-level problems that occur interpersonally (i.e., between people). However, the context of racism (e.g., Mills, 1997) and intersectional oppression (e.g., Collins, 1990) affects the causes, meaning making, and outcomes of Black male–perpetrated sexual violence against Black women and girls—known as *cultural betrayal sexual trauma* (current book). Moreover, societal inequality creates the existence and meaning of cultural betrayal sexual trauma as a community-oriented harm (e.g., Gómez & Gobin, 2022). Therefore, intersectional oppression and cultural betrayal sexual trauma against Black women and girls are not simply interpersonal harms. Instead, the harm is additionally societal and institutional in nature. Therefore, structural healing through substantive systems-level change is required (e.g., Grzanka, 2020a; Neblett, 2022).

Necessary for structural healing is *dreamstorming*, a concept I came up with in 2019: to think, write, and dream a different world for ourselves. More than simple brainstorming or daydreaming, dreamstorming is the process of envisioning liberation, as well as the paths it would take to create and inhabit a world of true freedom. Instead of getting stifled by the current state of the world, dreamstorming allows us to envision worlds where equality and peace are endemic. Moreover, dreamstorming guides us to the steps we, as individuals and as a collective, can take to march toward our dreamstormed world, empowering us to engage in institutional courage (Freyd, 2014b) now. In doing so, we go beyond change via triaging at the individual, interpersonal, and/or microlevel, such as conceptualizing individual therapy as the only avenue to heal from violence and oppression within a world that remains evermore violent and oppressive. Instead, dreamstorming pushes us to think structurally about absence; a dreamstormed world of freedom would be living in the absence of any and all individual and systemic oppressions and violence, including violation of the self, psychological imprisonment, reduced physical and logistical mobility, and fear.

I open this chapter with critical visioning regarding emotionality in institutional change work. I then provide a review of the literature on institutional betrayal (e.g., Smith & Freyd, 2014) and cowardice (L. S. Brown, 2021). Next, I introduce Freyd's (2014b) concept of institutional courage and outline steps, examples, and outcomes of institutional courage that can benefit Black women and girls. I then delineate realistic processes of structural healing by providing institutional examples of betrayal, courage, and dreamstorming across settings in health care, a university, and a nonprofit coalition. In the What This Can Actually Look Like section, I relay a real-life example of institutional courage from community–lawyer collaborations in Los Angeles, California (Cummings,

2021a), that provides lessons for psychologists and allied mental health professionals. Then, I discuss how to avoid barriers to systemic change, regarding dealing with White mediocrity, inequality in organizations, scope and limitations of measures of progress, and problematizing power. Finally, I close with a message of hope for using institutional courage to change the world, followed by summary bullet points of lessons from the current chapter.

CRITICAL VISIONING: EMOTIONALITY IN INSTITUTIONAL CHANGE WORK

> Who must do the hard things? Those who can.... Who must do the impossible things? Those who care. (Carolyn R. Payton, 1984, p. 397, taken from Asian philosophy)

I often interpret institutions' cowardly inaction as "X Institution does not care about, value, or prioritize Y," as in "University X does not care about retaining marginalized faculty." In doing so, I am providing an explanation for how an institution can profess values stated in its mission, vision, and advertisements, while no tangible evidence exists that demonstrates those values (Ahmed, 2012). An example of this is universities that profess to care about the importance of racially diversifying their faculty body while failing to hire stellar scholars of color year after year (Gómez, 2020b, 2022f).

Other interpretations of institutions' cowardice exist, which directly and perhaps deliberately avoid such "caring" language. For example, institutional inaction can be explained through the existence of a gap between policies and managerial discretion. As such, policies include those both related and unrelated to legal compliance, whereas managerial discretion refers to leaders' choices on if and how the leaders and the organization itself are held accountable to those policies (Edelman, 1992). In plain terms, institutional inaction can be explained by the distance between stated norms and behavioral practices. In this latter interpretation, changemakers can identify the complex and nuanced interplay between institutional actors and each other, institutional bureaucracy, and policies, thereby identifying practical solutions to close the norms–practices gap (e.g., Kim, 2021).

Cultural Betrayal Trauma Theory Lens

> [A Black feminist ethic of caring is] talking with the heart; appropriateness with emotions, because emotion indicates that the speaker believes in the validity of the argument. (Patricia Hill Collins, 1999/2000, p. 266)

For the cultural betrayal trauma theory (CBTT) lens, I pull not from the specifics of the theory itself but rather from its foundation as a Black feminist, empirical framework. In lieu of the harmful myth of objectivity, Black feminist work promotes Afrocentric feminist epistemology, including the ethic of caring (Collins, 1991/2000). According to Collins (1991/2000), the ethic of caring breaks down the White, Eurocentric epistemic separation between intellect and emotion. This White, Eurocentric epistemic separation can include, for instance, a theoretical and practical distinction between thoughts and feelings. Within an ethic of caring, however, one's heart, morality, and humanity are necessarily intertwined with one's intellectual thought processes and conclusions. Additionally, as an empirically testable theory, CBTT research provides evidence for and against its postulates, in addition to theorizing the harm of cultural betrayal trauma. Therefore, a CBTT lens undergirds the expectation that emotions inform intellect, with rhetoric, such as institutional norms, being measured against the institutions' actual practices.

The Tension and My Critical Visioning

> You always told me it takes time. . . . How much time do you want for your progress? (James Baldwin, 1989, in *James Baldwin: The Price of the Ticket*)

The tension occurs under explicit and implicit calls to suppress Black feminist emotionality in favor of White, Eurocentric rationality in order to understand institutions' inaction (Gómez, 2014). In dominant spaces, so-called rationality is oppressively euphemistic for operating devoid of ethics, morals, and emotions while punishing marginalized others who express these traits alongside true rationality. Such punishing behavior is antithetical to institutional equity, however, because violent oppression is not a feelingless experience (see Gutiérrez y Muhs et al., 2012; Niemann et al., 2020); therefore, a mandate for an emotionless response to violent oppression is unreasonable, unfair, and another instantiation of such oppression. My critical visioning privileges Black feminist emotionality, as grounded emotions can and should be used to engender motivation, problem-solving, and structural change. Thus, identifying the norms–practices gap within institutions happens within a deliberate ethic of caring (Collins, 1991/2000).

Moreover, the interpretation of institutions as "caring" can be beneficial. Far from inanimate objects, institutions are filled with people who do have emotions, ethics, morals, motivations, values, priorities, courage, and cowardice, which they use to create, uphold, disrupt, and recreate institutional norms and practices. My critical visioning allows for such humanity, while additionally framing the institutional problems I discuss in this chapter within the appropriate sense of urgency.

Plainly, it has been more than 400 years of anti-Blackness, including human rights violations, on the land currently known as the United States of America (Hannah-Jones, 2021); more than 150 years since Black women have publicly identified the problems of intersectional oppression and sexual violence (e.g., see Sojourner Truth and Anna Julia Cooper, as cited in Crenshaw, 1989; Combahee River Collective, 1977, as cited in K. Taylor, 2017; A. Walker, 1982); more than 50 years since Black feminists' initial critiques of White feminists' racism in their movement for women's liberation (e.g., Combahee River Collective, 1977, as cited in K. Taylor, 2017; hooks, 1981/2015); more than a decade since the first inauguration of the one and only U.S. president, Barack Obama, who was not a White man—though he was a man nonetheless (M. Phillips, 2009); and more than 2 years since the January 6, 2021, insurrection of the U.S. Capitol with the goal of overthrowing the electoral-college certification of President Biden and Vice President Harris (e.g., Dastagir, 2021; McShane, 2021).

The contemporary ravages of structural racism (e.g., D. D. King et al., 2022), intersectional oppression (e.g., Collins, 1990), sexual abuse (e.g., Bryant-Davis et al., 2009) through cultural betrayal, (intra)cultural pressure (e.g., Gómez & Gobin, 2020a), oppression in therapy (e.g., Sue, 1978), violent silencing, and more are evidenced in every aspect of Black women's and girls' lives. Exhausting is the common refrain of citing past true or mythical racial progress to avoid current engagement in actual equity (Eberhardt, 2021, in conversation with Richeson; Richeson, 2020). An example of this refrain comes from my first faculty position:

> When I joined the faculty in 2019, the department had a one-credit, pass/no pass ethics and diversity seminar course for clinical psychology graduate students, which met for only 50 minutes each week. This seminar was the only psychology graduate course with a specified focus on diversity of any kind. When I voiced concern about this not being enough education in diversity-related topics, I was told . . . we are lucky that diversity is offered as central in any course. (Gómez, 2022c)

The wait has been long, with the demands for patience wearing thin (e.g., Fleming, 2022). The unacceptable rate of progress across over 400 years can be at least partially explained by those at the top of the racial hierarchy (Mills, 1997)—known as White people—not behaviorally, and in many cases not even personally, caring about how many other people are actively being crushed under the oppression they perpetrate and collude with (for examples within psychology, see Gómez, 2022d, 2015g; Gómez, Smith, et al., 2016; Hoffman et al., 2015). Therefore, to those with White, Eurocentric rationality perspectives, the question of institutional change is this: How much time do you need to discover how to make your institution's stated norms match its practices? The question from a Black feminist ethic is this: How will you find, and then channel, the amount of care required to finally and courageously do the right thing? From both stances: When will enough be enough?

INSTITUTIONAL BETRAYAL AND COWARDICE

> The most common way people give up their power is by thinking they don't have any. (Alice Walker, n.d.-b, as cited in Goodreads, 2023b)

Institutional betrayal (C. P. Smith & Freyd, 2014) is the apparently isolated and/or systemic actions or inactions within an institution that harm its dependent members. An example of institutional betrayal is a university forcefully accessing the therapy records of a victimized student to use the information in a lawsuit (e.g., Gómez, 2022h; Kingkade, 2015; Pryal, 2022). Institutional cowardice is a type of institutional betrayal that is "a knowing or consciously motivated act, an intentional decision to go in a particular direction and allow a vulnerable person or persons to be harmed" (L. S. Brown, 2021, p. 242). Hallmarks of institutional cowardice are absences, such as refraining from providing an apology, ceasing all contact with and support of a victim of institutional betrayal, and doing nothing at all under the guise of following the rules. Similar to how (intra)cultural pressure additionally harms Black women and girls who have endured cultural betrayal sexual trauma (Gómez, 2019e), institutional betrayal negatively affects victims above and beyond the impact of the original harm (Adams-Clark & Freyd, 2021; Adams-Clark et al., 2020; Ahern, 2018; Andresen et al., 2019; Cromer et al., 2018; Freyd & Birrell, 2013; Gómez, 2015d, 2015g; Gómez & Freyd, 2014, 2019; Gómez, Noll, et al., 2021; Gómez, Smith, et al., 2014, 2016; Holland et al., 2018; Holliday & Monteith, 2019; Lind et al., 2020; Monteith et al., 2016, 2021; Pyke, 2018; Reinhardt et al., 2016; Rosenthal et al., 2016; Sall & Littleton, 2022; Smidt et al., 2021; C. P. Smith, 2017; C. P. Smith & Freyd, 2013, 2014, 2017; C. P. Smith et al., 2014, 2016; Tamaian et al., 2017; Wright et al., 2017). Therefore, institutional actors must engage in behaviors—including through systemic design of policy and implementation of practices—that address, and ultimately prevent, institutional betrayal (e.g., Klest et al., 2020; Pope, 2015).

INSTITUTIONAL COURAGE

> [Institutional courage] is an institution's commitment to seek the truth and engage in moral action, despite unpleasantness, risk, and short-term cost. It is a pledge to protect and care for those who depend on the institution. It is a compass oriented to the common good of individuals, institutions, and the world. It is a force that transforms institutions into more accountable, equitable, effective places for everyone. (Jennifer J. Freyd, Founder of Center for Institutional Courage, as cited in Institutional Courage, n.d.)

As the antidote to institutional betrayal and cowardice, institutional courage (Freyd, 2014b, 2018; Freyd & Smidt, 2019) requires that institutional actors and the institution itself promote equitable justice. Institutional courage can address diverse harms across a variety of institutions (e.g., Gómez et al., 2023). Institutional courage can provide structural prevention and healing for the systemic harms against Black women and girls, including racism, sexism, intersectional oppression, sexual violence, cultural betrayal, (intra)cultural pressure, violent silencing, and harm in therapy. Importantly, institutional courage is so named because engaging in it can be difficult and at times costly due to subsequent institutional betrayal.

I have adapted the table of institutional reparations from Gómez, Smith, and colleagues (2016), which includes one or more examples and verifiable outcomes of each institutional courage (Freyd, 2014b, 2018) step. I further organize institutional courage steps that can benefit Black women and girl survivors of intersectional oppression and cultural betrayal sexual trauma: Class 1: Operations; Class 2: Assessments; and Class 3: Reparations. As such, the content of these tables operationalize institutional courage while providing diverse examples of how institutional courage can be applied across institutions for the systemic benefit of Black women and girls.

Similar to institutional betrayal, some aspects of institutional courage occur in the absence of discreet problematic events, such as through policy. Class 1: Operations (Table 7.1) describes multiple steps that can provide the foundation for an institutionally courageous organization, including operating with transparency; employing checks and balances; complying with laws and with the spirit of the laws; educating individuals, communities, and organizations about cultural betrayal and (intra)cultural pressure; incorporating social justice; addressing societal problems; and committing budgetary, time, and person-power resources to all institutional courage steps.

Also employed as a matter of course in organizations, Class 2: Assessments (Table 7.2) deals with organizations' continuous assessments that are general, as well as those that are specific to measurable progress, priorities, and potential for future institutional betrayals. Such assessments can identify problem areas

TABLE 7.1. Institutional Courage Class 1: Operations—To Benefit Black Women and Girls Across Institutions and Communities

Institutional courage	Example	Verifiable outcome(s)
Operate with transparency[a,b,c,d]	Share results of climate survey, as well as action plan, to members of the clinic (e.g., licensed clinicians, clients)	Number of accessible articles, presentations, books, educational materials, and other forms of mass communication that include complete and accurate information
Employ checks and balances[e,f]	Have checks and balances in power structures and diffuse highly dependent relationships at the law firm	Documented power structure; absence of singular, highly dependent relationships
Comply with laws[a] and with the spirit of the laws	Comply with laws that prohibit discrimination and sexual violence	Documented reduction in discrimination and cultural betrayal sexual trauma
Educate individuals, communities, and organizations[g] about cultural betrayal and (intra)cultural pressure	Disseminate information to clinicians, clients, and the general public about institutional betrayal,[b,h] cultural betrayal, and (intra)cultural pressure, including how to combat denial through empowerment	Publications for professional and lay audiences, conference presentations, community events, etc.
Incorporate social justice[a,h,i]	Combat intersectional oppression,[j] secondary marginalization,[k] and more in all organizational endeavors	Content of institutional courage steps, including self-assessments, publications, apologies, etc.
Address societal problems[j]	Use the power of the clinic to provide individual, group, and community psychoeducation about cultural betrayal sexual trauma and (intra)cultural pressure	Content of programming, therapy, clinician education, etc.

TABLE 7.1. Institutional Courage Class 1: Operations—To Benefit Black Women and Girls Across Institutions and Communities (*Continued*)

Institutional courage	Example	Verifiable outcome(s)
Commit resources to all institutional courage steps[j]	Dedicate centralized (not add-on) resources to all institutional courage steps	Budget, time allocation, and person-power resources

[a] *Zwischenmenschilcher und institutioneller verrat [Interpersonal and Institutional Betrayal]* (pp. 82-90), by J. M. Gómez, C. P. Smith, and J. J. Freyd, 2014, Asanger Verlag. [b] "Institutional Betrayal," by C. P. Smith and J. J. Freyd, 2014, *American Psychologist, 69*(6), 575-587 (https://doi.org/10.1037/a0037564). [c] *Avoiding Judicial Betrayal of Child Witnesses: Implications From Betrayal Trauma Theory*, by J. J. Freyd, 2013, paper presentation at Roger Williams University. [d] *Institutional Betrayal*, by J. J. Freyd, 2014a, plenary address at the 31st Annual Meeting of the International Society for the Study of Trauma & Dissociation (ISSTD). [e] © J J. Freyd, 2022. [f] *Sexual Harassment of Women: Climate, Culture, and Consequences in Academic Sciences, Engineering, and Medicine*, by National Academies of Sciences, Engineering & Medicine, 2018, The National Academies Press. [g] *Blind to Betrayal: Why We Fool Ourselves We Aren't Being Fooled*, by J. J. Freyd and P. Birrell, 2013, John Wiley and Sons. [h] *From Buzzword to Clinical Psychology: An Invitation to Take Intersectionality Seriously* (pp. 244-261), by P. R. Grzanka, 2020, *Women & Therapy, 43*(3-4), 244-261 (https://doi.org/10.1080/02703149.2020.1729473). [i] "Mapping the Margins: Intersectionality, Identity Politics, and Violence Against Women of Color," by K. Crenshaw, 1991, *Stanford Law Review, 43*(6), 1241-1299 (https://doi.org/10.2307/1229039). [j] "When Sexual Assault Victims Speak Out, Their Institutions Often Betray Them," by J. J. Freyd, 2018, *The Conversation* (https://theconversation.com/when-sexual-assault-victims-speak-out-their-institutions-often-betray-them-87050). [k] "Dangerous Safe Havens: Institutional Betrayal Exacerbates Sexual Trauma," by C. P. Smith and J. J. Freyd, 2013, *Journal of Traumatic Stress, 26*(1), 119-124 (https://doi.org/10.1002/jts.21778).

that the organization can devote resources. Assessments are considered institutionally courageous because of the difficulty in having to know and then address how an organization and its members, including oneself, may be harmful.

Finally, Class 3: Reparations (Table 7.3) shows organizations' institutionally courageous responses to institutional betrayal that engender healing. Such reparations include bearing witness to those harmed, understanding the problem from the perspective of those harmed, acknowledging wrongdoing, apologizing, cherishing the whistleblower, and correcting/retracting false statements. These institutional courage steps can also serve as secondary prevention, thus altering the institutionally betraying trajectory of the organization into one of institutional courage.

Taken together, these classes of institutional courage—Operations, Assessments, and Reparations—provide preemptive, as opposed to solely reactive, institutional norms and practices that serve the institution itself, as well as the members who trust and/or depend on it. In the next section, I revisit these classes of institutional courage through real-life examples of institutional betrayal, institutional courage, and dreamstorming in settings across health care, university, and nonprofit coalition.

TABLE 7.2. Institutional Courage Class 2: Assessments—To Benefit Black Women and Girls Across Institutions and Communities

Institutional courage	Example	Verifiable outcome(s)
Conduct self-assessments: general[a,b,c,d]	Use the Institutional Betrayal Questionnaire[e] and other measures to conduct anonymous surveys that assess the harm experienced by Black women and girls within the department	Studies completed, with results informing creating and/or adapting policies
Conduct self-assessments: measurable progress[f,g]	Engage in thorough and honest appraisals of the university's progress in addressing violence and oppression, as well as effectively working with Black female faculty, staff, and students in culturally competent and trauma-informed manners	The norms-practices gap is eliminated; changes to policy are enforceable;[c] when professionals violate policy, they are held accountable[c]
Conduct self-assessments: priorities[h]	Create a document that includes the specific actions that the nonprofit organization takes to meet the goals of its mission; identify goals that are missing or deprioritized at various levels of leadership; revise the document accordingly; create an action plan to implement changes; make said changes	Documents created; actions taken
Conduct self-assessments: potential for additional institutional betrayals[b,h]	Assess discrimination, retaliation, violence, and institutional betrayal[b] throughout the clinic (e.g., in leadership, among clinicians, against clients)	Studies completed, with data informing creating and/or adapting policies

[a] *Institutional Betrayal*, by J. J. Freyd, 2014a, plenary address at the 31st Annual Meeting of the International Society for the Study of Trauma & Dissociation (ISSTD). [b] *Blind to Betrayal: Why We Fool Ourselves We Aren't Being Fooled*, by J. J. Freyd and P. Birrell, 2013, John Wiley and Sons. [c] *Zwischenmenschilcher und institutioneller verrat [Interpersonal and Institutional Betrayal]* (pp. 82–90), by J. M. Gómez, C. P. Smith, and J. J. Freyd, 2014, Asanger Verlag. [d] "Institutional Betrayal," by C. P. Smith and J. J. Freyd, 2014, *American Psychologist*, 69(6), 575–587 (https://doi.org/10.1037/a0037564). [e] "Dangerous Safe Havens: Institutional Betrayal Exacerbates Sexual Trauma," by C. P. Smith and J. J. Freyd, 2013, *Journal of Traumatic Stress*, 26(1), 119–124 (https://doi.org/10.1002/jts.21778). [f] "Institutional Betrayal Makes Violence More Toxic" [Op-Ed], by J. M. Gómez and J. J. Freyd, August 22, 2014, *The Register-Guard* (Eugene, Oregon), p. A9. [g] *The Hoffman Report and the American Psychological Association: Meeting the Challenge of Change* (pp. 1–9), by K. S. Pope, 2016, Wiley. [h] "Psychological Pressure: Did the APA Commit Institutional Betrayal?" [Op-Ed], by J. M. Gómez, 2015, *Eugene Weekly* (Eugene, Oregon) (https://www.eugeneweekly.com/2015/08/06/psychological-pressure/).

TABLE 7.3. Institutional Courage Class 3: Reparations—To Benefit Black Women and Girls Across Institutions and Communities

Institutional courage	Example	Verifiable outcome(s)
Bear witness to victims' harms[a,b,c,d,e,f]	Create accessible opportunities for diverse victimized Black women and girls to have their cultural betrayal, (intra)cultural pressure, oppression, and/or institutional betrayal be heard; respond well to such disclosures[e]	Accessible meetings (can include teleconferences, community events), where deidentified notes are taken, with permission, that document the harm reported; Class 3: Reparations enacted
Understand the problem[g,h,i]	Use a Black woman's conceptualization of the intersectional oppression she experienced at work as the truth, while linking the harm to systems of oppression	Public statements that are cocreated with the targeted individual, while using their definition of the problem and the harm
Acknowledge wrongdoing[a,f]	Publicly acknowledge all interpersonal and systemic harms committed within and outside the community center against Black women and girls, without minimizing or denying key actions or inactions	Public communications
Apologize[a,c,f,j]	Apologize to Black women and girls for the violence one has perpetrated as a member of the Black church	Documentation of apologies
Cherish the whistleblower[a,f,j,k,l]	Publicly thank individuals who spoke out about cultural betrayal sexual trauma (e.g., Drew Dixon,[m] Sherri Sher[m]); publicly encourage and reward reports of wrongdoing	Documented communications that support individuals who identified problems within the Black community; clear processes for communicating potential wrongdoing; transparent structures that indicate how information from whistleblowers will inform actions and policies

(continues)

TABLE 7.3. Institutional Courage Class 3: Reparations—To Benefit Black Women and Girls Across Institutions and Communities (*Continued*)

Institutional courage	Example	Verifiable outcome(s)
Correct and/or retract false statements[n]	Publicly correct statements that dismissed or discredited reports of wrongdoing[j] in at least the same avenues of original publications, if not broader venues	Publications, films, conference presentations, community events, etc.

[a] *Blind to Betrayal: Why We Fool Ourselves We Aren't Being Fooled*, by J. J. Freyd and P. Birrell, 2013, John Wiley and Sons. [b] *A Betrayal Trauma Perspective on Domestic Violence* (pp. 185–207), by M. Platt, J. Barton, and J. J. Freyd, 2009, Greenwood Press. [c] "The Psychology of Judicial Betrayal," by C. P. Smith, J. M. Gómez, and J. J. Freyd, 2014, *Roger Williams University Law Review*, 19, 451–475. [d] "When Sexual Assault Victims Speak Out, Their Institutions Often Betray Them," by J. J. Freyd, 2018, *The Conversation* (https://theconversation.com/when-sexual-assault-victims-speak-out-their-institutions-often-betray-them-87050). [e] "The Impact of Skills Training on Responses to the Disclosure of Mistreatment," by. M. M. Foynes and J. J. Freyd, *Psychology of Violence*, 1(1), 66–77 (https://doi.org/10.1037/a0022021). [f] *Avoiding Judicial Betrayal of Child Witnesses: Implications From Betrayal Trauma Theory*, by J. J. Freyd, 2013, paper presentation at Roger Williams University. [g] "Learning From the Outsider Within: The Sociological Significance of Black Feminist Thought," by P. H. Collins, *Social Problems*, 33(6), S14–S32 (https://doi.org/10.2307/800672). [h] *Black Feminist Thought: Knowledge, Consciousness, and the Politics of Empowerment*, by P. H. Collins, Routledge. [i] © L. Hassoun Ayoub and J. M Gómez, 2022. [j] *Zwischenmenschilcher und institutioneller verrat [Interpersonal and Institutional Betrayal]* (pp. 82–90), by J. M. Gómez, C. P. Smith, and J. J. Freyd, 2014, Asanger Verlag. [k] "Steps to Strengthen Ethics in Organizations: Research Findings, Ethics Placebos, and What Works," by K. S. Pope, *Journal of Trauma & Dissociation*, 16(2), 139–152 (https://doi.org/10.1080/15299732.2015.995021). [l] "Institutional Betrayal," by C. P. Smith and J. J. Freyd, 2014, *American Psychologist*, 69(6), 575–587 (https://doi.org/10.1037/a0037564). [m] *On the Record* [Film], directed by K. Dick and A. Ziering, 2020, HBO Max Original. [n] *The Hoffman Report and the American Psychological Association: Meeting the Challenge of Change* (pp. 1–9), by K. S. Pope, 2016, Wiley.

INSTITUTIONAL EXAMPLES: PATHWAYS FROM BETRAYAL TO COURAGE TO LIBERATION

Change is constant. That means the winning is temporary. That's why we need liberation. (adrienne marie brown, personal communication, 2018)

Individual efforts are interconnected and even structural and systemic in nature insofar as they provide droplets into what will become oceans of equality. Based on true stories, I chart the path from institutional betrayal to courage across a health care setting, a university, and a nonprofit organization. In doing so, I provide real-world examples of an original institutionally betraying harm that is followed by institutional betrayal in the response. I then imagine the institutionally courageous antidote to that harmful response. In each setting, I close with dreamstorming of what the situation would look like if the world were what we envision: truly free, equal, and peaceful for all.

Health Care: Whose Body Is It Anyway?

Black women find themselves in a bind, in which health care is necessary at times while simultaneously being a site of historical and present racist medical abuses (e.g., Burke, 2021; Washington, 2006). For Nikiya, a Black woman in her late 30s, her fear of authority stemmed from the prior cultural betrayal sexual trauma she endured at the hands of her father and other Black males. Doctors' offices represented similar sites where she was at the mercy of people in authority who often did not treat her as human. It was with this fear that Nikiya summoned the will to go to a new gynecologist to get her intrauterine device (IUD) replaced. Shared with permission, below is the complaint she filed to the state medical board against the White woman doctor:

> Dr. _____ came into the exam room to meet with me while on a conference call that was on speakerphone. She performed an IUD removal and insertion with . . . [a] nurse. . . . She inserted the speculum without warning. She removed the IUD without telling me beforehand—resulting in shock and pain. (After removal, she said something to the effect of, "You may feel pain as I remove it.") She inserted the IUD without telling me, which was painful. She inserted her finger in my vagina without telling me. (She told me she would do an exam or check, but not that that process would include vaginal penetration.)
>
> Entering my body without consent and without warning are violations tantamount to assault.
>
> After the procedure, she asked if I wanted pain relievers. The pain relievers included those that may cause me anaphylactic reactions. I gave this information to the nurse during this visit. Dr. _____'s unawareness of this pertinent medical history is dangerous.
>
> Impact: I have felt violated since this visit. . . . I have cried and hyperventilated on numerous occasions. I have had difficulty sleeping. I feel panic when thinking of returning to this doctor's office in one month for the follow-up ultrasound, even though the Dr. would not conduct the ultrasound herself. My fear is that I will be violated again, either by the technician doing the ultrasound or by Dr. _____ if the ultrasound's findings require follow-up by Dr. _____. In order to not be violated again, I have chosen not to return to this doctor or any other gynecologist for fear of being violated. This puts my physical health at risk—not doing the follow-up appointment or subsequent annual visits in the near future. I am making the choice in order to protect myself from the physical and psychological harm of being violated. I am filing this complaint in the hope that it will be taken seriously so that other women are not violated by Dr. _____.

In filing the complaint, Nikiya felt proud of herself for rejecting shame in lieu of placing the blame on the institutionally betraying doctor. She also sought more information that indicated to her that she was not alone, as Tarana Burke, founder of the #MeToo movement, had had a somewhat similar experience with a White woman doctor (see Burke, 2021, pp. 99–103).

Her positive sentiment, however, was short-lived. The medical board informed her that there was "insufficient basis to authorize an investigation of your complaint." Nikiya was perplexed. How could her detailed description not even warrant an investigation into what happened? In this case, the doctor committed the first institutional betrayal. The medical board committed the second. With a disclosure of a violation that Nikiya described, an investigation can only not be warranted if (a) such violation is deemed appropriate care or (b) the patient, a Black woman, is presumed to be wholeheartedly unreliable. Though such devaluation of Black women and their bodies can be perhaps expected within American health care (e.g., Washington, 2006), it is nevertheless profoundly painful.

In a last attempt, Nikiya relayed her complaint to the doctor's office itself. As systemic discrimination would have it, this resulted in the remaining institutional betrayals, with the office responding with the following (excerpt):

> Please be assured that the issues you raised were taken very seriously. . . . it was determined that neither Dr. _____ nor the office associate . . . recall any concerns raised by you on the day of your visit . . . the comprehensive review identified that you had engaged in the informed consent process. . . . As part of the review, the appropriate use of communication devices was reviewed . . . the team could not substantiate that your "body was entered without consent and without warning" . . . although Dr. _____ and the entire review team wishes to extend a sincere apology that you have expressed you felt that way. . . please be assured that a review of medication reconciliation processes has taken place with the staff. . . . It is strongly recommended that you seek health care to assist you with any health issues.

The final institutional betrayals came in the above response from the doctor's office. A striking component is what is present and absent in the reference to the violation itself. What is present is a fundamental lack of understanding of consent. Consent is an ongoing process. Consent to a procedure at the outset does not give the doctor the right to access one's body at any time and in any way throughout the remainder of the visit. Doing so is akin to suggesting that because a girlfriend consented to sex with her boyfriend, he was justified in anally raping her 30 minutes into the sexual encounter because she had originally given consent to sex. That is absurd.

Additionally present is no apparent understanding of trauma responses, with victim-blaming being issued that Nikiya did not communicate concerns during the visit. The doctor entered the room on the phone while Nikiya was near tears already out of fear. The doctor did not notice. Nikiya did communicate prior to the procedure that she was frightened, to which the doctor gave no response. When the violations occurred, Nikiya was scared into silence—and pain. Three violations happened: the removal of the IUD, the insertion of the new IUD, and the digital penetration of her vagina. Nikiya was too traumatized to say anything. Importantly, Nikiya also did not say to the doctor that talking on the phone during an office visit was inappropriate. Nevertheless, the office reviewed proper phone use. However, they did not do the same regarding the violations.

What is also absent in the doctor's office's institutionally betraying response is any remediation for the violations. Of note, remediation was indicated for cell phone use and medication policy, but not for how to not violate patients. Within the context of the doctor being distracted on the telephone and the patient's body belonging to herself, it would objectively appear that the patient's perception has an increased likelihood of accuracy. An absence of any education or remediation to this aspect of the complaint is deplorable.

With these three compounding sets of institutional betrayals, the harm against Nikiya was compounded as well. She was first violated and then dismissed, disbelieved, and blamed, while she was courageous enough to formally defend herself twice. The final recommendation from the doctor's office to seek health care is frightening given the context. What the medical board and the doctor's office communicated is that any doctor can violate patients at any time, with the office recommending Nikiya return to such sites of violence. Nikiya knows she will need to go to the doctor again in her life, and that knowledge fills her with dread and panic. The medical model would suggest that Nikiya is pathological (for a nonpathologizing understanding of human beings' distress, see Gómez, Lewis, et al., 2016). I will unequivocally say it is the system and our society that are disordered, not Nikiya.

Institutional Courage

The BITTEN framework of trauma-informed health care suggests "interpreting patients' interactions with healthcare providers and the healthcare system as a whole in light of their interpersonal and institutional trauma histories . . . to more fully embody trauma-informed healthcare" (Selwyn et al., 2021, p. 336). In line with Class 1's operations of institutional courage (see Table 7.1), the entire medical staff would be educated in trauma-informed care, including what consent is and is not. Further education would be provided on how Black women's bodies have been sites of White people's violation at least partially due to intersectionally oppressive stereotypes (see DePrince & Gómez, 2020; Washington, 2006), with all medical staff monitoring their misperceptions and behaving equitably. Furthermore, Class 2's assessments of institutional courage (see Table 7.2) with staff and patients would include identifying other institutional betrayals and the potential for further institutional betrayals, while uncovering the clinic's priorities. This would increase the likelihood of preventing such White women–perpetrated, gender–cultural betrayal.

With that in mind, institutional courage after the first institutional betrayal in this case would have been Class 3's reparations of institutional courage (see Table 7.3). The medical board would have borne witness to Nikiya's harm by investigating her complaint in ways that privileged her perspective. Moreover, the doctor and the doctor's office as a whole would have apologized—not for Nikiya expressing she felt violated but for the doctor actually violating her within an office context in which such a violation was more likely to occur. In documenting the steps they were taking to prevent any similar behavior from happening in the future, the office would have expressed that they are working to ensure doctor's offices are safe for Nikiya and all patients in the future through engaging in education and holding all medical staff accountable for their violations.

Dreamstorm
In the liberated world, authority could be trusted. Nikiya would not have entered the doctor's office afraid because she would have had no reason to be. The society in which teachers and doctors abuse those under their care would no longer exist, with professionals being properly educated about how not to abuse their power (for examples, see Gómez, 2020b, 2020g, 2022c; Gómez, Noll, et al., 2021). Her absence of fear would be warranted, as the doctor enters the room with care, understanding, and respect for Nikiya and her body. The doctor explains the procedure step by step, asking if Nikiya has any questions. Following thoroughly answering her questions, the doctor asks Nikiya if she would like her to tell her what she will do just before she does it, such as, "Here is my hand on your knee, thigh, upper thigh . . . [*pause*] . . . I will now insert the speculum; it may be a little cold. Okay? [*waits for affirmative response before continuing*]." The doctor listens as Nikiya tells her that she would like this physical and verbal communication throughout the procedure. When Nikiya's body tenses upon the removal of the IUD, the doctor will check in with her, ensuring that she is okay before she proceeds. This respect for Nikiya's personhood and body will continue throughout the entire visit. Following the procedure, the doctor will say that a heating pad or other home remedy may help with any discomfort, given that Nikiya is unable to take ibuprofen due to the potential for anaphylaxis. Nikiya, having left the doctor's office following receiving psychologically and physically safe health care, will sleep soundly night after night.

Universities: Where There's No Will, There's a University

> Hope is important. But we must never use an idealized "hope" to justify inaction and backlash. (Jennifer A. Richeson, personal communication, 2022)

In the abstract, research-intensive universities are repositories of world-changing knowledge, in which professors' life work is uncovering such knowledge while ushering in the next generation of scholars. In reality, these same universities can be sites where the rule-following educational elite engage in shallow thinking while cloaked in cowardice (e.g., Gómez, 2020b). At Research University, Professor Black Man was a groundbreaking leader in his field for decades. During this same time, he was also famous for sexually harassing the Black women graduate students in his lab. Less of an open secret and more of an accepted, if hushed, reality, the Black women who had filed formal complaints at Research University lost their careers before they had even begun: Some were pushed out of their graduate programs, while others were left to drown by being excluded from research projects, fellowships, and professional development opportunities. Enduring violent silencing from Black faculty, staff, and fellow students, other victimized students remained silent to protect Professor Black Man and themselves: Blackness of any gender was still a rarity in the field, with overt discriminatory attacks on Black people's intellects continuing to bar many from the discipline. Though the problem was worse in some ways for Black women due to intersectional oppression, the focal point of the harm of discrimination was Black men.

With the #MeToo movement (Burke, 2021), however, came a new pressure for universities to disallow such sexual harassment. A formal complaint by one courageous Black women graduate student was the first of an onslaught in this new era, which resulted in Professor Black Man retiring just before his tenure was to be revoked by the board of trustees. The department held a gala for Professor Black Man's retirement, with professors continuing to assign his work in their classes for years to come. Over time, the folklore of Professor Black Man held a divisive tone: Either you were against racism, in which case, what happened to Professor Black Man was an abomination because Professor White Man in the neighboring department had been sexually assaulting undergraduates for years with no punishment whatsoever, or you were against sexual harassment, in which Professor Black Man's decades of sexual harassment and the department's silence were considered abhorrent. Despite Professor Black Man's victimized students also being Black, there was no space in the department to be both antiracist and antisexual violence; once again, enduring intersectional oppression deprioritized and occluded the Black women students and their victimization.

The institutional betrayals in this example are numerous: Professor Black Man's sexual harassment, the department's inaction combined with retaliation and violent silencing, departmental praise of the professor, and dividing social justice causes in ways that erase the Black women at the center of the harm (i.e., political intersectionality; Crenshaw, 1991). This example reminds us that opportunity does not end by getting in the door; opportunity needs to continue while we are inside. For instance, within graduate school, there need to be opportunities to learn and live freely, without being sexually harassed, discriminated against, or further harmed through retaliation.

Institutional Courage
Institutional courage could take multiple forms. A trauma-informed, functional accountability structure would be in place (e.g., see Table 7.1; see Gómez notes on the First Annual NASEM Action Collaborative to Prevent and Address Sexual Harassment in Higher Ed Public Summit, in Gómez, 2022h). As such, the first victimized student—and each student thereafter—would have been supported in deciding when and how to disclose (for discussion on the importance of victim choice in disclosure, see Freyd, 2022). Upon disclosure, Professor Black Man would have been held accountable through transparent procedures, while the victimized students received academic, professional, and personal resources as needed. Moreover, other sexually harassing/assaulting professors with more privilege would additionally be held accountable for their own institutional betrayal (see Table 7.3). The department, college, and university would undergo self-assessments, with findings informing education, policy, and practice at the department, university, and field at large (see Table 7.2). Professor Black Man's behavior would not be weaponized against innocent Black people in the department, the profession, or society, while simultaneously, the students' scholarly contributions would be appropriately exalted. In accordance with Class 3 reparations of institutional courage (see Table 7.3), leaders in the university would publicly and privately thank the victimized students who came forward, while apologizing for individual and institutional wrongdoing.

Dreamstorm
> If men rape because they are men—as . . . theorists have argued—women will always be forced to regard the police, courts and prisons as their only glimmer of hope. If . . . the incentives for rape are not a natural product of male anatomy or psychology, but are rather social in nature, the prospects of eradicating sexual violence will depend on changes of an entirely different order. (Angela Davis, 1981, p. 39)

In dreamstorming a free world, many things are different. Structurally, there is equality in society, in the field, and in this department, such that

Black people across genders are numerous and discrimination is absent. Therefore, (intra)cultural pressure and violent silencing are also missing because protecting the Black community is entirely unnecessary. Professor Black Man, the graduate students, and all the members of the department and university are educated formally and informally throughout their lives about the responsibility to not perpetrate sexual harassment, with Professor Black Man's faculty appointment requiring knowledge and understanding of the power of being a professor. Moreover, in the absence of societal oppression and violence against Black men, the psychological pull to power-over, abuse, and violate those with less institutional power is nonexistent. At the academic level, there are structures in place that guard against graduate advisors' singular power over their students, including mentorship committees (National Academies of Sciences, Engineering, and Medicine, 2018). There is national policy to protect individuals regarding sexual harassment (Albright et al., 2020), with regular campus climate surveys informing needed areas for increased attention (Merhill et al., 2021). If, within this context, Professor Black Man still has the desire to sexually harass, he receives corrective support that provides him with the tools to never perpetrate.

Nonprofit Coalition: Let's Not Do This Together

> These conflicts . . . raise critical issues of power. The problem is not simply that women who dominate the antiviolence movement are different from women of color but that they frequently have power to determine, either through material or rhetorical resources, whether the intersectional differences of women of color will be incorporated at all into the basic formulation of policy. (Kimberlé Crenshaw, 1991, p. 1265)

Coalition, including within a marginalized group (e.g., Black people across genders working to combat cultural betrayal sexual trauma against Black women and girls) and across oppressed and privileged groups, can be a vital feminist tool in eradicating oppression (e.g., Cole, 2008, 2009; Cole & Luna, 2010; Giddings, 1985; Grzanka, 2020a; Hondagneu-Sotelo & Pastor, 2021). This includes allyship for social justice, in which individuals work with oppressed communities to dismantle systemic inequality, while recognizing their own privilege and the complexity of intersectional oppression (Edwards, 2006; Jenkins, 2009). Nevertheless, social justice struggles can also fall victim to the same and different oppressions that the coalitions are working to dismantle.

In this example, a working group comprising Black and White professionals from across a nonprofit organization were working together to create a policy document for addressing sexual abuse in the community. All members agreed that specific attention should be paid to diversity, equity, and inclusion, given that the community members were primarily Black. In discussing the policy, Kenya, a seasoned victim advocate who was a Black self-identified transwoman, stated that White supremacy should be listed as one of the causes of sexual abuse, and therefore, the efforts to end such violence must include work toward dismantling structural racism.

Beth, an older White woman who was friends with the founder of the organization, objected, stating that *White supremacy* was the wrong language because she and many like her are not White supremacists. Kenya explained that the term was not synonymous with groups like the Ku Klux Klan and that race scholarship identifies White supremacy as structural racism (e.g., Mills, 1997). Beth then attempted to get support for her perspective from others at the meeting, including declaring that a Black person she knows doesn't use the term and that surely other White professionals at the table would have a hard time with that language. Some of the White people at the table agreed, while others remained silent.

Kenya then stated that the current conversation in which her perspective was discounted in favor of White people's comfort is an example of how White supremacy gets reinstantiated within organizations. Several White women had tears in their eyes, saying that Kenya's appraisal of them as racists was unfair and mean-spirited. Beth told Kenya that her comments constituted discrimination, which was antithetical to the work of the nonprofit. The chair of the working group then decided to end the meeting. Later that day, Beth sent an email to Kenya saying that she wanted to check in with her because it seemed that the meeting hurt her (Kenya's) feelings.

The above provides an example of institutional betrayal that is likely familiar to many who have worked in cross-racial groups with White people—particularly those who adopt a color-blind racial ideology (Neville et al., 2013; Yi et al., 2022). The way inequality manifests in organizations (e.g., Crenshaw, 1991; V. Ray, 2019) includes preserving homogenous White ideals, norms, and worldviews (McIntosh, 2009), with White people's comfort level being the primary concern. Additionally, Beth's invocation that "most people agree with" her as a White person is a reflection of the inequality within the space, as opposed to the validity of her argument. Because of the overrepresentation of White mediocrity (Mitchell, 2018), many discussions on violence, racism, intersectional oppression, "how things are done" and "what will be palatable for most people" are by definition not equal, not equitable, and at times, not even sensical. This means that structural healing—important, uncomfortable, humble, systemic change—requires that White people listen, learn, and deliberately not perpetrate the same White supremacist, power-over dynamics that harm many in the institution and society.

Institutional Courage

> Solidarity does not just naturally exist, but is strengthened through processes of working together in common efforts. (Chris Benner & Manuel Pastor, 2021, p. 161)

To be institutionally courageous, there would be an emphasis on equality as both a process and an outcome (Cummings, 2021a). With the stated assertion toward diversity, equity, and inclusion (DEI) being predictably a nonperformative (Ahmed, 2012), institutional courage would include a demonstrable commitment to DEI that was transparently evidenced through both the content of the policy and the process of creating the policy (see Table 7.1). Regarding Class 3 reparations (see Table 7.3), when Kenya explained the meaning of the term *White supremacy*, Beth could have borne witness and listened as if Kenya were the knower who had experience and expertise that was both valid and valued (e.g., Dotson, 2011). Furthermore, the White people who engaged in institutional cowardice (L. S. Brown, 2021) through their silence could have instead apologized for their colleague's behavior, bolstered Kenya's point, and amplified her status as a valued member of the group. Lastly, members of the group could put together a card thanking Kenya for her courage in this meeting.

Class 1 operational institutional courage could occur before the group was formed, including in the selection of the members of the working group. Friendship with the founder and any apparent expertise in sexual abuse would not have solidified Beth's place in the working group. Instead, an understanding of people, systems, privilege, and oppression would have been requirements for entry. This would include Beth and all White members continuously engaging in their antiracist work (e.g., Case, 2015; Combahee River Collective, 1977, as cited in K. Taylor, 2017; Fang & White, 2022; Kendi, 2019; for a guide on engaging in such work, see McIntosh, 2009). In this situation, White committee members would privilege Kenya's perspective on White supremacy and its instantiation in the meeting, given her standpoint includes distinct knowledge, wisdom, and insight (Collins, 1991/2000). Additionally, processes would be in place that delineate how conflicts of inequality would be handled, which include understanding how to receive critical feedback in ways that promote one's own growth and reduce the potential for harm against the oppressed (Gómez, 2020d, 2020f). In line with Class 2 assessments (see Table 7.2), this would include baseline and longitudinal self-assessments that could aid in identifying typical problem areas.

Though this example was strewn with institutional betrayal, it also already included institutional courage. As an institutional actor, Kenya spoke up initially and continuously on the importance of labeling White supremacy as a cause of sexual abuse within a work environment that was neither welcoming nor understanding. In doing so, she partially reshaped and uplifted what this nonprofit is: not just a harbinger of oppression but a site of truth-telling for the benefit of the community that the nonprofit serves. As such, Kenya's institutional courage is admirable and powerful, as is her ability to reflect on the meeting in ways that reject the White supremacist meaning behind how Beth and others treated her. Because of her institutional courage, the nonprofit was transformed in the current moment and potentially beyond—depending on the existence of institutionally courageous future behavior of other members of the organization.

Finally, though she knew she would not send it, Kenya engaged in freewriting a response to Beth to regain her own sense of self and clarity on what had happened:

> Beth: Your behavior and your words towards me were totally and completely inappropriate, out of line, unacceptable, and yes hurtful. That harm from you impacted me and likely impacted our Black colleagues in particular very hard. Any reconciliation would require you to actually understand what you did—including the depth of harm—why you did it, and how you could avoid repeating such behavior in the future. In my opinion, any reconciliation would also be done at the same scope as the harm: You did this in front of all of us in that meeting, not privately to me. Therefore, you would need to engage in demonstrative acknowledgment of wrongdoing followed by an apology to all of us in that meeting, not privately to me. I am a professional, a Black woman, and a human being. Your behavior today showed a complete absence of respect for me on all those fronts. My hope for you would be that you critically, deeply, and honestly interrogate what drove you to such behavior, apologize to all of us for that behavior, and take corrective actions to prevent that kind of behavior in the future. My hope for myself is that I remember that both your bigotry and your bigoted behavior belong to you, and not me.

Dreamstorm

In my dreamstorming is an ideal world in which neither sexual abuse nor White supremacy exists, therefore relegating this working group obsolete. However, to the extent that freedom and liberation need to be continuously sought after and protected (e.g., Cummings, 2021a; Freire, 1970), a working group on sexual abuse policy is still needed. Fundamentally, a transdisciplinary understanding of White supremacy and its impact on every aspect of life would be understood in the mainstream. The common defensive refrain for White people of "everyone I know agrees with me" would actually include an *everyone* that is truly diverse, where knowledge necessarily incorporates critically interrogating systems of power, while meetings never include power-over attempts of such epistemic exclusion (e.g., Buchanan et al., 2021) and oppression (e.g., Dotson, 2011). In that way, the rhetorical use of a collective *we* that provides a comfortable inclusive farce for the most powerful while violently silencing the oppressed would simply never again leave White women's mouths.

Further, Whiteness is not needed to legitimate Black perspectives, though such validation is equitably granted because Black people are conceptualized and treated as if we and our perspectives are inherently worthy of thought, consideration, and respect. Such validation would be evident in selection processes, with diverse communities sharing the power to promote change. Therefore, instead of devolving into soul-crushing events, such coalitions would promote growth and healing through shared respect, solidarity, equality, and unity that understand and incorporate difference (e.g., Crenshaw, 1991).

WHAT THIS COULD ACTUALLY LOOK LIKE

> Freedom or Liberation . . . is not a gift. . . . It must be pursued constantly and responsibly. (Paolo Freire, 1970, p. 35)

I have previously provided information on how and why efforts for institutional change fail (for more, see Ahmed, 2012), as well as examples of institutional betrayal (e.g., C. P. Smith & Freyd, 2014) and trajectories toward institutional courage (e.g., Freyd, 2018) and dreamstorming liberation. However, there is a multitude of institutional courage in the world, including the following: Birth Detroit, an organization whose mission is to midwife safe, quality, loving care through pregnancy, birth, and beyond (Birth Detroit, 2021); Center for Institutional Courage, a nonprofit organization that conducts transformative research and education on institutional betrayal and institutional courage (Center for Institutional Courage, n.d.); Dance Theatre of Harlem, a leading dance institution, with a racially diverse ballet company and world-class school, that engages in community education and outreach (Dance Theatre of Harlem, 2023); 90by30, a community–campus partnership dedicated to reducing child abuse in Lane County, Oregon, by 90% by 2030 (90by30, n.d.); and We, As Ourselves, a collaborative campaign to change the conversation about sexual violence and its impact in the Black community (We, As Ourselves, 2021). There are also relatively simple examples of institutional courage, such as over 90% of the 2021–2022 fellows at the Center for Advanced Study in the Behavioral Sciences (CASBS) at Stanford University signing an open letter in support of our colleague, Hakeem Jefferson, who was the target of racist attacks (Araral et al., 2021). I do not highlight the aforementioned institutions as global endorsements of the individuals, organizations, and fields involved, as institutions and people are complex and imperfect. However, I do point to them as organizations that, nevertheless, provide examples of engaging in institutional courage.

Important lessons for institutional courage can be found both within and outside the field of psychology. Below, I detail an example from a community-lawyer partnership in Los Angeles (Cummings, 2021a) to understand institutional courage. I further hope that this example provides both practical steps and radical hope for each of us to cocreate the institutions, societies, and the world that are worthy of us thriving in. Therefore, I give a brief background, including successes and limitations, followed by lessons learned and take-home messages for psychologists and allied mental health field professionals. Importantly, much of what I discuss below is in line with community organizing principles (e.g., Perlo & Feeley, 2018; Reisch, 2005; Speer & Hughey, 1995) that psychologists and allied professionals can use in their own work.

AN EQUAL PLACE: COMMUNITY-LAWYER COLLABORATIONS ON COMMUNITY BENEFITS AGREEMENTS IN CITY REDEVELOPMENT PROCESSES

Like social justice–oriented academic, research, and clinical/counseling psychologists (Grzanka & Cole, 2021) and other allied mental health field professionals, lawyers can exist on a tight rope of if and how to use their power to promote positive societal change. In law, there can be tension about whom lawyers are serving: the client versus society (Bell, 1975; Cummings, 2021a). Similarly, specific considerations exist regarding mental health professionals' roles and responsibilities related to that of their clients. However, in his book *An Equal Place: Lawyers in the Struggle for Los Angeles*, Scott L. Cummings (2021a) empirically and theoretically reinterprets a path for lawyers in affecting societal change based on their role in key movements in Los Angeles (LA) from the early 1990s through 2008. Psychologists and allied professionals can learn some key lessons from these lawyers.

Within the context of long-standing structural, oppressive displacement and impending racialized gentrification (Rucks-Ahidiana, 2021) in LA in the late 1990s, lawyers contributed their expertise to community efforts by crafting community benefits agreements (CBAs). According to Cummings (2021a), a CBA is a

> contract in which a developer agreed to provide specific levels of living wage jobs, affordable housing, environmental remediation, and other benefits in exchange for community support for project approvals and public subsidies. . . . CBAs . . . rested on a distinctive model of community organizing—leveraging the power of broad-based coalitions to extract benefits through negotiation, thereby avoiding litigation (though wielding its threat). (p. 165)

Further, lawyers "identified strategic points of legal leverage in the development process, advised coalitions on legal options, negotiated benefits with developers, and ultimately drafted—and helped to enforce—CBAs" (Cummings, 2021a, p. 165). Thus, CBAs are particularly important legal mechanisms to help protect racially marginalized communities in city redevelopment processes.

Like many social justice efforts and movements, the outcomes of CBAs in LA represent a mixed bag of successes and failures (Cummings, 2021a). Though often difficult to enforce, the CBAs institutionalized community benefits into city redevelopment processes, which served as *site fights*, or proof-of-concept institutional change mechanisms that, when successful, could be scaled up for larger, systemic reform. In those ways, CBAs were successful. Disappointingly, the scaling up via citywide policy adoption failed to come to fruition. Whereas an equitable reality would mean that local, state, and federal governmental policies and cultural norms dictated community protections, CBAs provided ad hoc, case-by-case solutions within a system that remained fundamentally unequal.

Lessons Learned

Lessons for academic, research, and clinical/counseling psychologists and allied mental health professionals come in two forms. The first is addressing power in working with lower-status individuals and communities. The second is advocating for change behind the scenes. My first lesson from Cummings's (2021a) description of CBAs in LA focuses on lawyers as a class of individual actors who have structural power over their clients. Though key distinctions in professional relationships exist, psychologists similarly have power over their junior faculty colleagues, students, clients, and others. Moreover, both fields have a history of domination over other forms of knowledge and social justice mobilizing. For instance, in dominant psychology, quantitative scientific research is conceptualized as the most legitimate way of knowing, whereas qualitative research, theorizing, and lived experiences are devalued (e.g., Buchanan et al., 2021). Such stances are mirrored in typical decision-making processes in which those with power make decisions unilaterally for those without power (Okun, n.d., in Gómez, 2022h).

On the contrary, Cummings (2021a) described lawyers in coalition with community partners in social movements as approaching their work with humility, while operating with deliberate awareness of their educational and class privilege. As evidence of the importance of diversity in professional fields, many of these lawyers were Latino, and therefore more culturally similar to community members in LA; such similarity may have provided these lawyers with a better understanding of and respect for the perspectives and needs of the community. These lawyers used their positions to cocreate "an equal place" (Cummings, 2021a) in which they saw their law contributions as neither dominant nor subjugated in the efforts for positive societal change. In other words, these lawyers did not place themselves above or below the community professionals and advocates they worked alongside. Instead, they understood themselves as horizontal collaborators with expertise different but equal to that of other members of their coalitions.

Psychologists and allied mental health professionals can approach their work with those with reduced power, such as students and clients, in ways similar to that of these lawyers. In line with trauma-informed care (e.g., Danylchuk, 2015), a collaborative approach that does not privilege psychologists' field knowledge over all other forms would avoid power-over mentor, advisor, and therapeutic approaches. Instead of placing themselves as the sole expert, psychologists would instead conceptualize themselves as having unique expertise to provide alongside that of the student and/or client. Such a stance is not synonymous with eschewing the responsibility of increased power or degrading one's own specified knowledge in the field. Rather than closing the door on one's own knowledge, this power-with stance instead encourages increased contributions from students and clients, in which one's professional knowledge is beneficially augmented and expanded. Pedagogically and therapeutically, this approach promotes growth, agency, and investment of those students and clients who have less power. Equitably and honestly, this behavior also places psychological knowledge and ourselves as professionals in our rightful, "equal place" (Cummings, 2021a) with those we work with and serve. On a metalevel, such an approach would appreciate the current example from law (Cummings, 2021a), as psychology would not be conceptualized as the only field with relevant knowledge for psychologists.

The second and final lesson from lawyers I will discuss is that of advocating for systems-level changes behind the scenes. Along with their community partners, lawyers strategized behind the scenes about avenues for successfully promoting change (Cummings, 2021a): Who on the other side is the person to connect with on X issue? What information from that person do we need to better understand their resistance to entering into an agreement? Who from our team should engage in discussion with that person? Is there anyone else we should hear from first or follow up with afterward? Such behind-the-scenes work already happens in psychology. Examples include a practicing psychologist advocating for their clients at their clinic and a psychology professor fighting for an overhaul of the White supremacist, exclusionary curricula in their graduate program.

Despite its current existence in our field, I highlight this lesson specifically because it contradicts the excuses cowardly psychologists and allied mental health professionals often make for why they do not engage in institutional courage: They are shy, they are meek, and they do not like the spotlight. However, those excuses do not match the tasks at hand given that so much institutionally courageous work happens outside of the public arena. Institutional courage happens in one-on-one meetings, over emails, in committee service, and much more. Though powerful and necessary in some situations, being a public superstar is not the only way to be institutionally courageous. Moreover, infantilizing ourselves as delicate flowers in comparison to one-dimensionally fearless changemakers is not a fair or accurate representation of ourselves or others.

Take-Home Messages for Psychologists and Allied Mental Health Professionals

There are many lessons psychologists and allied mental health professionals can learn from lawyers working in social movements to incorporate CBAs in city redevelopment processes (Cummings, 2021a). Two of those lessons are promoting equality in both process and outcome and advocating behind the scenes. In using the examples of the aforementioned lawyers who operated in equality-promoting ways while working toward equitable community benefits, psychologists and allied mental health professionals can engage in institutional courage within their spheres of influence to promote equity, equality, and inclusion on larger and larger scales.

AVOIDING BARRIERS TO SYSTEMIC CHANGE

Given the content of the current chapter, it could seem that transforming organizations into institutionally courageous ones should be relatively straightforward, such as the American Medical Association's (2021) public opposition to "excited delirium syndrome" (Obasogie, 2021) as a justification for police murdering Black people. However, given the apparent scarcity of institutional courage, I invariably often ask myself, Why is it so hard, if not impossible at times, for people and their organizations to just do the right thing? (for further discussion, see Pope, 2015). In this section, I highlight predictable problems that interfere with institutional courage: White mediocrity, the uneven power field, (im)measurable progress, and problematizing power. Importantly, in, around, and through these problems, we can be changemakers (for example, see Sarsour, 2020) who promote structural healing.

White Mediocrity

White mediocrity (e.g., Mitchell, 2018) is the term to describe White people's skills and performance that are average or subpar. Due to White supremacy that places White people at the top of the racial hierarchy (e.g., Mills, 1997), White individuals can advance in their careers despite not being qualified. Therefore, White mediocrity can be prevalent in elite places, including in higher education (e.g., Mitchell, 2018).

Definition
> There is an important difference between openness and naiveté. Not everyone has good intentions nor means me well. I remind myself I do not need to change these people, only recognize who they are. (Audre Lorde, n.d.-a, as cited in Goodreads, 2023a)

When working institutionally as a faculty member (e.g., Gómez, 2022h), I have found myself wondering if the institutional betrayal I am witnessing is due to malice, bigotry, and/or incompetence. For instance, in my first faculty position, we often had no process—transparent or otherwise—for making decisions, despite our responsibilities, including decision making related to faculty hires (Gómez, 2022f), graduate curricula (Gómez, 2022c), and graduate admissions (Gómez, 2022d; Gómez, Caño, et al., 2021). Obviously, decision-making processes that are haphazard and/or oppressive can lead to much harm (e.g., Gómez, 2020b, 2022d; Gutiérrez y Muhs et al., 2012; Niemann et al., 2020). Understanding why a graduate program would ostensibly continue its dysfunction for decades can be difficult. Is it aggressive laziness? A willful desire to perpetuate the status quo? A hope for processes to be as unfair and inequitable as possible? Perhaps there are times when the answer to all of the above is yes. However, it would be a mistake to underestimate the prevalence and level of White mediocrity (Mitchell, 2013, 2015, 2018, 2020) in the academy.

Due to the benefits of structural racism (V. Ray, 2019), many subpar White people have risen to the top of their professions, including in academia. Therefore, obvious, practical matters, such as known and used decision-making processes, are absent, while the ability for deep, critical thought on complex issues of oppression, privilege, abuse of power, and one's role in each is impossible. At times, this White mediocrity is accompanied by know-your-place aggression, which is the aggression that some White people show to stellar marginalized individuals (Mitchell, 2018). Know-your-place aggression (Mitchell, 2018) is the underlying sentiment that if you are marginalized, (a) you should just be grateful to be here at all; (b) you should not dare be comfortable, think you belong, and/or share your brilliance with others; and (c) you should instead know your place—as a guest who is only conditionally accepted into their world (Inside Higher Ed., 2022). This know-your-place aggression (e.g., Mitchell, 2013) creates a bind for marginalized scholars, who are punished when they are presumed to not be good enough, while paradoxically also being punished when they show themselves to be too good (Gómez, 2020b).

Importance

> [For White people,] the bar for transcending awfulness is low. (Scott L. Cummings, 2021b)

Why is White mediocrity important to understand and at times expect? First, if you do not know the world around you, you will employ inappropriate strategies for institutional change and structural healing. For instance, if you are assuming that you are around hardworking, deep-thinking professors, you will use strategies that require other faculty to engage in hard work and deep thought. If those professors are capable of neither and/or are steeped in institutional indifference or callousness (Annmarie Caño, personal communication, May 6, 2022), then your strategies on those fronts will fail. If you could instead understand that simplistic explanations that bolster a goal of prestige among peer institutions are more palatable, for instance, you are more likely to use those strategies and thus be successful in implementing change. Second, you can identify how the system promotes epistemic oppression (e.g., Dotson, 2011), thus pushing you to seek out the scholarship that your colleagues claim does not exist. Third, as highlighted by Mitchell (2018), it is dangerous to misinterpret know-your-place aggression as fact, internalizing their discriminatory treatment as appropriate. This is vital for your own personal sanity and professional longevity (Gómez, 2020b). Fourth, you can express the importance of White people holding themselves and each other to higher standards (e.g., Mitchell, 2018). Fifth, you can monitor when it is time to leave and find a new place that will be able to appreciate and utilize you, your efforts, and your life's work. Finally, you can begin to restructure in yourself, your colleagues, your superiors, and your students the skills necessary to be institutionally courageous, including honoring humility, engaging with respect, presuming competence of marginalized and lower-status individuals (Gómez, 2020b, 2022h), creating equal places in both processes and outcomes, and drawing inspiration from those who are oppressed in domains in which you are privileged (Cummings, 2021b).

Uneven Power Field

> What does it mean when there are whole domains . . . that are practicing agnotology (Schiebinger and Proctor's term for the production of ignorance)? . . . It is an active reproduction of the violent racial order performed as if passive, natural, and obvious. . . . [It is] terrifying. (Julie Livingston, personal communication, 2022)

In discussions of promoting equity and equality on systemic levels, the following sentiment inevitably emerges: Why can't we just learn from and do what the other side is doing? Those in power seem to keep winning, so if we can just learn their strategies, then we can win too. In addition to derailing action that could result in progress, such a thought stems from a fundamental misunderstanding of the existence and impact of structural inequality. This sentiment comes from the faulty premise that there is an equal playing field from which we begin. However, the reality is that the present state of society and our institutions are not a neutral baseline (Mills, 1997). Thus, we are not beginning our institutionally courageous work within a race-neutral psychological science profession, a race-neutral academia writ large, or a race-neutral society. Given the racial hierarchy in society (Mills, 1997) and organizations (Ray, 2019), it is not enough to suppose abstractly that people of color are of equal value; instead, there needs to be fundamental change of the systems that are predicated on racial (and intersectional) privilege, hierarchy, and oppression (Crenshaw, 1991; Mills, 1997).

Within this uneven power field, the Power Side operates under a certain set of conditions, while the marginalized side exists under different restrictions. Specifically, the Power Side is called on to ignore, not think, not change, and by and large, not do anything, with any mindless action resulting in continuing downstream *with* the current of inequality. Conversely, the Marginalized Side is called on to identify the problem (Ahmed, 2014), face it head-on, think, change, and do everything to travel upstream *against* the current of inequality.

To illustrate this, we can use the image of being on a raft in a river. If you're on the Power Side, everyone is the same: same culture, same worldviews, and same goals. If you do nothing, then you are still moving downstream with the current. If you start paddling, then you are moving ever faster toward your "White supremacist downstream destination" because you are going with the current.

However, things on the Marginalized Side are different. There is a heterogeneous mix of people with different cultures, worldviews, and priorities for which goals should be pursued first. When you stop working for a moment, your raft does not remain in the same place; it gets pulled downstream and further away from "destination equality upstream." When you start to paddle upstream using the same oar as the power side, you quickly realize it is not enough; you gain an inch toward destination equality upstream as you paddle with all your might, but then you lose 3 feet to the downstream in the blink of an eye. Moreover, the different people on the raft each have different ideas on the best way to make it to destination equality upstream. Some suggest trying the power side's oar again; others say that additional oars should be used; and still others suggest that success will only happen once you get in the water, with people both pulling and pushing the front and back of the raft, respectively. In-fighting, frustration, learned helplessness, and anger ensue: We are supposed to all be on the same side, but we have different ways of working, and despite all our efforts, it appears we get no closer to our destination equality upstream.

To add insult to oppressive injury, the Power Side says to the Marginalized Side, "Why don't you just enjoy the river? It's so pristine here, so peaceful. Light breeze. Even though there's no discernible current, you continue to insist on needing to paddle upstream. Why? Everything is comfortable here. What are you even whining about? It's as if nothing is ever good enough for you. It's not as if there's even a storm here. Just an inconsequential body of water."

Predictably, perceiving a problem has meant that your perceptions have become the problem (Ahmed, 2014). Specifically, identifying the current of inequality while fighting for structural change results in gaslighting and disrespect from members of the Power Side, who may be on the same river but exist within an entirely different context. Therefore, we on the Marginalized Side cannot use the same tools in the same way as those who sit perched on the ease and epistemological ignorance that comes from privilege (Lorde, 1984; Mills, 1997). We instead must do the different, harder work consistently, with our failures indicating the depth and breadth of inequality, not individual or group incompetence. Instead of, or perhaps in addition to, being overwhelming, clarity regarding this differential context can provide hope: We are not aimlessly incompetent but rather righteously working toward greater gains despite the odds against us.

(Im)measurable Progress

> Instead of viewing success as advancing . . . change that constitutes a decisive victory . . . appreciate that struggle is an unending process in which wins must be defended and extended over time. (Scott L. Cummings, 2021a, p. 490)

A barrier to morale and institutional change trajectory is how we understand success. Put simply, how do we know whether we have succeeded in structural change? The answer to what appears to be such a simple question depends on at least two things: (a) the time horizon (when you ask): what you have determined as your end point in time; and (b) the benchmark (what you measure): what you have defined as "success" (Cummings, 2021b).

First, it is important to appropriately frame the time horizon. Outcomes should not be assessed only directly after a win, such as a change in policy. Simultaneously, end points cannot be projected solely by decades. Why? Success is never stable (Cummings, 2021a; Freire, 1970). At any given point, the needle could be moving farther away from equality even when the overall trajectory is bending toward justice (Martin Luther King, Jr., as cited in Ellis, 2011). Therefore, long-term transformation is necessary, with care being given to the contexts and times when success, or lack thereof, is measured.

Second, the benchmark of success—that is, what counts as success—additionally needs careful consideration. If only 100% change counts as success, then for all our lifetimes, we will remain defeated. For instance, with the current book, I would love for every Black woman and girl who has endured cultural betrayal sexual trauma to know fully and completely that it was not their fault and that they are a valued member of the Black community and world at large—with all intersectional oppression and sexual abuse ultimately ceasing to exist. If those total and complete eradications are the only things that will count as success, then I will overlook how this book affected an individual's healing or promoted one institutional change. The reality is nuanced: Even though I have not 100% won, I also have not unilaterally failed.

There are levels of degrees within the small and large scales of measurement, with different points in time capturing different metrics of success. Thus, a small-wins model of change provides concrete and doable actions that produce measurable results that motivate further actions (Correll, 2017); this approach then can have ripple effects of institutional change that continue across time (Correll, 2017; Nishiura Mackenzie, in Gómez et al., 2023). These small wins then fold into larger institutional and societal change. That change affects people, one individual after another. Therefore, change and structural healing are, in fact, happening. Perhaps equally as important, acknowledging and relishing our successes provide us with hope. Our work, our pain, our tears, and our perseverance have not been for naught. What we do matters. We ourselves matter (Gómez, in Asmelash, 2022). Provided we are paying attention, our world is strewn with small, medium, and large wins all around us.

Problematizing Power

> Rethinking Black women's activism uncovers a new vision of Black women's empowerment that is distinct from existing models of power as domination. . . . African-American women have overtly rejected theories of power based on domination in order to embrace an alternative vision of power based on a humanist vision of self-actualization, self-definition, and self-determination. (Patricia Hill Collins, 1991/2000, p. 224)

I have noticed a troubling dialectic within the interface between my work and how it is received in the world. As my research becomes more accepted, it receives stamps of approval from powerful places that provide funding, invite me for plenary talks, and more. Those same institutions hold power at least partially due to White supremacy and elitism: Neither everyone nor all work gets to be included in these exclusionary spaces. Inclusion in these exclusive spaces signals value and status for the work and for myself as a scholar. Confusingly, of course, my work highlights structural inequality and its related harms, which are the same oppressive harms that elitism reinstantiates (e.g., gatekeeping to higher education; Gómez, 2022d). Within this dialectic, I have been questioning whether power—including our ability to be successful when we institutionally fight the good fight—relies on segregation, elitism, and domination. Is there a way to have power without an oppressive hierarchy? Can there be a top if there is no bottom? Should there be?

Like many before me (e.g., Benner & Pastor, 2021; Collins, 1991/2000; Davis, 1989; hooks, 1989; Lorde, 1984; Steady, 1981), I have thought about the need to transform the topography and landscape of power—specifically, disaggregating it from domination and instead using power as "an expression of collective determination" (Benner & Pastor, 2021, p. 166), such as power-with approaches (Miller & Stiver, 1997). For instance, by claiming one's own power and developing relational coalitions of power (Hondagneu-Sotelo & Pastor, 2021), we can disrupt and deflate some of the power-by-domination granted by White supremacy (Kraus & Torrez, 2020) by shaping institutions' social agenda and meaning, including determining which issues get priority and how those issues are culturally understood (Healey & Hinson, 2013).

In this context, I have further wondered whether power that is shared within a marginalized group in the absence of secondary marginalization (Cohen, 2009) can result in increased solidarity and institutional success. Or is there only loss for the relatively powerful and gain for the relatively oppressed when there are power shifts? How do we disrupt toxic domination while retaining respect for difference and avoiding hegemony? Further, how can we dismantle viewing power solely through the lens of a hierarchical domination?

Though social structures, such as race, gender, and class, are embedded within power (Kraus & Torrez, 2020), being a leader through prestige and respect, as opposed to domination, is linked with better-perceived health (Knight, 2022). Moreover, the existence of power—such as that granted to elder members of the community—may not be problematic *necessarily*, provided abuses of power and abusing others while in positions of power do not occur. Given the need for leadership and the complexity of power, I carry three axioms for institutionally courageous work toward structural healing and change: (a) leaders are needed; (b) each of us can humbly lead within our spheres of influence; and (c) power—including the pure success, efficiency, oppression, and corruption that power can engender—needs to be consistently and persistently grappled with and redefined.

Capstone

> The change is never good enough, but it is hope. (Jorge Delva, personal communication, 2022)

What we face is the power of the dialectic: The structural healing and societal change we desperately need and courageously work toward remains out of our reach, while smaller, iterative wins occur constantly and dramatically. For instance, I grew up as a Black girl in the 1990s knowing very well that the same Black solidarity that I contributed to would not be extended to me in any experience of cultural betrayal sexual trauma (Gómez, in Asmelash, 2022). The overt (intra)cultural pressure to keep these problems in-house was only matched by the violent silencing that such experiences would not be meaningfully discussed, much less prioritized, in the Black community (Gómez, 2020i). Though cultural betrayal sexual trauma is still happening 25 years later, so is awareness, as evidenced by my article "The Unique Harm of Sexual Abuse in the Black Community" (Gómez, 2019h), being read more than 638,600 times as of February 2023. For us to have a realistic appraisal of the world in which we live combined with dreamstorming motivation for the world we want, we must hold the dialectic: No, the change we are witnessing is not enough, and yes, the change is radical, meaningful, and oh, so very valuable nonetheless.

In doing so, each of us individually and collectively engaging in institutional courage (Freyd, 2018) has bravery, humility, critical thought, and ongoing correction against how our efforts may be reifying a hierarchically oppressive world that we are working to eradicate. We further do not wait for permission or acceptance of our presence. Moreover, if the world, or any corner of it, is not ready for us, we persevere anyway. This perseverance includes steps at destabilizing and ultimately eradicating the White Read (Bowleg, 2021) through (a) embracing our experiential knowledge base (McCarty, 2022); (b) holding sacred our referential knowledge (McCarty, 2022); (c) privileging and amplifying our own knowledge and space; (d) having an ethic of caring self-determination, and standpoint (Collins, 1991/2000) throughout the entire process of systemic change; and (e) revolutionarily transforming our institutions iteratively through each and every act of institutional courage.

To do so, we can learn from our ancestors, such as Mr. Arthur Mitchell, cofounder and former artistic director of Dance Theatre of Harlem. The following is my remembrance of Mr. Mitchell in reference to myself:

> Mr. Mitchell buck[ed] against the system. Of just you cannot, cannot wait for things to be equal enough and for oppression to be eradicated. And wait for me to walk in the room as a Black woman and have people assume I'm a professor before I get up to speak. I cannot wait for those things to happen. I have to just do it anyways. And I think it's the biggest lesson from [Mr. Mitchell] and then from what he's done with Dance Theatre of Harlem, that you just do it anyways.

And when you're doing it anyways, change is happening. Things do become more equal by your presence of just kind of pretending that you belong and that people want you here. Even when you're not sure that's true, because of racism or sexism. (Gómez, 2020h)

In bucking against the system, I have learned lessons that sustain me in this work for the long haul: (a) Create and review as necessary my personal list of things that make me feel hopeful; (b) know that it is okay to step away from change-making work to recharge my soul with rest and joy; (c) identify the narcissism and self-elevation of thoughts, such as "only I can do X" and "if I don't do this, no one will"; (d) know that pain is an expected part of the journey in change-making; (e) behave within my priorities, refusing to give up aspects of myself and my life that are important to me; (f) know that trust and partnerships need to be earned instead of automatically assumed due to shared identities, as professors, Black people, and so forth; and (g) remember that each change and each human life, including my own, matters. Finally, whereby culture sustains inequality (Valentino & Vaisey, 2022), I cry, *may we never forgo dreamstorming, as our efforts must impactfully transcend generations.*

SUMMARY BULLET POINTS

1. Though there are individual- and interpersonal-level components, intersectional oppression and cultural betrayal sexual trauma include structural harms; therefore, structural solutions are required for both prevention efforts and institutional change.

2. Radical institutional change and institutional courage combine a Black feminist ethic of caring with grounded emotions engendering motivation, problem-solving, and structural change.

3. Institutions, including institutional actors, have power to both harm (institutional betrayal and cowardice) and help (institutional courage).

4. Adapted to benefit Black women and girls who experience intersectional oppression and cultural betrayal sexual trauma are institutional courage steps in three classes: Class 1: Operations; Class 2: Assessments; and Class 3: Reparations.

5. Institutional courage within the current world and dreamstorming for a better world are both necessary behavioral and psychological exercises when embarking on structural healing.

6. In coalition work, addressing power and reinstantiations of inequality is paramount, with equality being important in both the process and outcome of efforts.

7. Institutional courage work can be done in the forefront (e.g., protests, leadership) and behind the scenes (e.g., meetings, policy change).

8. In lieu of striving for equal opportunity to dominate and oppress, we must dismantle the cultural bases of group oppression to promote a peaceful equality.

9. White mediocrity, extant inequality, unclear metrics of success, and toxic use of power can impede institutional change and structural healing.

10. Our pursuits for freedom, liberation, equality, and peace transcend generations, with small, medium, and large wins being garnered each and every day.

CONCLUSION

What Does It All Mean? From Micro- to Macrolevel Change

> **CHAPTER AT A GLANCE**
>
> In this chapter, I write a capstone that summarizes the book through (a) amplifying Black women and girls' humanity; (b) discussing equality and equity within social justice efforts; (c) identifying structural solutions to the problems identified within each chapter; and (d) discussing the book's (at least) two paradigm shifts within trauma psychology—with an emphasis on structural, instead of individual, change and a focus on healing, instead of solely harm.

We reject pedestals, queenhood, and walking ten paces behind. To be recognized as human, levelly human, is enough.
—Combahee River Collective, 1977, as cited in K. Taylor, 2017, p. 19

The impetus for this book is the humanity, love, and respect I have as a Black woman for fellow Black women and girls. As such, I began this book in dedication

---

https://doi.org/10.1037/0000362-008
The Cultural Betrayal of Black Women and Girls: A Black Feminist Approach to Healing From Sexual Abuse, by J. M. Gómez
Copyright © 2023 by the American Psychological Association. All rights reserved.

to all the Black women and girls—alive and departed from this life—who have experienced the violating and violent indignities of cultural betrayal sexual trauma. I expressed hope in a continuous overhaul of the aspects of the world that breathe life into violence and oppression through dreamstorming and cocreating a better, more peaceful, and more equal world for us. Consequently, in the first half of the book, I provided basic research on White supremacy, anti-Black racism, intersectional oppression, sexual abuse, cultural betrayal trauma, (intra)cultural pressure, and violent silencing. As such, Black women and girls were centered, while the causes of our struggle were externalized: Anti-Black racism and intersectional oppression (Chapter 2) are largely structural, whereas cultural betrayal sexual trauma and its aftermath (Chapters 3 and 4) are mostly contextual and cultural—with interpersonal, structural, and societal influences. In the second half of the book, I applied this knowledge to culturally competent trauma therapy (Chapter 5), radical healing in the Black community (Chapter 6), and institutional courage to change the world as we know it (Chapter 7). Throughout the book, I have sought to present a person-centered, Black feminist perspective on understanding Black women and girls in the context of racism, intersectional oppression, cultural betrayal sexual trauma, violent silencing, healing, hope, Black solidarity, strength, and vulnerability.

FREEDOM FIGHTING

> If Black women were free, it would mean that everyone else would have to be free since our freedom would necessitate the destruction of all systems of oppression. (Combahee River Collective, 1977, as cited in K. Taylor, 2017, pp. 22–23)

Any fight for freedom must have freedom within it (Combahee River Collective, 1977, as cited in K. Taylor, 2017). In other words, we cannot accept strategies that work toward a peaceful world by restricting the freedoms of people in the process. For instance, it is a harmful reification of the status quo to work toward abuse-free environments in which we restrict women's freedoms (e.g., where they go and what they wear; e.g., Hill, 2021), while reducing men to sexually violent caricatures who warrant no greater expectation than absent-minded proclivities to rape (Davis, 1978, as cited in Davis, 1981). Put simply, the hypothesized ends of freedom cannot justify such oppressive means (Combahee River Collective, 1977, as cited in K. Taylor, 2017). Furthermore, we cannot be striving for our equal ability to dominate and oppress. We must instead dismantle the cultural bases of such group oppression, thus resulting in equality that promotes peace while rejecting domination (hooks, 1981/2015, 1984/2015).

EQUITY IN SOCIAL JUSTICE EFFORTS

> In order to survive, those of us for whom oppression is as American as apple pie have always had to be watchers. (Audre Lorde, 1984, p. 114)

Continuing a world in which White people, including White women, oppress, degrade, and disrespect Black women in academic, professional, personal, and social justice spaces must be abandoned. Such processes are insulting, are unwarranted, and do not actually get us closer to the liberation we so desperately need. As in research about inequalities (Hicken et al., 2018), practicing relationally equitable dialogues, coalitions, and collaborative work requires a shared understanding that both structural inequality and prejudicial malice exist, with White people as the beneficiaries—and at times, perpetrators—of both. When, instead, White people in relative or absolute positions of institutional power obstinately refuse to acknowledge and address the unequal context and the prejudice that justifies and upholds such inequality, then the hierarchical social order reproduces the same oppression within these profoundly unequal dialogues, coalitions, and collaborative efforts.

White people's common yet faulty assumption in cross-racial dialogues is that all perspectives hold equal merit. Therefore, both sides—White people and all people of color—need to listen to each other to gain understanding, with the ultimate goal being consensus. Such an assumption ignores the fact that people of color, including Black people, by survival necessity are trained in White people's humanity, worldviews, and systems, while simultaneously White people are similarly ingratiated in their own perspectives and not the realities of Black people (e.g., M. L. King, 1968). This supposition of an even power field ignores the importance of standpoint (Collins, 1986, 1991/2000, 1997): The perspectives of those Black women and girls who have knowledge, insight, and wisdom about inequalities and intersectional oppressions should be privileged over the oppressive ignorance of powerful White people. Such privileging is difficult, however, because it requires White people interrupt their own prejudice, abandon the conceptualization of themselves as wholly good people (McIntosh, 2009), and refrain from explosive attacks against the marginalized (Dewey, 1966). Doing so would result in processes of equality—*we are all the same*—being discarded in favor of those of equity, in which the realization of foundational inequality informs interpersonal and structural corrections that promote opportunity and fairness (Morgan, 2019). Responsibility for equity lands on White people who have societal, and many times institutional, positions of power.

Importantly, the unequal and violently oppressive status quo will continue in all spaces in which White people fail to intellectually and emotionally understand the basic fundamentals of inequality, including how centralizing their own perspectives and feelings to the exclusion of all marginalized others is an instantiation of inequality. Put simply, a faulty premise of current structural and cultural equality across races undermines the effectiveness of all the efforts toward future equality. As such, the charge is given to White people to finally and humbly expect and demand more of themselves and each other. Where such cross-racial equity exists, true human solidarity can flourish (Collins, 1991/2000).

RADICAL CHANGE

> Persistence is a fundamental requirement of this journey from silence to language to action. (Patricia Hill Collins, 1991/2000, p. 112)

While individual and community oriented, my approach belies the need for structural change. It is the structural forces of intersectional oppression and violence that negatively affect Black women and girl survivors, while also infecting the systems, such as mental health care and the field of psychology, that are ostensibly designed to aid in help and healing, as expressed in Table 1. In the current book, the concepts, harms, and avenues for healing and transformation for Black women and girls branch across individual, familial, community, institutional, cultural, and societal levels. Vitally, however, is that structural inequality needs to be understood as the tree that bears the harmful fruit of racism, intersectional oppression, cultural betrayal sexual trauma, and violent silencing. Therefore, I consolidate chapter-by-chapter information from the book in Table 1 by providing a formulaic template for actionable sample steps to take as we dreamstorm a new world. With this table, I hope to crystallize a primary message of the book: Structural inequality, oppressions, and violence enacted upon individual Black women and girls must be addressed through structural means. Such a framing does not remove the responsibility or agency of the individual, particularly as oppression and resistance occur on individual, community, and systemic levels (Collins, 1991/2000). However, it does reorient the locus of the problem—and therefore, the locus of the solutions—away from Black women and girls as individuals and onto the familial, institutional, cultural, and societal collectives, Black and not.

Structural understanding of problems and solutions can be overwhelming: If so many aspects of each part of our professional and personal lives are marred by inequality and its diverse instantiations, then where do we even begin to advocate for change? The hopeful side is predicated on that same ubiquity of inequality: Precisely because inequality is everywhere (e.g., DePrince, 2022a,

TABLE 1. Structural Solutions to Individualized Harms

Harm
Societal, Cultural, Institutional, Community, Familial, Interpersonal, Individual
Violent Silencing

Chapter: Topics	Sample structural solutions
Chapter 2: Anti-Black racism,[a] White supremacy,[a] intersectional oppression,[b] intersectionality [c]	Dismantle White supremacy and patriarchy systemically and culturally
Chapter 3: Secondary marginalization,[d] sexual abuse, outcomes, "the rape problem"	Engage in cultural change promoting gender equality in the Black community
Chapter 4: Cultural betrayal trauma theory[e]: (intra)cultural trust, cultural betrayal, cultural betrayal trauma, (intra)cultural pressure, (intra)cultural support, abuse and cultural outcomes, posttraumatic growth	Advocate for societal equality, while simultaneously leveraging (intra)cultural trust and support to promote community healing
Chapter 5: Individually and structurally culturally competent trauma therapy, relational cultural theory,[f] liberation health framework[g]	Overhaul curricula and practicums in graduate education that currently promote decontextualized, pathologizing frameworks of human beings and their mental health difficulties
Chapter 6: Individual- and group-level radical healing,[g] including restorative justice principles,[h] responding supportively to disclosures of cultural betrayal sexual trauma, the roles of Black men and the Black family, and finding liberation through freewriting	Foster Black spaces to learn, grow, connect, and heal individually and together, while working to abolish violent White spaces
Chapter 7: Institutional betrayal,[i] institutional cowardice,[j] institutional courage,[k] dreamstorming,[l] concrete tactics for institutional transformation, barriers to institutional change (White mediocrity/know-your-place aggression,[m] role of inequality, difficulty in measuring progress, problems in power)	Conduct and apply research that identifies individual and institutional factors that promote and reward institutional courage

[a] *The Racial Contract*, by C. W. Mills, 1997, Cornell University Press. [b] *Black Feminist Thought in the Matrix of Domination* (pp. 221-238), by P. H. Collins, 1990, Routledge. [c] "Mapping the Margins: Intersectionality, Identity Politics, and Violence Against Women of Color," by K. Crenshaw, 1991, *Stanford Law Review*, 43(6), 1241-1299 (https://doi.org/10.2307/1229039). [d] *The Boundaries of Blackness: AIDS and the Breakdown of Black Politics*, by C. J. Cohen, 2009, University of Chicago Press. [e] *The Cultural Betrayal of Black Women and Girls: A Black Feminist Approach to Healing From Sexual Abuse*, by J. M. Gómez, 2023, American Psychological Association. [f] *Toward a New Psychology of Women*, by J. B. Miller, 1976, Beacon Press. [g] *Social Justice in Clinical Practice: A Liberation Health Framework for Social Work*, by D. Belkin Martinez and A. Fleck-Henderson, 2014, Routledge. [h] "Toward a Psychological Framework of Radical Healing in Communities of Color," by B. H. French, J. A. Lewis, D. V. Mosley, H. Y. Adames, N. Y. Chavez-Dueñas, G. A. Chen, and H. A. Neville, 2020, *The Counseling Psychologist*, 48(1), 14-46 (https://doi.org/10.1177/0011000019843506). [i] "Institutional Betrayal," by C. P. Smith and J. J. Freyd, 2014, *American Psychologist*, 69(6), 575-587 (https://doi.org/10.1037/a0037564). [j] *The Little Book of Restorative Justice*, by H. Zehr, 2002, Good Books. [k] "Institutional Cowardice: A Powerful, Often Invisible Manifestation of Institutional Betrayal," by L. S. Brown, 2021, *Journal of Trauma & Dissociation*, 22(3), 241-248 (https://doi.org/10.1080/15299732.2020.1801307). [l] © Jennifer M. Gómez, 2019. [m] "Identifying White Mediocrity and Know-Your-Place Aggression: A Form of Self-Care," by K. Mitchell, 2018, *African American Review*, 51(4), 253-262 (https://doi.org/10.1353/afa.2018.0045).

2022b), we can take each opportunity in every corner of our lives to make a difference that can positively affect Black women and girls as individuals and as a population. For example, if we want Black women and girls to be treated properly in therapy, we can change how we treat Black female psychology doctoral students (for an example of prejudicial treatment, see Gómez, 2014) while educating ourselves and our trainees on culturally competent trauma therapy (Chapter 5). When we do not want Black women and girls to be suicidal after being raped, we can learn how to listen more supportively to disclosures, while carrying the burden of humanizing the Black male perpetrator(s) (Chapter 6). Further, in creating spaces for true Black solidarity, we can call Black men in (e.g., Gómez, 2020f)—holding them accountable for their benefits, and at times, perpetration and perpetuation, of sexism, while expecting more equitable, peaceful, and courageous behavior from them (Chapter 6; see 1984 conversation between James Baldwin and Audre Lorde, as cited in The Culture, 2018). Finally, because we want Black women and girls to live in worlds where we are peacefully respected, all of us can engage in institutional courage when we witness White people's discrimination against them (Chapter 7). Therefore, far from being hopeless, the systemic problems outlined in this book create openings for far-reaching, long-lasting structural change that happens one person, one effort, one conversation, one family, one policy change, one community, one doctoral program, one clinic, one institution, one university, one government, and one society at a time (Gómez, as cited in Asmelash, 2022). Therefore, through dreamstorming equality and equity in both the process and the outcome (Cummings, 2021a), we can inch closer to freedom each day.

BLACK WOMEN AND GIRLS: OUR HUMANITY

> Portraying Black women solely as passive, unfortunate recipients of racial and sexual abuse stifles notions that Black women can actively work to . . . bring about changes in our lives. Similarly, presenting African-American women solely as heroic figures who easily engage in resisting oppression on all fronts minimizes the very real costs of oppression and can foster the perception that Black women need no help because we can "take it." Black feminist thought's emphasis on the ongoing interplay between Black women's oppression and Black women's activism presents the matrix of domination as responsive to human agency.
> (Patricia Hill Collins, 1991/2000, p. 237)

I would like to close this book where I began: with the humanity, love, and respect I have as a Black woman for fellow Black women and girls. Within my work, I have leveraged my outsider-within perspective (Collins, 1991/2000) to personalize the pain of life, while documenting the multifaceted and interconnected harms of intersectional oppression, cultural betrayal sexual trauma, (intra)cultural pressure, and violent silencing. To do so, I bravely forged alternative paradigms, including using Black feminist epistemologies that indict the unequal, violent contexts faced by us Black women and girls who live them.

With this book come at least two additional paradigm shifts within trauma psychology. The first is the emphasis on structural change. Since the interpersonal, familial, community, cultural, institutional, and societal contexts of abuse, trauma, and violence are causally impactful, then solutions must include those contexts. It no longer remains acceptable to feign interest in the importance of context while continuing to pathologize the lives of Black women and girls by constructing different theoretical, empirical, clinical, and pharmaceutical ways that we should change.

Interfacing with this emphasis on broader systemic change is an explicit focus on healing. As Black women and girls, we are not damned to reside underneath the oppressions and abuse heaved upon us. As such, documenting our harm without amplifying the hope, laughter, joy, love, and connection of our lives is now irresponsible, inaccurate, and destructive. Therefore, this book represents my reappraisal of the role of the matrix of domination (Collins, 1991/2000) in my own work: It does bind us, hurt us, abuse us, dismiss us, and attempt to erase us by killing our very essences while demanding our internalized collusion with its oppression. Simultaneously, we keep dreamstorming throughout our full lives, creating individual, interpersonal, and structural healing pathways to exist distinctly beyond what we have endured. In doing so, we intimately experience the "both/and" dialectic that dominates Black feminist thought (Collins, 1991/2000): Within both oppression and resistance, we self-define a cocreated consciousness (Collins, 1991/2000) where freedom and liberation—instead of domination—breathe life and possibility into us all.

References

Aaliyah. (2001). Never no more [Song]. On *Aaliyah*. Blackground Records; Virgin Records.

Adames, H. Y., & Chavez-Dueñas, N. Y. (2017). *Cultural foundations and interventions in Latino/a mental health: History, theory, and within group differences*. Routledge.

Adames, H. Y., Chavez-Dueñas, N. Y., Lewis, J. A., Neville, H. A., French, B. H., Chen, G. A., & Mosley, D. V. (2022). Radical healing in psychotherapy: Addressing the wounds of racism-related stress and trauma. *Psychotherapy*. Advance online publication. https://doi.org/10.1037/pst0000435

Adams-Clark, A., Gómez, J. M., & Barlow, M. R. (2022). Adaptive dissociation: A response to interpersonal, institutional, and cultural betrayal. In M. Dorahy & S. Gold (Eds.), *Dissociation and the dissociative disorders book* (pp. 98–110). Routledge. https://doi.org/10.4324/9781003057314-9

Adams-Clark, A., Gómez, J. M., Gobin, R. L., Noll, L. K., & Delker, B. (2020). Impact of interpersonal, family, cultural, and institutional betrayal on adult survivors of abuse. In R. Geffner, V. Vieth, V. Vaughan-Eden, A. Rosenbaum, L. K. Hamberger, & J. White (Eds.), *Handbook of interpersonal violence across the lifespan* (pp. 1–27). Springer/National Partnership to End Interpersonal Violence Across the Lifespan (NPEIV). https://doi.org/10.1007/978-3-319-62122-7_310-1

Adams-Clark, A. A., & Freyd, J. J. (2021). COVID-19-related institutional betrayal associated with trauma symptoms among undergraduate students. *PLOS ONE, 16*(10), Article e0258294. https://doi.org/10.1371/journal.pone.0258294

Ahern, K. (2018). Institutional betrayal and gaslighting: Why whistle-blowers are so traumatized. *Journal of Perinatal & Neonatal Nursing, 32*(1), 59–65. https://doi.org/10.1097/jpn.0000000000000306

Ahmed, S. (2012). *On being included: Racism and diversity in institutional life*. Duke University Press.

Ahmed, S. (2014). *The problem of perception*. https://feministkilljoys.com/2014/02/17/the-problem-of-perception/

Akbar, M. (2017). *Urban trauma: A legacy of racism*. Publish Your Purpose Press.

Albright, S. D., Gómez, J. M., & Martinez, C. B. (2020, October). *Sexual harassment and the sciences: How the data can inform local and national policy* [Poster presentation]. National Academies of Sciences, Engineering, and Medicine (NASEM) 2nd Annual Public Summit of the Action Collaborative to Prevent Sexual Harassment in Higher Education, Madison, WI, United States.

Alexander, J. C., Eyerman, R., Giesen, B., Smelser, N. J., & Sztompka, P. (2004). *Cultural trauma and collective identity*. University of California Press.

Alexander, M. (2010). *The new Jim Crow: Mass incarceration in the age of color blindness*. The New Press.

Almeida, R. V., Dolan-Del Vecchio, K., & Parker, L. (2008). *Transformative family therapy: Just families in a just society*. Pearson Education.

American Medical Association. (2021). *New AMA policy opposes "excited delirium" diagnosis*. https://www.ama-assn.org/press-center/press-releases/new-ama-policy-opposes-excited-delirium-diagnosis

American Psychiatric Association. (2013). *Diagnostic and statistical manual for mental disorders* (5th ed.).

American Psychological Association. (2017a). *Ethical principles of psychologists and code of conduct*. https://www.apa.org/ethics/code/ethics-code-2017.pdf

American Psychological Association. (2017b). *Multicultural guidelines: An ecological approach to context, identity, and intersectionality*. https://www.apa.org/about/policy/multicultural-guidelines.pdf

American Psychological Association Council of Representatives. (2021a). *Apology to people of Color for APA's role in promoting, perpetuating, and failing to challenge racism, racial discrimination, and human hierarchy in U.S.* https://www.apa.org/about/policy/racism-apology

American Psychological Association Council of Representatives. (2021b). *Role of psychology and APA in dismantling systemic racism against people of color in U.S.* https://www.apa.org/about/policy/dismantling-systemic-racism

American Psychological Association Guideline Development Panel for the Treatment of PTSD in Adults. (2017). *Clinical practice guideline for the treatment of posttraumatic stress disorder (PTSD) in adults*. https://www.apa.org/ptsd-guideline/ptsd.pdf

Anca, R. (2022, December 16). For many boys and men, sexual assault and abuse is a very real issue. *Giddy*. https://getmegiddy.com/boys-men-sexual-assault

Andresen, F. J., Monteith, L. L., Kugler, J., Cruz, R. A., & Blais, R. K. (2019). Institutional betrayal following military sexual trauma is associated with more severe depression and specific posttraumatic stress disorder symptom clusters. *Journal of Clinical Psychology, 75*(7), 1305–1319. https://doi.org/10.1002/jclp.22773

Annamma, S. A., Connor, D., & Ferri, B. (2013). Dis/ability critical race studies (DisCrit): Theorizing at the intersections of race and dis/ability. *Race, Ethnicity and Education, 16*(1), 1–31. https://doi.org/10.1080/13613324.2012.730511

Anzaldúa, G., & Moraga, C. (1981). *This bridge called my back: Writings of radical women of color*. Persephone Press.

Araral, E., Aronowitz, R., Bednar, J., Beliso-De Jesús, A. M., Bernstein, M., Chen, S., Cummings, S. L., Danescu-Niculescu-Mizil, C., de Renzio, P., Evans, G. W., Finn, M., Gómez, J. M., Guilhamon, L., Houpt, S. O., Kessler, A., Kligler-Vilenchik, N., Laikwan, P., Lansing, J. S., Levenson, T., . . . Walker, E. (2021, November). Open letter of support for professor Hakeem Jefferson. *Google Blogspot.* https://openletter4profhakeemjefferson.blogspot.com/2021/11/open-letter-of-support-for-prof-hakeem.html

Archer, D. (2021). *Anti-racist psychotherapy: Confronting systemic racism and healing racial trauma.* Each One Teach One Publications.

Arjini, N. (2019). Imani Perry's liberation feminism. *The Nation.* https://www.thenation.com/article/archive/imani-perry-liberation-feminism-beyonce-lorraine-hansberry/

Armstrong, E. A., Gleckman-Krut, M., & Johnson, L. (2018). Silence, power, and inequality: An intersectional approach to sexual violence. *Annual Review of Sociology, 44,* 99–122. https://doi.org/10.1146/annurev-soc-073117-041410

Asante, M. K. (1987). *The Afrocentric idea.* Temple University Press.

Asmelash, L. (2022, October 27). In 5 years of #MeToo, here's what's changed—and what hasn't. *CNN.* https://www.cnn.com/2022/10/27/us/metoo-five-years-later-cec/index.html

Association of Black Psychologists. (2022). *Official statement: The APA apology; Unacceptable.* https://abpsi.org/wp-content/uploads/2021/11/ABPsi-Full-Statement.pdf

Avery, B. (1989). Black women's health: A conspiracy of silence. *Sojourner,* 15–16.

Bailey, M. (2016). Misogynoir in medical media: On Caster Semenya and R. Kelly. *Catalyst: Feminism, theory, technoscience, 2*(2), 1–31. https://doi.org/10.28968/cftt.v2i2.28800

Baldwin, J. (1989). *James Baldwin: The price of the ticket.* https://www.pbs.org/wnet/americanmasters/james-baldwin-film-james-baldwin-the-price-of-the-ticket/2632/

Beck, E., Kropf, N. P., & Blume Leonard, P. (2011). *Social justice and restorative justice: Skills for dialogue, peacemaking, and reconciliation.* Oxford University Press.

Belgrave, F. Z., & Allison, K. W. (2018). *African American psychology: From Africa to America.* Sage.

Beliso-De Jesús, A. (2022, March 16). *Excited delirium syndrome: Police violence, Black and Latinx death, and Afro-Cuban spiritualism* [Paper presentation]. Stanford University Center for Advanced Study in the Behavioral Sciences (CASBS) Research Seminar Series, Stanford, CA, United States.

Belkin Martinez, D. (2014). The liberation health model: Theory and practice. In D. Belkin Martinez & A. Fleck-Henderson (Eds.), *Social justice in clinical practice: A liberation health framework for social work* (pp. 9–29). Routledge. https://doi.org/10.4324/9781315813073

Belkin Martinez, D., & Fleck-Henderson, A. (Eds.). (2014). *Social justice in clinical practice: A liberation health framework for social work.* Routledge. https://doi.org/10.4324/9781315813073

Belkin Martinez, D., Hamilton, G., & Toraif, N. (n.d.). Understanding structural and institutional racism. *Boston University School of Social Work: The Network of Professional Education*. https://thenetwork.bu.edu/offering/understanding-structural-institutional-racism/

Bell, D. A., Jr. (1975). Serving two masters: Integration ideals and client interests in school desegregation litigation. *The Yale Law Journal, 85*, 470–517.

Benner, C., & Pastor, M. (2021). *Solidarity economics: Why mutuality and movements matter*. Wiley.

Bent-Goodley, T. B. (2001). Eradicating domestic violence in the African American community: A literature review and action agenda. *Trauma, Violence & Abuse, 2*(4), 316–330. https://doi.org/10.1177/1524838001002004003

Bent-Goodley, T. B. (2009). A black experience-based approach to gender-based violence. *Social Work, 54*(3), 262–269. https://doi.org/10.1093/sw/54.3.262

Bent-Goodley, T. B. (2017). Living our core values [Editorial]. *Social Work, 62*(4), 293–295. https://doi.org/10.1093/sw/swx046

Bent-Goodley, T. B., & Gómez, J. M. (in press). Sexual assault: Cultural context and social work response. In T. B. Bent-Goodley (Ed.), *Responding to interpersonal violence: The social work response*. National Association of Social Workers.

Bent-Goodley, T. B., St. Vil, N., & Rodgers, S. (2012). African American women and sexual violence. In J. Postmus (Ed.), *Encyclopedia of sexual violence and abuse*. ABC-CLIO.

Birrell, P. J. (2011). *Ethics and power: Navigating mutuality in therapeutic relationships*. Wellesley Centers for Women.

Birrell, P. J., & Freyd, J. J. (2006). Betrayal trauma: Relational models of harm and healing. *Journal of Trauma Practice, 5*(1), 49–63. https://doi.org/10.1300/J189v05n01_04

Birth Detroit. (2021). *Birth Detroit: Midwifing safe, quality, loving care*. https://www.birthdetroit.com/about

Black Lives Matter Foundation, Inc. (n.d.). *The Black Lives Matter Movement*. https://blacklivesmatter.com/about/

Blee, K. M. (2008). *Women of the Klan: Racism and gender in the 1920s*. University of California Press.

Blumenfeld, W. J. (1992). *Homophobia: How we all pay the price*. Beacon Press. https://case.edu/lgbt/safe-zone/heterosexism-homophobia

Bones, P., & Mathew, S. M. (2020). The power (threat) of White women: A content analysis of gender, race, and context in police calls on racial minorities in America. *Journal of Liberal Arts & Humanities, 1*(7), 1–11.

Bonilla-Silva, E. (2021). What makes systemic racism systemic? *Sociological Inquiry, 91*(3), 513–533. https://doi.org/10.1111/soin.12420

Bowlby, J. (1969). *Attachment and loss: Vol. 1. Attachment*. Basic Books.

Bowleg, L. (2008). When black + lesbian + woman ≠ black lesbian woman: The methodological challenges of qualitative and quantitative intersectionality research. *Sex Roles, 59*, 312–325. https://doi.org/10.1007/s11199-008-9400-z

Bowleg, L. (2020). We're not all in this together: On COVID-19, intersectionality, and structural inequality. *American Journal of Public Health (1971), 110*(7), 917–917. https://doi.org/10.2105/AJPH.2020.305766

Bowleg, L. (2021). "The master's tools will never dismantle the master's house": Ten critical lessons for Black and other health equity researchers of color. *Health Education & Behavior, 48*(3), 237–249. https://doi.org/10.1177/10901981211007402

Boykin, C. M. (2022). Constructs, tape measures, and mercury. *Perspectives on Psychological Science*. Advance online publication. https://doi.org/10.1177/17456916221098078

Bozarth, K., Western, G., & Jones, J. (2020). *Black women best: The framework we need for an equitable economy*. Roosevelt Institute. https://rooseveltinstitute.org/publications/black-women-best-the-framework-we-need-for-an-equitable-economy/

Branch, E. H., & Jackson, C. (2020). *Black in America: The paradox of the color line* (1st ed.). Wiley.

Branscombe, N. R., Ellemers, N., Spears, R., & Doosje, B. (1999). The context and content of social identity threat. In N. Ellemers, R. Spears, & B. Doosje (Eds.), *Social identity: Context, commitment, content* (pp. 35–58). Blackwell Science.

Bronfenbrenner, U. (1979). *The ecology of human development: Experiments by nature and design*. Harvard University Press.

brown, a. m., & Imarisha, W. (2015). *Octavia's brood: Science fiction stories from social justice movements*. AK Press. https://doi.org/10.1037/11752-000

Brown, L. S. (2008). *Cultural competence in trauma therapy: Beyond the flashback*. American Psychological Association. https://doi.org/10.1037/11752-000

Brown, L. S. (2021). Institutional cowardice: A powerful, often invisible manifestation of institutional betrayal. *Journal of Trauma & Dissociation, 22*(3), 241–248. https://doi.org/10.1080/15299732.2020.1801307

Brown, M., Ray, R., Summers, E., & Fraistat, N. (2017). #SayHerName: A case study of intersectional social media activism. *Ethnic and Racial Studies, 40*(11), 1831–1846. https://doi.org/10.1080/01419870.2017.1334934

Brans, C. M., & Trimble, C. (2001). Rising tide: Taking our place as young feminist psychologists. *Women & Therapy, 23*(2), 19–36. https://doi.org/10.1300/J015v23n02_03

Bryant, T. (2022). *Homecoming: Overcome fear and trauma to reclaim your whole, authentic self*. Penguin Random House.

Bryant-Davis, T. (2005). *Thriving in the wake of trauma: A multicultural guide*. Praeger Publishers/Greenwood Publishing Group.

Bryant-Davis, T., Adams, T., Alejandre, A., & Gray, A. A. (2017). The trauma lens of police violence against racial and ethnic minorities. *Journal of Social Issues, 73*(4), 852–871. https://doi.org/10.1111/josi.12251

Bryant-Davis, T., Chung, H., Tillman, S., & Belcourt, A. (2009). From the margins to the center: Ethnic minority women and the mental health effects of sexual assault. *Trauma, Violence & Abuse, 10*(4), 330–357. https://doi.org/10.1177/1524838009339755

Bryant-Davis, T., & Comas-Díaz, L. (Eds.). (2016). *Womanist and mujerista psychologies: Voices of fire, acts of courage*. American Psychological Association. https://doi.org/10.1037/14937-000

Bryant-Davis, T., & Moore-Lobban, S. J. (2020). Black minds matter: Applying liberation psychology to Black Americans. In L. Comas-Díaz & E. Torres Rivera (Eds.), *Liberation psychology: Theory, method, practice, and social justice* (pp. 189–206). American Psychological Association. https://doi.org/10.1037/0000198-011

Bryant-Davis, T., & Ocampo, C. (2005). Racist incident–based trauma. *The Counseling Psychologist, 33*(4), 479–500. https://doi.org/10.1177/0011000005276465

Buchanan, N. T., & Fitzgerald, L. F. (2008). Effects of racial and sexual harassment on work and the psychological well-being of African American women. *Journal of Occupational Health Psychology, 13*(2), 137–151. https://doi.org/10.1037/1076-8998.13.2.137

Buchanan, N. T., & Ormerod, A. J. (2002). Racialized sexual harassment in the lives of African American women. *Women & Therapy, 25*(3–4), 107–124. https://doi.org/10.1300/J015v25n03_08

Buchanan, N. T., Perez, M., Prinstein, M. J., & Thurston, I. B. (2021). Upending racism in psychological science: Strategies to change how science is conducted, reported, reviewed, and disseminated. *American Psychologist, 76*(7), 1097–1112. https://doi.org/10.1037/amp0000905

Buchanan, N. T., & Wiklund, L. O. (2020). Why clinical science must change or die: Integrating intersectionality and social justice. *Women & Therapy, 43*(3–4), 309–329. https://doi.org/10.1080/02703149.2020.1729470

Buchanan, N. T., & Wiklund, L. O. (2021). Intersectionality research in psychological science: Resisting the tendency to disconnect, dilute, and depoliticize. *Research on Child and Adolescent Psychopathology, 49*(1), 25–31. https://doi.org/10.1007/s10802-020-00748-y

Buggs, S. G., Pittman Claytor, C., García, S. J., Imoagene, O., Keith, V., Khoshneviss, H., Lee, C., Mayorga-Gallo, S., Ray, V. E., & Roth, W. D. (2020). Systemic anti-black racism must be dismantled: Statement by the American Sociological Association section on racial and ethnic minorities. *Sociology of Race and Ethnicity, 6*(3), 289–291. https://doi.org/10.1177/2332649220941019

Burke, T. (2021). *Unbound: My story of liberation and the birth of the Me Too movement*. Macmillan.

Burstow, B. (2003). Toward a radical understanding of trauma and trauma work. *Violence Against Women, 9*(11), 1293–1317. https://doi.org/10.1177/1077801203255555

Burstow, B. (2005). A critique of posttraumatic stress disorder and the *DSM*. *Journal of Humanistic Psychology, 45*(4), 429–445. https://doi.org/10.1177/0022167805280265

Bush, B. (1986). "The family tree is not cut": Women and cultural resistance in slave family life in the British Caribbean. In G. Y. Okhiro (Ed.), *In resistance:*

Studies in African, Caribbean and Afro-American history (pp. 117–132). University of Massachusetts Press.

Butler, P. (2021, June). Black transhuman liberation. In M. Hope (Moderator), *Black and free: Freedom and liberation in the 21st century* [Webinar]. Invited panelist at University of Michigan National Center for Institutional Diversity 2nd Annual Juneteenth Webinar. https://lsa.umich.edu/ncid/news-events/all-events/black-and-free.html

Cade Bambara, T. B. (Ed.). (1970). *The Black woman: An anthology*. New American Library.

Campbell, R. (2009). Science, social change, and ending violence against women: Which one of these is not like the others? *Violence Against Women, 15*(4), 434–439. https://doi.org/10.1177/1077801208330696

Carlson, G. (2021). Silenced: How America's love affair with the NDA protects workplace predators. *Stanford University Clayman Conversations*. https://gender.stanford.edu/events/clayman-conversations-silenced-how-americas-love-affair-nda-protects-workplace-predators

Carpenter-Song, E., Chu, E., Drake, R. E., Ritsema, M., Smith, B., & Alverson, H. (2010). Ethno-cultural variations in the experience and meaning of mental illness and treatment: Implications for access and utilization. *Transcultural Psychiatry, 47*(2), 224–251. https://doi.org/10.1177/1363461510368906

Carter, S. E., Mekawi, Y., & Harnett, N. G. (2022). It's about racism, not race: A call to purge oppressive practices from neuropsychiatry and scientific discovery. *Neuropsychopharmacology*. Advance online publication. https://doi.org/10.1038/s41386-022-01367-5

Case, K. A. (2015). White practitioners in therapeutic ally-ance. An intersectional privilege awareness training model. *Women & Therapy, 38*(3–4), 263–278. https://doi.org/10.1080/02703149.2015.1059209

Case, K. A. (Ed.). (2017). *Intersectional pedagogy: A model for complicating identity and social justice*. Routledge.

Center for Institutional Courage. (n.d.). *Center for Institutional Courage*. https://www.institutionalcourage.org/the-call-to-courage

Centers for Disease Control and Prevention. (2020). *Introduction to COVID-19 racial and ethnic health disparities*. https://www.cdc.gov/coronavirus/2019-ncov/community/health-equity/racial-ethnic-disparities/index.html

Chatterjee, A., Glasgow, L., Bullard, M., Sabir, M., Hamilton, G., Chassler, D., Stevens-Watkins, D. J., Goddard-Eckrich, D., Rodgers, E., Chaya, J., Rodriguez, S., Gutnick, D. N., Oga, E. A., Salsberry, P., & Martinez, L. S. (2022). Placing racial equity at the center of substance use research: Lessons from the HEALing communities study. *American Journal of Public Health, 112*(2), 204–208. https://doi.org/10.2105/AJPH.2021.306572

Chioneso, N. A., Hunter, C. D., Gobin, R. L., McNeil Smith, S., Mendenhall, R., & Neville, H. A. (2020). Community healing and resistance through storytelling: A framework to address racial trauma in Africana communities. *The Journal of Black Psychology, 46*(2–3), 95–121. https://doi.org/10.1177/0095798420929468

Cho, S., Crenshaw, K. W., & McCall, L. (2013). Toward a field of intersectionality studies: Theory, applications, and praxis. *Signs: Journal of Women in Culture and Society, 38*(4), 785–810. https://doi.org/10.1086/669608

Cloitre, M. (2015). The "one size fits all" approach to trauma treatment: Should we be satisfied? *European Journal of Psychotraumatology, 6*(1), 27344. https://doi.org/10.3402/ejpt.v6.27344

Cohen, E. S. (2001). The complex nature of ageism: What is it? Who does it? Who perceives it? *The Gerontologist, 41*(5), 576–577.

Cohen, C. J. (2009). *The boundaries of blackness: AIDS and the breakdown of black politics*. University of Chicago Press.

Cokley, K. (2007). Critical issues in the measurement of ethnic and racial identity: A referendum on the state of the field. *Journal of Counseling Psychology, 54*(3), 224–234. https://doi.org/10.1037/0022-0167.54.3.224

Cokley, K., Krueger, N., Cunningham, S. R., Burlew, K., Hall, S., Harris, K., Castelin, S., & Coleman, C. (2022). The COVID-19/racial injustice syndemic and mental health among Black Americans: The roles of general and race-related COVID worry, cultural mistrust, and perceived discrimination. *Journal of Community Psychology, 50*(6), 2542–2561. https://doi.org/10.1002/jcop.22747

Cole, E. R. (2008). Coalitions as a model for intersectionality: From practice to theory. *Sex Roles, 59*, 443–453. https://doi.org/10.1007/s11199-008-9419-1

Cole, E. R. (2009). Intersectionality and research in psychology. *American Psychologist, 64*(3), 170–180. https://doi.org/10.1037/a0014564

Cole, E. R. (2020). Demarginalizing women of color in intersectionality scholarship in psychology: A Black feminist critique. *Journal of Social Issues, 76*(4), 1036–1044. https://doi.org/10.1111/josi.12413

Cole, E. R., & Luna, Z. T. (2010). Making coalitions work: Solidarity across difference within U.S. feminism. *Feminist Studies, 35*, 71–98.

Coles, S. M., & Pasek, J. (2020). Intersectional invisibility revisited: How group prototypes lead to the erasure and exclusion of Black women. *Translational Issues in Psychological Science, 6*(4), 314–324. https://doi.org/10.1037/tps0000256

Collins, P. H. (1986). Learning from the outsider within: The sociological significance of Black feminist thought. *Social Problems, 33*(6), S14–S32. https://doi.org/10.2307/800672

Collins, P. H. (1989). A comparison of two works on black family life. *Signs: Journal of Women in Culture and Society, 14*(4), 875–884. https://doi.org/10.1086/494548

Collins, P. H. (1990). Black feminist thought in the matrix of domination. In *Black feminist thought: Knowledge, consciousness, and the politics of empowerment* (pp. 221–238). Routledge.

Collins, P. H. (1991/2000). *Black feminist thought: Knowledge, consciousness, and the politics of empowerment*. Routledge.

Collins, P. H. (1997). Comment on Hekman's "Truth and method: Feminist standpoint theory revisited": Where's the power? *Signs: Journal of Women in Culture and Society, 22*(2), 375–381. https://doi.org/10.1086/495162

Collins, P. H. (2022). Black feminist sociology: An interview with Patricia Hill Collins. In Z. Luna & W. L. Pirtle (Eds.), *Black feminist sociology: Perspectives and praxis* (pp. 19–31). Routledge.

Comas-Díaz, L. (2007). Ethnopolitical psychology: Healing and transformation. In E. Aldarondo (Ed.), *Advancing social justice through clinical practice* (pp. 91–118). Erlbaum.

Comas-Díaz, L., & Torres Rivera, E. (Eds.). (2020). *Liberation psychology: Theory, method, practice, and social justice*. American Psychological Association. https://doi.org/10.1037/0000198-000

Combahee River Collective. (1995). Combahee River Collective statement. In B. Guy-Sheftall (Ed.), *Words of fire: An anthology of African American feminist thought* (pp. 232–240). New Press.

Community Healing Network [@CHNWorld_]. (2022, July 7). *What is #Emotional Emancipation?* [Tweet]. Twitter. https://twitter.com/CHNWorld_/status/1545030344692334592

Comstock, D. L., Hammer, T. R., Strentzsch, J., Cannon, K., Parsons, J., & Salazar, G. I. I. (2008). Relational-cultural theory: A framework for bridging relational, multicultural, and social justice competencies. *Journal of Counseling and Development, 86*(3), 279–287. https://doi.org/10.1002/j.1556-6678.2008.tb00510.x

Correia & Puth, PLLC. (2016). *University of Oregon employees resolve Title IX and whistleblower claims for $425,000*. https://www.correiaputh.com/news/university-oregon-employees-resolve-title-ix-whistleblower-claims-425000/

Correll, S. J. (2017). SWS 2016 feminist lecture: Reducing gender biases in modern workplaces; A small wins approach to organizational change. *Gender & Society, 31*(6), 725–750. https://doi.org/10.1177/0891243217738518

Crenshaw, K. (1991). Mapping the margins: Intersectionality, identity politics, and violence against women of color. *Stanford Law Review, 43*(6), 1241–1299. https://doi.org/10.2307/1229039

Crenshaw, K., Gotanda, N., Peller, G., & Thomas, K. (1995). *Critical race theory*. The New Press.

Crenshaw, K. W. (1989). Demarginalizing the intersection of race and sex: A Black feminist critique of antidiscrimination doctrine, feminist theory, and antiracist politics. *University of Chicago Legal Forum, 139*, 139–167.

Crenshaw, K. W. (2012). From private violence to mass incarceration: Thinking intersectionally about women, race, and social control. *UCLA Law Review, 59*(6), 1418–1472.

Crenshaw, K. W. (2019). We still have not learned from Anita Hill's testimony. *UCLA Women's Law Journal, 26*(1), 17–20. https://doi.org/10.5070/L3261044346

Crenshaw, K. W., & Ritchie, A. J. (2015). Say her name: Resisting police brutality against Black women. *African American Policy Forum.* https://www.aapf.org/_files/ugd/1187fd_7db4f9a2e9e94cce9ac6c03b290916d4.pdf

Cromer, L. D., Vasquez, L., Gray, M. E., & Freyd, J. J. (2018). The relationship of acculturation to historical loss awareness, institutional betrayal, and the intergenerational transmission of trauma in the American Indian experience. *Journal of Cross-Cultural Psychology, 49*(1), 99–114. https://doi.org/10.1177/0022022117738749

The Culture. *Revolutionary hope: A conversation between James Baldwin and Audre Lorde.* (2018). https://theculture.forharriet.com/2014/03/revolutionary-hope-conversation-between.html

Cummings, S. L. (2021a). *An equal place: Lawyers in the struggle for Los Angeles.* Oxford University Press. https://doi.org/10.1093/oso/9780190215927.001.0001

Cummings, S. L. (2021b, December). *Lawyers and movements: Legal mobilization in transformative times* [Paper presentation]. Stanford University Center for Advanced Study in the Behavioral Sciences (CASBS) Research Seminar Series, Stanford, CA, United States.

Dance Theatre of Harlem. (2023). *Who we are.* https://www.dancetheatreofharlem.org/who-we-are/

Danylchuk, L. S. (2015). The training of a trauma therapist: Bringing it home. *Journal of Trauma & Dissociation, 16*(1), 1–6. https://doi.org/10.1080/15299732.2014.930804

Dastagir, A. (2021, February 2). Alexandria Ocasio-Cortez is explaining something about trauma. Experts say we should listen. *USA Today.* https://www.usatoday.com/story/life/health-wellness/2021/02/02/alexandria-ocasio-cortez-trauma-and-why-survivors-cant-just-forget/4355687001/

Davis, A. (1985). *Violence against women and the ongoing challenge to racism.* Kitchen Table/Women of Color Press.

Davis, A. (1989). *Women, culture, and politics.* Random House.

Davis, A. Y. (1981). Rape, racism and the capitalist setting. *The Black Scholar, 12*(6), 39–45. https://doi.org/10.1080/00064246.1981.11414219

D'Cruz, H., Gillingham, P., & Melendez, S. (2007). Reflexivity, its meanings and relevance for social work: A critical review of the literature. *British Journal of Social Work, 37*(1), 73–90. https://doi.org/10.1093/bjsw/bcl001

DeBlaere, C., Brewster, M. E., Sarkees, A., & Moradi, B. (2010). Conducting research with LGB people of color: Methodological challenges and strategies. *The Counseling Psychologist, 38*(3), 331–362. https://doi.org/10.1177/0011000009335257

Delker, B. C. (2019). When self-care is not enough: Reflections on how to make trauma-intensive clinical work more sustainable. *Dignity: A Journal of Sexual Exploitation and Violence, 4*, 1–17. https://doi.org/10.23860/dignity.2019.04.01.06

Delker, B. C., Smith, C. P., Rosenthal, M. N., Bernstein, R. E., & Freyd, J. J. (2018). When home is where the harm is: Family betrayal and posttraumatic outcomes in young adulthood. *Journal of Aggression, Maltreatment & Trauma, 27*(7), 720–743. https://doi.org/10.1080/10926771.2017.1382639

DePrince, A., & Gómez, J. M. (2020). Weinstein trial begs a question: Why is the pain of women and minorities often ignored? *The Conversation.* https://theconversation.com/weinstein-trial-begs-a-question-why-is-the-pain-of-women-and-minorities-often-ignored-131640

DePrince, A. P. (2022a). *Every 90 seconds: Our common cause ending violence against women.* Oxford University Press. https://doi.org/10.1093/oso/9780197545744.001.0001

DePrince, A. P. (2022b). Translating scientific knowledge about trauma into action. *Journal of Trauma & Dissociation, 23*(3), 205–211. https://doi.org/10.1080/15299732.2022.2041225

DePrince, A. P., & Freyd, J. J. (2002). The harm of trauma: Pathological fear, shattered assumptions, or betrayal. In J. Kauffman (Ed.), *Loss of the assumptive world: A theory of traumatic loss* (pp. 71–82). Brunner-Routledge.

Dewey, J. (1966). *The middle works of John Dewey, 1899–1924: Vol. 9. 1916, democracy and education* (J. Boydston, Ed.). Southern Illinois University Press.

Dichter, M. E. (2015). *Women's experiences of abuse as a risk factor for incarceration: A research update.* VAWnet, National Online Resource Center on Domestic Violence. https://vawnet.org/sites/default/files/materials/files/2016-09/AR_IncarcerationUpdate.pdf

Dick, K., & Ziering, A. (Directors). (2020). *On the record* [Film]. HBO Max Original.

Dotson, K. (2011). Tracking epistemic violence, tracking practices of silencing. *Hypatia, 26*(2), 236–257. https://doi.org/10.1111/j.1527-2001.2011.01177.x

Dotson, K. (2012). A cautionary tale: On limiting epistemic oppression. *Frontiers, 33*(1), 24–47. https://doi.org/10.5250/fronjwomestud.33.1.0024

Dotson, K. (2014). Conceptualizing epistemic oppression. *Social Epistemology, 28*(2), 115–138. https://doi.org/10.1080/02691728.2013.782585

Dressler, W. W., Oths, K. S., & Gravlee, C. C. (2005). Race and ethnicity in public health research: Models to explain health disparities. *Annual Review of Anthropology, 34,* 231–252. https://doi.org/10.1146/annurev.anthro.34.081804.120505

Dreyer, B. P., Trent, M., Anderson, A. T., Askew, G. L., Boyd, R., Coker, T. R., Coyne-Beasley, T., Fuentes-Afflick, E., Johnson, T., Mendoza, F., Montoya-Williams, D., Oyeku, S. O., Poitevien, P., Spinks-Franklin, A. A. I., Thomas, O. W., Walker-Harding, L., Willis, E., Wright, J. L., Berman, S., . . . Stein, F. (2020). The death of George Floyd: Bending the arc of history toward justice for generations of children. *Pediatrics, 146*(3), Article e2020009639. Advance online publication. https://doi.org/10.1542/peds.2020-009639

Dukes, K. N., & Gaither, S. E. (2017). Black racial stereotypes and victim blaming: Implications for media coverage and criminal proceedings in cases of police violence against racial and ethnic minorities. *Journal of Social Issues, 73*(4), 789–807. https://doi.org/10.1111/josi.12248

Durkee, M. I., & Gómez, J. M. (2022). Mental health implications of the acting white accusation: The role of cultural betrayal and ethnic-racial identity among Black and Latina/o emerging adults. *American Journal of Orthopsychiatry, 92*(1), 68–78. https://doi.org/10.1037/ort0000589

Eaton, A. A., Grzanka, P. R., Schlehofer, M. M., & Silka, L. (2021). Public psychology: Introduction to the special issue. *American Psychologist, 76*(8), 1209–1216. https://doi.org/10.1037/amp0000933

Eberhardt, J. (2021). The magnitude of our mythology. *Association for Psychological Science.* https://www.psychologicalscience.org/observer/magnitude-mythology

Eberhardt, J. L. (2020). *Biased: Uncovering the hidden prejudice that shapes what we see, think, and do.* Penguin Books.

Edelman, L. B. (1992). Legal ambiguity and symbolic structures: Organizational mediation of civil rights law. *American Journal of Sociology, 97*(6), 1531–1576. https://doi.org/10.1086/229939

Educational Testing Service (ETS). (2022). Graduate Record Examination (GRE): Guide to the use of scores. https://www.ets.org/pdfs/gre/gre-guide-to-the-use-of-scores.pdf

Edwards, K. E. (2006). Aspiring social justice ally identity development: A conceptual model. *NASPA Journal, 43*(4), 39–60. https://doi.org/10.2202/1949-6605.1722

Ellis, D. (2011). The arc of the moral universe is long, but it bends towards justice. *The White House.* https://obamawhitehouse.archives.gov/blog/2011/10/21/arc-moral-universe-long-it-bends-toward-justice

Ennis, W. (2021). Midsummer musings: Simone Biles is the G.O.A.T. *The Dartmouth.* https://www.thedartmouth.com/article/2021/07/midsummer-musings-simone-biles-is-the-g-o-a-t

Evening Standard. *How author created film character Precious through her own sexual abuse.* (2012, April 10). https://www.standard.co.uk/lifestyle/how-author-created-film-character-precious-through-her-own-sexual-abuse-6735992.html

Fang, A. H., & White, S. (2022). Historical information and beliefs about racial inequality. *Politics, Groups, and Identities.* Advance online publication. https://doi.org/10.1080/21565503.2022.2104167

Feagin, J. R. (2001). White supremacy and Mexican Americans: Rethinking the Black–White paradigm. *Rutgers Law Review, 54,* 959.

Feminist Campus Team. (2017). Institutional cultural betrayal: The loss of HBCU pride. *Feminist Campus.* https://feministcampus.org/institutional-cultural-betrayal-the-loss-of-hbcu-pride/

Fine, M. (1984). Coping with rape: Critical perspectives on consciousness. *Imagination, Cognition and Personality, 3*(3), 249–267. https://doi.org/10.2190/1F1E-KUVH-6T3K-DPN8

Fine, M., & Torre, M. E. (2019). Critical participatory action research: A feminist project for validity and solidarity. *Psychology of Women Quarterly, 43*(4), 433–444. https://doi.org/10.1177/0361684319865255

Fisher, D. R., Dow, D. M., & Ray, R. (2017). Intersectionality takes it to the streets: Mobilizing across diverse interests for the Women's March. *Science Advances, 3*(9), eaao1390. https://doi.org/10.1126/sciadv.aao1390

Fitzgerald, K. J. (2017). Understanding racialized homophobic and transphobic violence. In *violence Against Black bodies* (pp. 53–70). Routledge. https://doi.org/10.4324/9781315408705-5

Fleming, J. B., Jr. (2022). *Black patience: Performance, civil rights, and the unfinished project of emancipation*. New York University Press. https://doi.org/10.18574/nyu/9781479806874.001.0001

Fook, J. (1993). *Radical casework: A theory of practice*. Allen & Unwin.

Foynes, M. M., & Freyd, J. J. (2011). The impact of skills training on responses to the disclosure of mistreatment. *Psychology of Violence, 1*(1), 66–77. https://doi.org/10.1037/a0022021

Freire, P. (1970). *Pedagogy of the oppressed*. Herder and Herder.

Freire, P. (1974). *Education for critical consciousness*. Continuum.

Freire, P. (1992). *Pedagogy of hope*. Bloomsbury.

Freire, P. (1996). *Letters to Christina: Reflections of my life and work*. Routledge.

French, B. H., Lewis, J. A., Mosley, D. V., Adames, H. Y., Chavez-Dueñas, N. Y., Chen, G. A., & Neville, H. A. (2020). Toward a psychological framework of radical healing in communities of color. *The Counseling Psychologist, 48*(1), 14–46. https://doi.org/10.1177/0011000019843506

Freyd, J., & Birrell, P. (2013). *Blind to betrayal: Why we fool ourselves we aren't being fooled*. John Wiley & Sons.

Freyd, J. J. (n.d.). *We are making a call to courage*. Center for Institutional Courage. https://www.institutionalcourage.org/the-call-to-courage

Freyd, J. J. (1996). *Betrayal trauma: The logic of forgetting childhood abuse*. Harvard University Press.

Freyd, J. J. (1997). II. Violations of power, adaptive blindness and betrayal trauma theory. *Feminism & Psychology, 7*(1), 22–32. https://doi.org/10.1177/0959353597071004

Freyd, J. J. (2014a, October). *Institutional betrayal*. Plenary address at the 31st Annual Meeting of the International Society for the Study of Trauma and Dissociation (ISSTD), Long Beach, CA, United States.

Freyd, J. J. (2014b). Official campus statistics for sexual violence mislead [Op-Ed]. *Al Jazeera America*. http://america.aljazeera.com/opinions/2014/7/college-campus-sexualassaultsafetydatawhitehousegender.html

Freyd, J. J. (2018). When sexual assault victims speak out, their institutions often betray them. *The Conversation*. https://theconversation.com/when-sexual-assault-victims-speak-out-their-institutions-often-betray-them-87050

Freyd, J. J. (2022). *Compelled disclosure: The problem with "mandated reporting" of sexual violence on college campuses; A compilation of articles and resources*. https://dynamic.uoregon.edu/jjf/disclosure/requiredreporting.html

Freyd, J. J., & Smidt, A. M. (2019). So you want to address sexual harassment and assault in your organization? *Training* is not enough; *Education* is necessary.

Journal of Trauma & Dissociation, 20(5), 489–494. https://doi.org/10.1080/15299732.2019.1663475

Fricker, M. (2007). *Epistemic injustice: Power and the ethics of knowing.* Oxford University Press. https://doi.org/10.1093/acprof:oso/9780198237907.001.0001

Fricker, M. (2017). Evolving concepts of epistemic injustice. In I. J. Kidd, J. Medina, & G. Pohlhaus, Jr. (Eds.), *Routledge handbook of epistemic injustice* (pp. 53–60). Routledge. https://doi.org/10.4324/9781315212043-5

Giddings, P. (1985). *When and where I enter: The impact of Black women on race and sex in America.* Morrow.

Ginwright, S. A. (2010). *Black youth rising: Activism and radical healing in urban America.* Teachers College Press.

Ginwright, S. A. (2016). *Hope and healing in urban education: How urban activists and teachers are reclaiming matters of the heart.* Routledge.

Gobin, R. L. (2019). *The self-care prescription: Powerful tools to manage stress, reduce anxiety, and enhance well-being.* Althea Press.

Gobin, R. L., & Allard, C. B. (2016). Associations between sexual health concerns and mental health symptoms among African American and European American women veterans who have experienced interpersonal trauma. *Personality and Individual Differences, 100,* 37–42. https://doi.org/10.1016/j.paid.2016.02.007

Gobin, R. L., & Gómez, J. M. (2020). The cultural context of sexual assault and its consequences among ethnic minority women. In R. Geffner, V. Vieth, V. Vaughan-Eden, A. Rosenbaum, L. K. Hamberger, & J. White (Eds.), *Handbook of interpersonal violence across the lifespan.* Springer/National Partnership to End Interpersonal Violence Across the Lifespan (NPEIV). https://doi.org/10.1007/978-3-319-62122-7_216-1

Gómez, J. M. (n.d.-a). All's well that doesn't begin well: The positive impact of (intra)cultural support on Black young women's posttraumatic growth following cultural betrayal sexual trauma [Manuscript in preparation].

Gómez, J. M. (n.d.-b). *HOPE Lab.* https://jmgomez.org/hope-lab/

Gómez, J. M. (n.d.-c). The impact of (intra)cultural trust and pressure for Black female cultural betrayal sexual trauma survivors [Manuscript in preparation].

Gómez, J. M. (2012). Cultural betrayal trauma theory: The impact of culture on the effects of trauma. In *Blind to Betrayal.* https://web.archive.org/web/20221006011353/https://sites.google.com/site/betrayalbook/betrayal-research-news/cultural-betrayal

Gómez, J. M. (2014). Ebony in the ivory tower: Dismantling the stronghold of racial inequality from the inside out. In K. J. Fasching-Varner, R. Reynolds, K. Albert, & L. Martin (Eds.), *Trayvon Martin, race, and American justice: Writing wrong* (pp. 113–117). Sense Publishers. https://doi.org/10.1007/978-94-6209-842-8_21

Gómez, J. M. (2015a). The aesthetics of social justice: Appearance sidetracks our internal processes [Op-Ed]. *Eugene Weekly* (Eugene, Oregon). https://www.eugeneweekly.com/2015/10/15/the-aesthetics-of-social-justice/

Gómez, J. M. (2015b). Conceptualizing trauma: In pursuit of culturally relevant research. *Trauma Psychology Newsletter (American Psychological Association Division 56), 10,* 40–44.

Gómez, J. M. (2015c). *Email to Oregon Board of Psychologist Examiners regarding psychologists accessing Jane Doe university therapy records.* Gómez Social Justice & Institutional Change Collection. Open Science Framework. https://osf.io/f9vwh

Gómez, J. M. (2015d). Microaggressions and the enduring mental health disparity: Black Americans at risk for institutional betrayal. *The Journal of Black Psychology, 41*(2), 121–143. https://doi.org/10.1177/0095798413514608

Gómez, J. M. (2015e). Rape, Black men, and the degraded Black woman: Feminist psychologists' role in addressing within-group sexual violence. *The Feminist Psychologist: Newsletter for the Society of the Psychology of Women (American Psychological Association Division 35), 42*(2), 12–13.

Gómez, J. M. (2015f, February 9). Dear President Coltrane [Op-Ed]. *Daily Emerald* (Eugene, Oregon). https://www.dailyemerald.com/opinion/guest-viewpoint-dear-president-coltrane/article_fb211bc1-a40b-50d6-bcb4-42ef4cf2503f.html

Gómez, J. M. (2015g, August 6). Psychological pressure: Did the APA commit institutional betrayal? [Op-Ed]. *Eugene Weekly* (Eugene, Oregon). https://www.eugeneweekly.com/2015/08/06/psychological-pressure/

Gómez, J. M. (2015h, October 21). Inequality plays a role in campus sexual violence [Op-Ed]. *The Register-Guard* (Eugene, Oregon). https://www.registerguard.com/article/20151021/OPINION/310219958

Gómez, J. M. (2016, June 23). Black, raped, shamed, and supported: Our responses to rape can build or destroy our community. *The Black Commentator, 659.* https://www.blackcommentator.com/659/659_campus_rape_gomez_guest.html

Gómez, J. M. (2017). Does ethno-cultural betrayal in trauma affect Asian American/Pacific Islander college students' mental health outcomes? An exploratory study. *Journal of American College Health, 65*(6), 432–436. https://doi.org/10.1080/07448481.2017.1341896

Gómez, J. M. (2018, December 6). Black women and #MeToo: The violence of silencing. *The Black Commentator, 767.* https://blackcommentator.com/767/767_guest_gomez_black_women_and_metoo.html

Gómez, J. M. (2019a, January 8). *Cultural betrayal trauma in "violence against women"* [Film]. YouTube. https://youtu.be/UZ9G0AjSJeU

Gómez, J. M. (2019b, October). *Cultural betrayal trauma theory: Sexual abuse, solidarity, and healing in the Black community* [Keynote presentation]. Motor City Singers' Space Presents Soul Train: Mental Health Moment, Detroit, MI, United States.

Gómez, J. M. (2019c). Group dynamics as a predictor of dissociation for Black victims of violence: An exploratory study of cultural betrayal trauma theory. *Transcultural Psychiatry, 56*(5), 878–894. https://doi.org/10.1177/1363461519847300

Gómez, J. M. (2019d). High betrayal adolescent sexual abuse and non-suicidal self-injury: The role of depersonalization in emerging adults. *Journal of Child Sexual Abuse, 28*(3), 318–332. https://doi.org/10.1080/10538712.2018.1539425

Gómez, J. M. (2019e). Isn't it all about victimization? (Intra)cultural pressure and cultural betrayal trauma in ethnic minority college women. *Violence Against Women, 25*(10), 1211–1225. https://doi.org/10.1177/1077801218811682

Gómez, J. M. (2019f, September 13). Navigating the dialectic of privilege and oppression. *Inside Higher Ed Conditionally Accepted Blog.* https://www.insidehighered.com/advice/2019/09/13/balancing-sense-both-oppression-and-privilege-new-faculty-member-color-opinion

Gómez, J. M. (2019g). *Self-care and longevity in research and clinical work regarding trauma & inequality.* Gómez HOPE Lab Professional Development Series. Open Science Framework. https://osf.io/wpg62

Gómez, J. M. (2019h, May 13). The unique harm of sexual abuse in the Black community. *The Conversation.* https://theconversation.com/the-unique-harm-of-sexual-abuse-in-the-black-community-114948

Gómez, J. M. (2019i). What's in a betrayal? Trauma, dissociation, and hallucinations among high-functioning ethnic minority emerging adults. *Journal of Aggression, Maltreatment & Trauma, 28*(10), 1181–1198. https://doi.org/10.1080/10926771.2018.1494653

Gómez, J. M. (2019j). What's the harm? Internalized prejudice and intra-racial trauma as cultural betrayal among ethnic minority college students. *American Journal of Orthopsychiatry, 89*(2), 237–247. https://doi.org/10.1037/ort0000367

Gómez, J. M. (2019k, January 31). Who's betraying who? R. Kelly, sexual violence, and the dismissal of Black women and girls. *Google Blogspot.* https://culturalbetrayalrkellyblackfemales.blogspot.com

Gómez, J. M. (2020a). *Ethics, anti-oppression, and responsibility in trauma and inequality research.* Gómez HOPE Lab Professional Development Series. Open Science Framework. https://osf.io/wpg62

Gómez, J. M. (2020b). Exposure to discrimination, cultural betrayal, and intoxication as a Black female graduate student applying for tenure-track faculty positions. In Y. F. Niemann, G. Gutierrez y Muhs, & C. G. Gonzalez, *Presumed incompetent II: Race, class, power, and resistance of women in academia* (pp. 204–214). University Press of Colorado. https://doi.org/10.7330/9781607329664.c019

Gómez, J. M. (2020c). It hurts when you're close: High betrayal sexual trauma, dissociation, and suicidal ideation in young adults. *Violence and Victims, 35*(5), 712–723. https://doi.org/10.1891/VV-D-19-00150

Gómez, J. M. (2020d). *Notes on process in cross-racial coalition for anti-racism professional development.* Gómez Social Justice & Institutional Change Collection. Open Science Framework. https://osf.io/f9vwh

Gómez, J. M. (2020e). *Publishing work that centralizes inequality: Efficiency and self-care amidst rejections.* Gómez HOPE Lab Professional Development Series. Open Science Framework. https://osf.io/wpg62

Gómez, J. M. (2020f, February 21). Scholars should hold themselves accountable for discrimination in academe. *Inside Higher Ed Conditionally Accepted Blog*. https://www.insidehighered.com/advice/2020/02/21/scholars-should-hold-themselves-accountable-discrimination-academe-opinion

Gómez, J. M. (2020g). Trainee perspectives on relational cultural therapy and cultural competency in supervision of trauma cases. *Journal of Psychotherapy Integration, 30*(1), 60–66. https://doi.org/10.1037/int0000154

Gómez, J. M. (2020h, September). Transitioning from ballerina to professor: Lessons learned from Arthur Mitchell and Dance Theatre of Harlem [Audio podcast episode]. In *Count 9*. https://anchor.fm/count9/episodes/Ep--9---Jennifer-M--Gmez--Ph-D---Assistant-Professor--Researcher--and-Trauma-Psychologist-ejj0kc

Gómez, J. M. (2020i, February). *Yell! From R. Kelly to Kobe Bryant: Why is it so hard to discuss sexual abuse in the Black community? A research perspective from cultural betrayal trauma theory* [Panelist]. BBC Women's Hour Radio Show. https://www.bbc.co.uk/sounds/play/m000g4fr

Gómez, J. M. (2021a, March). Arts as healing from cultural betrayal and sexual violence. In A. Scobie, *In conversation: Arts and healing, Part 1* [Video]. Invited panelist at the Michigan Opera Theatre at Home Series, Detroit, MI, United States. YouTube. https://www.youtube.com/watch?v=4Tq_JvvM_Yg

Gómez, J. M. (2021b, March). Arts as healing from cultural betrayal and sexual violence. In A. Scobie, *In conversation: Arts and healing, Part 2* [Video]. Invited panelist at the Michigan Opera Theatre at Home Series, Detroit, MI, United States. YouTube. https://www.youtube.com/watch?v=f_aX0-AWMJU

Gómez, J. M. (2021c). Cultural betrayal as a dimension of traumatic harm: Violence and PTSS among ethnic minority emerging adults. *Journal of Child & Adolescent Trauma, 14*(3), 347–356. https://link.springer.com/article/10.1007/s40653-020-00314-0

Gómez, J. M. (2021d). Does gender matter? An exploratory study of cultural betrayal trauma and hallucinations in Latino undergraduates at a predominantly White university. *Journal of Interpersonal Violence, 36*(3–4), NP1375–1390NP. https://doi.org/10.1177/0886260517746942

Gómez, J. M. (2021e). Gendered sexual violence: Betrayal trauma, dissociation, and PTSD in diverse college students [Special issue]. *Journal of Aggression, Maltreatment, & Trauma, 30*(5), 625–640. https://doi.org/10.1080/10926771.2020.1783737

Gómez, J. M. (2021f). When solidarity hurts: (Intra)cultural trust, cultural betrayal sexual trauma, and PTSD in culturally diverse minoritized youth transitioning to adulthood. *Transcultural Psychiatry, 59*(3), 292–301. https://doi.org/10.1177/13634615211062970

Gómez, J. M. (2021g). Who is okay? The harm of one-dimensional appraisals of women scholars during COVID-19 and beyond. *The ADVANCE Journal, 2*(3). https://doi.org/10.5399/osu/ADVJRNL.2.3.7

Gómez, J. M. (2022a). Campus sexual harassment, other violence, and racism, oh my! Evidence from Black women undergraduates for a culturally competent university approach to Title IX. *Feminist Criminology, 17*(3), 368–383. https://doi.org/10.1177/15570851211062574

Gómez, J. M. (2022b). Campus sexual violence, gender, and mental health in diverse undergraduate/graduate students. *Journal of Aggression, Maltreatment, & Trauma, 31*(8), 981–995. https://doi.org/10.1080/10926771.2022.2043972

Gómez, J. M. (2022c). Diversity wanted! Utilizing transdisciplinary scholarship on structural inequality to educate psychology graduate students [Special issue]. *Social Justice Pedagogy: Diversity, Equity, & Inclusion in the Teaching of Psychology.* Advance online publication. https://doi.org/10.1177/00986283211061687

Gómez, J. M. (2022d). Epistemic oppression, construct validity, and scientific rigor: Commentary on Woo et al. (2022). *Perspectives on Psychological Science.* https://doi.org/10.1177/17456916211072830

Gómez, J. M. (2022e). Gender, campus sexual violence, cultural betrayal, institutional betrayal, and institutional support in U.S. ethnic minority college students: A descriptive study. *Violence Against Women, 28*(1), 93–106. https://doi.org/10.1177/1077801221998757

Gómez, J. M. (2022f). *I am not just a body but also a soul: The power of erasure amidst hypervisibility on a faculty search committee* [Accepted manuscript version]. https://doi.org/10.31234/osf.io/6y7tj

Gómez, J. M. (2022h). *Table of contents.* Gómez Social Justice & Institutional Change Collection. Open Science Framework. https://osf.io/f9vwh

Gómez, J. M. (in press). Black feminist activism from the ivory tower: Cultural betrayal, sexual abuse, and healing for Black women and girls. In M. Marcel & E. Joachimpillai, *Scapegoats to citizens: This era of Black activism.*

Gómez, J. M., Caño, A., & Baltes, B. B. (2021). Who are we missing? Examining the Graduate Record Examination quantitative score as a barrier to admission into psychology doctoral programs for capable ethnic minorities. *Training and Education in Professional Psychology, 15*(3), 211–218. https://doi.org/10.1037/tep0000336

Gómez, J. M., & Freyd, J. J. (2014, August 22). Institutional betrayal makes violence more toxic [Op-Ed]. *The Register-Guard* (Eugene, Oregon), p. A9. https://www.registerguard.com/article/20140822/OPINION/308229834

Gómez, J. M., & Freyd, J. J. (2018). Psychological outcomes of within-group sexual violence: Evidence of cultural betrayal. *Journal of Immigrant and Minority Health, 20*(6), 1458–1467. https://doi.org/10.1007/s10903-017-0687-0

Gómez, J. M., & Freyd, J. J. (2019). Betrayal trauma. In J. J. Ponzetti (Ed.), *Macmillan encyclopedia of intimate and family relationships: An interdisciplinary approach* (pp. 79–82). Cengage Learning Inc.

Gómez, J. M., Freyd, J. J., Delva, J., Tracy, B., Nishiura Mackenzie, L., Ray, V., & Weathington, B. (2023). Institutional courage in action: Racism, sexual violence, & concrete institutional change. *Journal of Trauma & Dissociation, 24*(2), 157–170. https://doi.org/10.1080/15299732.2023.2168245

Gómez, J. M., & Gobin, R. L. (2020a). Black women and girls and #MeToo: Rape, cultural betrayal, and healing. *Sex Roles, 82*(1–2), 1–12. https://doi.org/10.1007/s11199-019-01040-0

Gómez, J. M., & Gobin, R. L. (2020b, June 29). Russell Simmons, rape, and the myth of "toxic femininity": What Black men can do to be part of the solution. *Blavity.* https://blavity.com/russell-simmons-rape-and-the-myth-of-toxic-feminity-what-black-men-can-do-to-be-part-of-the-solution

Gómez, J. M., & Gobin, R. L. (2022). *"It will always feel worse because it comes with that added 'betrayal'": Black young women survivors' reactions to cultural betrayal trauma theory.* PsyArXiv. https://doi.org/10.31234/osf.io/hfe6z

Gómez, J. M., Gobin, R. L., & Barnes, M. L. (2021). Discrimination, violence, and healing within marginalized communities. *Journal of Trauma & Dissociation, 22*(2), 135–140. https://doi.org/10.1080/15299732.2021.1869059

Gómez, J. M., & Johnson, L. (2022). *Assessing "friendly fire": The development and validation of the Cultural Betrayal Multidimensional Inventory for Black American Young Adults (CBMI-BAYA).* PsyArXiv. https://doi.org/10.31234/osf.io/vea7p

Gómez, J. M., & Johnson-Freyd, S. (2015, October 25). *Condemned to dance: Cultural betrayal trauma theory* [Video]. YouTube. https://www.youtube.com/watch?v=X_QwbCkb_m8

Gómez, J. M., Kaehler, L. A., & Freyd, J. J. (2014). Are hallucinations related to betrayal trauma exposure? A three-study exploration. *Psychological Trauma: Theory, Research, Practice, and Policy, 6*(6), 675–682. https://doi.org/10.1037/a0037084

Gómez, J. M., Lewis, J. K., Noll, L. K., Smidt, A. M., & Birrell, P. J. (2016). Shifting the focus: Nonpathologizing approaches to healing from betrayal trauma through an emphasis on relational care [Special section]. *Journal of Trauma & Dissociation, 17*(2), 165–185. https://doi.org/10.1080/15299732.2016.1103104

Gómez, J. M., Noll, L. K., Adams-Clark, A. A., & Courtois, C. A. (2021). When colleagues betray: The harm of sexual boundary violations in psychotherapy extends beyond the victim. In A. (L.) Steinberg, J. L. Alpert, & C. A. Courtois (Eds.), *Sexual boundary violations in psychotherapy: Facing therapist indiscretions, transgressions, and misconduct* (pp. 297–315). American Psychological Association. https://doi.org/10.1037/0000247-017

Gómez, J. M., & Partridge, T. (2022). *But is it okay? The need to still ask Black/African American mothers about violence exposure during the COVID-19 worldwide pandemic.* https://doi.org/10.31234/osf.io/pa6ek

Gómez, J. M., Smith, C. P., & Freyd, J. J. (2014). Zwischenmenschlicher und institutioneller verrat [Interpersonal and institutional betrayal]. In R. Vogt (Ed.), *Verleumdung und Verrat: Dissoziative Störungen bei schwer traumatisierten Menschen als Folge von Vertrauensbrüchen* (pp. 82–90). Asanger Verlag.

Gómez, J. M., Smith, C. P., Gobin, R. L., Tang, S. S., & Freyd, J. J. (2016). Collusion, torture, and inequality: Understanding the actions of the American Psychological Association as institutional betrayal [Editorial]. *Journal of*

Trauma & Dissociation, 17(5), 527–544. https://doi.org/10.1080/15299732.2016.1214436

Gómez, J. M., Zounlome, N. O. O., & Noll, L. K. (2022). Development and initial validation of the Betrayal Blindness Questionnaires (BBQs): Past memory, current memory, and rotating betrayal blindness questionnaires. *Journal of Aggression, Maltreatment, & Trauma*. Advance online publication. https://doi.org/10.1080/10926771.2022.2112339

Goodreads. (2023a). Audre Lorde quotable quote. *Goodreads*. https://www.goodreads.com/quotes/1199797-there-is-an-important-difference-between-openness-and-na-vet-not

Goodreads. (2023b). Alice Walker quotable quotes. *Goodreads*. https://www.goodreads.com/quotes/15083-the-most-common-way-people-give-up-their-power-is

Gray, C. (2016). Senate unanimous in bill protecting student medical records. *The Lund Report*. https://www.thelundreport.org/content/senate-unanimous-bill-protecting-student-medical-records

Greco, A. N., Wharton, R. M., & Brand, A. (2016). Demographics of scholarly publishing and communication professionals. *Learned Publishing, 29*(2), 97–101. https://doi.org/10.1002/leap.1017

Green, S. (2017). *Violence against Black women: Many types, far-reaching effects*. Institute for Women's Policy Research.

Grills, C. (2013). The context, perspective, and mission of ABPsi past and present. *The Journal of Black Psychology, 39*(3), 276–283. https://doi.org/10.1177/0095798413480685

Grollman, E. A. (2018). Black, queer, and beaten: On the trauma of graduate school. In A. X. C. H. Nowakowski & J. E. Sumerau (Eds.), *Negotiating the emotional challenges of conducting deeply personal research in health* (pp. 159–171). Routledge.

Gross, K. (2015). African American women of color mass incarceration and the politics of protection. *The Journal of American History, 102*(1), 25–33. https://doi.org/10.1093/jahist/jav226

Grzanka, P. R. (2018). Intersectionality and feminist psychology: Power, knowledge, and process. In C. B. Travis & J. W. White (Eds.), *Handbook of the psychology of women: Vol 1. History, theory, and battlegrounds* (pp. 585–602). American Psychological Association. https://doi.org/10.1037/0000059-030

Grzanka, P. R. (Ed.). (2019). *Intersectionality: Foundations and frontiers* (2nd ed.). Routledge.

Grzanka, P. R. (2020a). From buzzword to critical psychology: An invitation to take intersectionality seriously. *Women & Therapy, 43*(3–4), 244–261. https://doi.org/10.1080/02703149.2020.1729473

Grzanka, P. R. (2020b). *From buzzword to critical psychology: An invitation to take intersectionality seriously mini-talk* [Video]. YouTube. https://www.youtube.com/watch?feature=youtu.be&v=7OwsLWRo2jE&app=desktop

Grzanka, P. R., & Cole, E. R. (2021). An argument for bad psychology: Disciplinary disruption, public engagement, and social transformation. *American Psychologist, 76*(8), 1334–1345. https://doi.org/10.1037/amp0000853

Grzanka, P. R., & Moradi, B. (2021). The qualitative imagination in counseling psychology: Enhancing methodological rigor across methods. *Journal of Counseling Psychology, 68*(3), 247–258. https://doi.org/10.1037/cou0000560

Guthrie, R. V. (1976). *Even the rat was white*. Harper and Row/Pearson Education.

Guthrie, R. V. (2004). *Even the rat was white: A historical view of psychology*. Pearson Education.

Gutiérrez y Muhs, G., Niemann, Y. F., González, C. G., & Harris, A. P. (2012). *Presumed incompetent: The intersections of race and class for women in academia*. University Press of Colorado.

Hall, E. V., Hall, A. V., Galinsky, A. D., & Phillips, K. W. (2019). MOSAIC: A model of stereotyping through associated and intersectional categories. *Academy of Management Review, 44*(3), 643–672. https://doi.org/10.5465/amr.2017.0109

Hames-García, M. R. (2000). "Who are our own people?" Challenges for a theory of social identity. In P. M. L. Moya & M. R. Hames-García (Eds.), *Reclaiming identity: Realist theory and the predicament of postmodernism* (pp. 102–129). University of California Press.

Hames-García, M. R. (2011). *Identity complex: Making the case for multiplicity*. University of Minnesota Press. https://doi.org/10.5749/minnesota/9780816649853.001.0001

Hamilton, P. (2020). "Now that I know what you're about": Black feminist reflections on power in the research relationship. *Qualitative Research, 20*(5), 519–533. https://doi.org/10.1177/1468794119891583

Hannah-Jones, N. (2021). *The 1619 project: A new origin story*. Random House One World.

Hargons, C. (2020). *A daily journal for Black women who want to respond to racism, but don't want to be called angry: First of all. . . .* Center for Healing Racial Trauma.

Harrell, S. P. (2000). A multidimensional conceptualization of racism-related stress: Implications for the well-being of people of color. *American Journal of Orthopsychiatry, 70*(1), 42–57. https://doi.org/10.1037/h0087722

Harris, J. C., Karunaratne, N., & Gutzwa, J. A. (2021). Effective modalities for healing from campus sexual assault: Centering the experiences of women of color undergraduate student survivors. *Harvard Educational Review, 91*(2), 248–272. https://doi.org/10.17763/1943-5045-91.2.248

Harris, J. R. A., Haskins, N., Parker, J., & Lee, A. (2021). Womanist theology and relational cultural theory: Counseling religious Black women. *Journal of Creativity in Mental Health*, 1–19. Advance online publication. https://doi.org/10.1080/15401383.2021.1999359

Hassoun Ayoub, L., Partridge, T., & Gómez, J. M. (2022). Two sides of the same coin: A mixed methods study of Black mothers' experiences with violence, stressors, parenting, and coping during the pandemic. *Journal of Social Issues.* Advance online publication. https://doi.org/10.1111/josi.12526

Hattery, A. J., Smith, E., Magnuson, S., Monterrosa, A., Kafonek, K., Shaw, C., Mhonde, R. D., & Kanewske, L. C. (2022). Diversity, equity, and inclusion in research teams: The good, the bad, and the ugly. *Race and Justice.* Advance online publication. https://doi.org/10.1177/21533687221087373

Healey, R., & Hinson, S. (2013). *The three faces of power.* Grassroots Policy Project. https://grassrootspowerproject.org/analysis/the-three-faces-of-power/

Henrich, J., Heine, S. J., & Norenzayan, A. (2010). Most people are not WEIRD. *Nature, 466*(7302), 29–29. https://doi.org/10.1038/466029a

Herman, J. (1997). *Trauma and recovery* (2nd ed.). Basic Books.

Hernández, T. K. (2022). *Racial innocence: Unmasking Latino anti-Black bias and the struggle for equality.* Beacon Press.

Hetey, R. C., & Eberhardt, J. L. (2018). The numbers don't speak for themselves: Racial disparities and the persistence of inequality in the criminal justice system. *Current Directions in Psychological Science, 27*(3), 183–187. https://doi.org/10.1177/0963721418763931

Hettler, B. (1976). *The six dimensions of wellness model.* National Wellness Institute. https://members.nationalwellness.org/resource/resmgr/pdfs/sixdimensionsfactsheet.pdf

Hicken, M. T., Kravitz-Wirtz, N., Durkee, M., & Jackson, J. S. (2018). Racial inequalities in health: Framing future research. *Social Science & Medicine, 199*, 11–18. https://doi.org/10.1016/j.socscimed.2017.12.027

Hickson, J. M., Paul, R. J., Perkins, A. C., Anderson, C. R., & Pittman, D. M. (2022). Sankofa: A testimony of the restorative power of Black activism in the self-care practices of Black activists. *The Journal of Black Psychology, 48*(3–4), 448–474. https://doi.org/10.1177/00957984211015572

Hill, A. (1997). *Speaking truth to power.* Penguin Random House.

Hill, A. (2021). *Believing: Our thirty-year journey to end gender violence.* Penguin Random House.

Hill, L. (1998). Everything is everything [Song]. On *The miseducation of Lauryn Hill.* Ruffhouse Records and Columbia Records.

Hilliard, T. O. (1978). Psychology, law, and the black community. *Law and Human Behavior, 2*(2), 107–131. https://doi.org/10.1007/BF01040387

Hine, D. C. (1989). Rape and the inner lives of Black women in the Middle West. *Signs: Journal of Women in Culture and Society, 14*(4), 912–920. https://doi.org/10.1086/494552

Hislop, M. (2020). "I love this country, but sometimes I not sure where I am": Black immigrant women, sexual violence, and Afropessimistic justice in New York v. Strauss-Kahn and Chimamanda Ngozi Adichie's *Americanah. Law and Literature.* Advance online publication. https://doi.org/10.1080/1535685X.2019.1688546

Hlavka, H. R., & Mulla, S. (2021). *Bodies in evidence: Race, gender, and science in sexual assault adjudication.* New York University Press. https://doi.org/10.18574/nyu/9781479809639.001.0001

Hoang, K. K. (2022). Theorizing from the margins: A tribute to Lewis and Rose Laub Coser. *Sociological Theory, 40*(3), 203–223. https://doi.org/10.1177/07352751221106199

Hoffman, D. H., Carter, D. J., Viglucci Lopez, C. R., Benzmiller, H. L., Guo, A. X., Yasir Latifi, S., & Craig, D. C. (2015). *Report to the special committee of the board of directors of the American Psychological Association: Independent review relating to APA ethics guidelines, national security interrogations, and torture—revised September 4, 2015*. https://www.apa.org/independent-review/revised-report.pdf

Holland, K. J., & Bedera, N. (2019). "Call for help immediately": A discourse analysis of resident assistants' responses to sexual assault disclosures. *Violence Against Women, 26*(11), 1383–1402. https://doi.org/10.1177/1077801219863879

Holland, K. J., Cortina, L. M., & Freyd, J. J. (2018). Compelled disclosure of college sexual assault. *American Psychologist, 73*(3), 256–268. https://doi.org/10.1037/amp0000186

Holliday, R., & Monteith, L. L. (2019). Seeking help for the health sequelae of military sexual trauma: A theory-driven model of the role of institutional betrayal. *Journal of Trauma & Dissociation, 20*(3), 340–356. https://doi.org/10.1080/15299732.2019.1571888

Hondagneu-Sotelo, P., & Pastor, M. (2021). *South Central dreams: Finding home and building community in south L.A.* New York University Press. https://doi.org/10.18574/nyu/9781479804023.001.0001

hooks, b. (2015). *Ain't I a woman: Black women and feminism*. South End Press/Routledge. (Original work published 1981)

hooks, b. (2015). *Feminist theory: From margin to center*. South End Press/Routledge. (Original work published 1984)

hooks, b. (1989). *Talking feminist: Thinking feminist, thinking Black*. South End Press.

hooks, b. (1994). *Teaching to transgress: Education as the practice of freedom*. Routledge.

Hope, E. C., & Spencer, M. B. (2017). Civic engagement as an adaptive coping response to conditions of inequality: An application of phenomenological variant of ecological systems theory (PVEST). In N. Cabrera & B. Leyendecker (Eds.), *Handbook on positive development of minority children and youth* (pp. 421–435). Springer. https://doi.org/10.1007/978-3-319-43645-6_25

Hope, M. (2021, June). *Black and free: Freedom and liberation in the 21st century*. University of Michigan National Center for Institutional Diversity Second Annual Juneteenth Webinar. https://lsa.umich.edu/ncid/news-events/all-events/black-and-free.html

Howard Valdivia, R. L., Ahrens, C. E., & Gómez, J. M. (2022). Violence victimization in Latina/o/x young adults: The multiplicative effects of cultural and high betrayal trauma. *Journal of Family Trauma, Child Custody & Child Development*. Advance online publication. https://doi.org/10.1080/26904586.2022.2066596

Hunt, J. (2018). *University of Nike: How corporate cash bought American higher education*. Melville House.

Hurston, Z. N. (1928/2015). *How it feels to be colored me*. https://www.wheelersburg.net/Downloads/Hurston.pdf (Original work published 1928)

Inside Higher Ed. (2022). *Conditionally Accepted Blog*. https://www.insidehighered.com/users/conditionally-accepted

Iruka, I. U., Gardner-Neblett, N., Telfer, N. A., Ibekwe-Okafor, N., Curenton, S. M., Sims, J., & Neblett, E. W. (2022). Effects of racism on child development: Advancing antiracist developmental science. *Annual Review of Developmental Psychology*. Advance online publication. https://doi.org/10.1146/annurev-devpsych-121020-031339

Jacobs, M. S. (2021). Sometimes they don't die: Can criminal justice reform measures help halt police sexual assault on Black women? *Harvard Journal of Law & Gender, 44*, 251.

Jenkins, T. (2009). A seat at the table that I set: Beyond social justice allies. *About Campus: Enriching the Student Learning Experience, 14*(5), 27–29. https://doi.org/10.1002/abc.305

Jilani, Z., Marzette, D., & Gómez, J. M. (2022). *Development and validation of the Cultural Betrayal Multidimensional Inventory for Desi and South Asian American Young Adults (CBMI-DSAYA)*.

Joseph, J. (2020). Transphobic femicide: An intersectional perspective. In J. Joseph & S. Jergenson (Eds.), *An international perspective on contemporary developments in victimology* (pp. 105–119). Springer. https://doi.org/10.1007/978-3-030-41622-5_8

Karlsson, M. E., & Zielinski, M. J. (2020). Sexual victimization and mental illness prevalence rates among incarcerated women: A literature review. *Trauma, Violence & Abuse, 21*(2), 326–349. https://doi.org/10.1177/1524838018767933

Kendi, I. X. (2016). *Stamped from the beginning*. Nation Books.

Kendi, I. X. (2019). *How to be an antiracist*. Penguin Random House.

Kim, M. M. (2021). *The wake up: Closing the gap between good intentions and real change*. Hachette.

King, D. D., Hall, A. V., Johnson, L., Carter, J., Burrows, D., & Samuel, N. (2022). Research on anti-Black racism in organizations: Insights, ideas, and considerations. *Journal of Business and Psychology*, 1–18. Advance online publication. https://doi.org/10.1007/s10869-022-09804-4

King, M. L., Jr. (1968). The role of the behavioral scientist in the civil rights movement. *Journal of Social Issues, 24*(1), 2–12. https://doi.org/10.1111/j.1540-4560.1968.tb01465.x

Kingkade, T. (2015). University of Oregon violated sexual assault victim's medical privacy, employees claim. *HuffPost*. https://www.huffpost.com/entry/university-of-oregon-medical-privacy_n_6641920

Klest, B., Smith, C. P., May, C., McCall-Hosenfeld, J., & Tamaian, A. (2020). COVID-19 has united patients and providers against institutional betrayal in health care: A battle to be heard, believed, and protected. *Psychological*

Trauma: Theory, Research, Practice, and Policy, 12(S1), S159–S161. https://doi.org/10.1037/tra0000855

Knight, E. L. (2022). Two routes to status, one route to health: Trait dominance and prestige differentially associate with self-reported stress and health in two US university populations. *Adaptive Human Behavior and Physiology*. Advance online publication. https://doi.org/10.1007/s40750-022-00199-3

Komarraju, M., & Cokley, K. O. (2008). Horizontal and vertical dimensions of individualism-collectivism: A comparison of African Americans and European Americans. *Cultural Diversity & Ethnic Minority Psychology, 14*(4), 336–343. https://doi.org/10.1037/1099-9809.14.4.336

Kraus, M. W., & Torrez, B. (2020). A psychology of power that is embedded in societal structures. *Current Opinion in Psychology, 33*, 86–90. https://doi.org/10.1016/j.copsyc.2019.07.018

Ladson-Billings, G. (2021). *Culturally relevant pedagogy: Asking a different question*. Teachers College Press.

Lane, C. (2022, July 19). A decisive blow to the serotonin hypothesis of depression. *Psychology Today*. https://www.psychologytoday.com/us/blog/side-effects/202207/decisive-blow-the-serotonin-hypothesis-depression

Last, B. (2020). Is racism a disease? *Nonsite.org, 33*. https://nonsite.org/is-racism-a-disease/

Laurencin, C. T., & McClinton, A. (2020). The COVID-19 pandemic: A call to action to identify and address racial and ethnic disparities. *Journal of Racial and Ethnic Health Disparities, 7*(3), 398–402. https://doi.org/10.1007/s40615-020-00756-0

Lear, J. (2008). *Radical hope: Ethics in the face of cultural devastation*. Harvard University Press.

Leath, S., Ball, P., Mims, L., Butler-Barnes, S., & Quiles, T. (2022). "They need to hear our voices": A multidimensional framework of Black college women's sociopolitical development and activism. *The Journal of Black Psychology, 48*(3–4), 392–427. https://doi.org/10.1177/00957984211016943

Leath, S., Quiles, T., Samuel, M., Chima, U., & Chavous, T. (2022). "Our community is so small": Considering intraracial peer networks in Black student adjustment and belonging at PWIs. *American Educational Research Journal*. Advance online publication. https://doi.org/10.3102/00028312221092780

Leonard, P. B. (2011). An introduction to restorative justice. In E. Beck, N. P. Kropf, & P. B. Leonard (Eds.), *Social work and restorative justice: Skills for dialogue, peacemaking, and reconciliation* (pp. 31–63). Oxford University Press.

Leroy, J., & Jenkins, D. (Eds.). (2021). *Histories of racial capitalism*. Columbia University Press. https://doi.org/10.7312/jenk19074

Lewis, J. A., & Grzanka, P. R. (2016). Applying intersectionality theory to research on perceived racism. In A. Alvarez, C. Liang, & H. Neville (Eds.), *The cost of racism for people of color: Contextualizing experiences of discrimination* (pp. 31–54). American Psychological Association. https://doi.org/10.1037/14852-003

Lind, M. N., Adams-Clark, A. A., & Freyd, J. J. (2020). Isn't high school bad enough already? Rates of gender harassment and institutional betrayal in high school and their association with trauma-related symptoms. *PLOS ONE, 15*(8), Article e0237713. https://doi.org/10.1371/journal.pone.0237713

Lindsey, T. B. (2022). *America, goddam: Violence, Black women, and the struggle for justice*. University of California Press.

Lorde, A. (1978). *The black unicorn*. Penguin Books Limited.

Lorde, A. (1983). There is no hierarchy of oppressions. *Bulletin: Homophobia and Education, 14*(3/4), 9. https://womenscenter.missouri.edu/wp-content/uploads/2013/05/THERE-IS-NO-HIERARCHY-OF-OPPRESSIONS.pdf

Lorde, A. (1984). *Sister outsider*. The Crossing Press.

Louie, P., & Upenieks, L. (2022). Vicarious discrimination, psychosocial resources, and mental health among Black Americans. *Social Psychology Quarterly*. Advance online publication. https://doi.org/10.1177/01902725221079279

Lynch, S. M., Frich, A., & Heath, N. W. (2012). Looking beneath the surface: The nature of women's experiences of interpersonal violence, treatment needs, and mental health. *Feminist Criminology, 7*(4), 381–400. https://doi.org/10.1177/1557085112439224

Lyons, H. Z., Bike, D. H., Johnson, A., & Bethea, A. (2011). Culturally competent qualitative research with people of African descent. *The Journal of Black Psychology, 38*(2), 153–171. https://doi.org/10.1177/0095798411414019

Mackler, D. (2008). *Take these broken wings: Recovery from schizophrenia without medication*. https://wildtruth.net/films-english/brokenwings/

Martin, E. P., & Martin, J. M. (1995). *Social work and the black experience*. National Association of Social Workers Press.

Martín-Baró, I. (1994). *Writings for a liberation psychology: Essays 1985–1989*. Harvard University Press.

Matsuzaka, S., Jamison, L., Avery, L. R., Schmidt, K. M., Stanton, A. G., & Debnam, K. (2022). Gendered Racial Microaggressions Scale: Measurement invariance across sexual orientation. *Psychology of Women Quarterly*. Advance online publication. https://doi.org/10.1177/03616843221118339

May, V. (2015). *Pursuing intersectionality, unsettling dominant imaginaries*. Routledge. https://doi.org/10.4324/9780203141991

McAdoo, H. P., & Younge, S. N. (2009). Black families. In H. A. Neville, B. M. Tynes, & S. O. Utsey (Eds.), *Handbook of African American psychology* (pp. 103–115). Sage.

McCarty, T. (2022). *Viable path for education: Relationality and relational accountability in Indigenous education and research—A meditation* [Paper presentation]. Stanford University Center for Advanced Study in the Behavioral Sciences (CASBS) Research Seminar Series, Stanford, CA, United States.

McClelland, S. I., Rubin, J. D., & Bauermeister, J. A. (2016). Adapting to injustice: Young bisexual women's interpretations of microaggressions. *Psychology of Women Quarterly, 40*(4), 532–550. https://doi.org/10.1177/0361684316664514

McDaniel, M. C., Zelenak, L., & Gómez, J. M. (2022). *Effect of White supremacy and hostile masculinity on White young people's blame attributions in a male-perpetrated acquaintance rape vignette.* PsyArXiv. https://psyarxiv.com/d6kwa

McGoron, L., Wargo Aikins, J., Trentacosta, C. J., Gómez, J. M., & Beeghly, M. (2022). School support, chaos, routines, and parents' mental health during COVID-19 remote schooling. *The School Psychologist, 37*(2), 173–182. https://doi.org/10.1037/spq0000467

McGuire, D. L. (2010). *At the dark end of the street: Black women, rape, and resistance—A new history of the civil rights movement from Rosa Parks to the rise of Black power.* Vintage.

McIntosh, P. (2009). White people facing race: Uncovering the myths that keep racism in place. Wellesley Centers for Women. https://www.nationalseedproject.org/images/documents/peggy/Peggy_McIntosh_White_People_Facing_Race.pdf

McQuaide, S. (1987). Beyond the logic of pessimism: A personal portrait of Bertha Capen Reynolds. *Clinical Social Work Journal, 15*(3), 271–280. https://doi.org/10.1007/BF00753606

McShane, J. (2021, February 2). In Alexandria Ocasio-Cortez, these survivors found a voice: "I felt with her the deeply vulnerable pain of telling someone." *The Lily*, a product of *The Washington Post*. https://www.thelily.com/in-alexandria-ocasio-cortez-these-survivors-found-a-voice-i-felt-with-her-the-deeply-vulnerable-pain-of-telling-someone/

Merhill, N. M., Bonner, K. A., & Baker, A. L. (Eds.). (2021). *Guidance for measuring sexual harassment prevalence using campus climate surveys.* National Academies of Sciences, Engineering, and Medicine. https://doi.org/10.17226/26346

Metzl, J. M., & Hansen, H. (2014). Structural competency: Theorizing a new medical engagement with stigma and inequality. *Social Science & Medicine, 103*, 126–133. https://doi.org/10.1016/j.socscimed.2013.06.032

Miller, J. B. (1976). *Toward a new psychology of women.* Beacon Press.

Miller, J. B. (1988). *Connections, disconnections and violations.* Wellesley Centers for Women.

Miller, J. B., Jordan, J., Stiver, I. P., Walker, M., Surrey, J. L., & Eldridge, N. A. (1999). *Therapists' authenticity.* Wellesley Centers for Women.

Miller, J. B., & Stiver, I. P. (1997). *The healing connection: How women form relationships in therapy and in life.* Beacon Press.

Mills, C. W. (1997). *The racial contract.* Cornell University Press.

Milner, H. R., IV. (2007). Race, culture, and researcher positionality: Working through dangers seen, unseen, and unforeseen. *Educational Researcher, 36*(7), 388–400. https://doi.org/10.3102/0013189X07309471

Mitchell, K. (2013). Love in action: Noting similarities between lynching then and anti-LGBT violence now. *Callaloo, 36*(3), 688–717. https://doi.org/10.1353/cal.2013.0167

Mitchell, K. (2015). Keep claiming space! *CLA Journal, 58*(3/4), 229–244.

Mitchell, K. (2018). Identifying white mediocrity and know-your-place aggression: A form of self-care. *African American Review, 51*(4), 253–262. https://doi.org/10.1353/afa.2018.0045

Mitchell, K. (2020). *From slave cabins to the White House: Homemade citizenship in African American culture.* University of Illinois Press.

Moncrieff, J., Cooper, R. E., Stockmann, T., Amendola, S., Hengartner, M. P., & Horowitz, M. A. (2022). The serotonin theory of depression: A systematic umbrella review of the evidence. *Molecular Psychiatry.* Advance online publication. https://doi.org/10.1038/s41380-022-01661-0

Monteith, L. L., Bahraini, N. H., Matarazzo, B. B., Soberay, K. A., & Smith, C. P. (2016). Perceptions of institutional betrayal predict suicidal self-directed violence among veterans exposed to military sexual trauma. *Journal of Clinical Psychology, 72*(7), 743–755. https://doi.org/10.1002/jclp.22292

Monteith, L. L., Holliday, R., Schneider, A. L., Miller, C. N., Bahraini, N. H., & Forster, J. E. (2021). Institutional betrayal and help-seeking among women survivors of military sexual trauma. *Psychological Trauma: Theory, Research, Practice, and Policy.* Advance online publication. https://psycnet.apa.org/doi/10.1037/tra0001027

Moodley, R., & West, W. (Eds.). (2005). *Integrating traditional healing practices into counseling and psychotherapy* (Vol. 22). Sage. https://doi.org/10.4135/9781452231648

Moon, S. H., & Sandage, S. J. (2019). Cultural humility for people of color: Critique of current theory and practice. *Journal of Psychology and Theology, 47*(2), 76–86. https://doi.org/10.1177/0091647119842407

Moore-Lobban, S. J., & Gobin, R. L. (2022). *The Black woman's guide to overcoming domestic violence.* New Harbinger Publications, Inc.

Moradi, B., & Grzanka, P. R. (2017). Using intersectionality responsibly: Toward critical epistemology, structural analysis, and social justice activism. *Journal of Counseling Psychology, 64*(5), 500–513. https://doi.org/10.1037/cou0000203

Morgan, S. (2019). *Inclusion, equality, equity.* BuzzARooney. https://thebuzzonhr.com/inclusion-equality-equity/

Moskowitz, A. (2011). Schizophrenia, trauma, dissociation, and scientific revolutions. *Journal of Trauma & Dissociation, 12*(4), 347–357. https://doi.org/10.1080/15299732.2011.573770

Mosley, D. V., Neville, H. A., Chavez-Dueñas, N. Y., Adames, H. Y., Lewis, J. A., & French, B. H. (2020). Radical hope in revolting times: Proposing a culturally relevant psychological framework. *Social and Personality Psychology Compass, 14*(1), Article e12512. https://doi.org/10.1111/spc3.12512

Motor City Singers' Space. (n.d.). *Motor City Singers' Space.* http://www.motorcitysings.com

Muller, C. (2021). Exclusion and exploitation: The incarceration of Black Americans from slavery to the present. *Science, 374*(6565), 282–286. https://doi.org/10.1126/science.abj7781

Myers, L. J. (1988). *Understanding an Afrocentric world view: Introduction to an optimal psychology*. Kendall & Hunt.

Myers, L. J. (2013). Restoration of spirit: An African-centered communal health model. *The Journal of Black Psychology, 39*(3), 257–260. https://doi.org/10.1177/0095798413478080

National Academies of Sciences, Engineering, and Medicine. (2018). *Sexual harassment of women: Climate, culture, and consequences in academic sciences, engineering, and medicine*. The National Academies Press.

National Organization of Sisters of Color Ending Sexual Assault. (2017). *National communities of color sexual assault organizations*. https://sisterslead.org/resources/national-communities-of-color-sexual-assault-organizations-2/

Neblett, E. W., Jr. (2022). Racism measurement and influences, variations on scientific racism, and a vision. *Social Science & Medicine*. Advance online publication. https://doi.org/10.1016/j.socscimed.2022.115247

Neeley, J. E. (2021). Addressing sexual assault in criminal justice, higher education and employment: What restorative justice means for survivors and community accountability. *Kansas Journal of Law & Public Policy, 31*, 1.

Neville, H., & Cokley, K. (2022). Introduction to special issue on the psychology of Black activism: The psychology of Black activism in the 21st century. *The Journal of Black Psychology, 48*(3–4), 265–272. https://doi.org/10.1177/00957984221096212

Neville, H. A., Awad, G. H., Brooks, J. E., Flores, M. P., & Bluemel, J. (2013). Color-blind racial ideology: Theory, training, and measurement implications in psychology. *American Psychologist, 68*(6), 455–466. https://doi.org/10.1037/a0033282

Neville, H. A., Ruedas-Gracia, N., Lee, B. A., Ogunfemi, N., Maghsoodi, A. H., Mosley, D. V., LaFromboise, T. D., & Fine, M. (2021). The public psychology for liberation training model: A call to transform the discipline. *American Psychologist, 76*(8), 1248–1265. https://doi.org/10.1037/amp0000887

Niemann, Y. F., Gutiérrez y Muhs, G., & González, C. G. (2020). *Presumed incompetent II: Race, class, power, and resistance of women in academia*. University Press of Colorado.

90by30. (n.d.). *90by30: Reduce child abuse 90% by 2030 in Lane County*. https://facebook.com/90by30

Nkimbeng, M., Taylor, J. L., Roberts, L., Winch, P. J., Commodore-Mensah, Y., Thorpe, R. J., Jr., Han, H. R., & Szanton, S. L. (2021). "All I know is that there is a lot of discrimination": Older African immigrants' experiences of discrimination in the United States. *Geriatric Nursing, 42*(1), 196–204. https://doi.org/10.1016/j.gerinurse.2020.08.002

Nobles, W. W. (1972). African philosophy: Foundations for Black psychology. In F. Windom Hayes (Ed.), *A turbulent voyage: Readings in African American studies* (pp. 280–292). Rowman & Littlefield Publishers.

Noll, L. K., & Gómez, J. M. (2013). Rotating betrayal blindness and the nonlinear path to knowing. In *Blind to betrayal*. https://web.archive.org/web/

20201022234230/https://sites.google.com/site/betrayalbook/betrayal-research-news/rotating-betrayal-blindness-and-the-non-linear-path-to-knowing

Obasogie, O. K. (2021). Excited delirium and police use of force. *Virginia Law Review, 107*(8), 1545–1620. https://www.virginialawreview.org/articles/excited-delirium-and-police-use-of-force/

Okun, T. (n.d.). White supremacy. *dRwORKS*. https://supportblackmesa.org/wp-content/uploads/2011/09/White-Supremacy-Culture-Tema-Okun2.pdf

Ondersma, S. J., Beatty, J. R., Svikis, D. S., Strickler, R. C., Tzilos, G. K., Chang, G., Divine, G. W., Taylor, A. R., & Sokol, R. J. (2015). Computer-delivered screening and brief intervention for alcohol use in pregnancy: A pilot randomized trial. *Alcoholism, Clinical and Experimental Research, 39*(7), 1219–1226. https://doi.org/10.1111/acer.12747

Orozco, R. A. (2012). Racism and power: Arizona politicians' use of the discourse of anti-Americanism against Mexican American studies. *Hispanic Journal of Behavioral Sciences, 34*(1), 43–60. https://doi.org/10.1177/0739986311430209

Page, J., & Soss, J. (2021). The predatory dimensions of criminal justice. *Science, 374*(6565), 291–294. https://doi.org/10.1126/science.abj7782

Pateman, C. (1988). *The sexual contract*. Stanford University Press.

Payton, C. R. (1984). Who must do the hard things? *American Psychologist, 39*(4), 391–397. https://doi.org/10.1037/0003-066X.39.4.391

Pennell, J., & Koss, M. P. (2011). Feminist perspectives on family rights: Social work and restorative justice practices for stopping abuse of women. In E. Beck, N. P. Kropf, & P. B. Leonard (Eds.), *Social work and restorative justice: Skills for dialogue, peacemaking, and reconciliation* (pp. 195–219). Oxford University Press.

Perlo, J., & Feeley, D. (2018). Applying community organizing principles to restore joy in work. *NEJM Catalyst*. https://catalyst.nejm.org/doi/full/10.1056/CAT.18.0165

Phillips, A. (2018). Students on alert after off campus sexual assault reported. *Local News 8*. https://www.localnews8.com/news/students-on-alert-after-off-campus-sexual-assault-reported/867554656

Phillips, M. (2009). President Barack Obama's inaugural address. *The White House*. https://obamawhitehouse.archives.gov/blog/2009/01/21/president-Barack-obamas-inaugural-address

Polletta, F. (2012, June). *Freedom is an endless meeting: Democracy in American social movements*. University of Chicago Press.

Pope, K. S. (2015). Steps to strengthen ethics in organizations: Research findings, ethics placebos, and what works. *Journal of Trauma & Dissociation, 16*(2), 139–152. https://doi.org/10.1080/15299732.2015.995021

Poteat, T., Millett, G. A., Nelson, L. E., & Beyrer, C. (2020). Understanding COVID-19 risks and vulnerabilities among black communities in America: The lethal force of syndemics. *Annals of Epidemiology, 47*, 1–3. https://doi.org/10.1016/j.annepidem.2020.05.004

Power, J., Gobeil, R., Beaudette, J. N., Ritchie, M. B., Brown, S. L., & Smith, H. P. (2016). Childhood abuse, non-suicidal self-injury, and suicide attempts: An exploration of gender differences in incarcerated adults. *Suicide and Life-Threatening Behavior, 46*(6), 745–751. https://doi.org/10.1111/sltb.12263

Pryal, K. R. G. (2022). When universities raid student therapy records. *The Chronicle of Higher Education.* https://www.chronicle.com/article/when-universities-raid-student-therapy-records

Purdie-Vaughns, V., & Eibach, R. P. (2008). Intersectional invisibility: The distinctive advantages and disadvantages of multiple subordinate-group identities. *Sex Roles, 59*(5–6), 377–391. https://doi.org/10.1007/s11199-008-9424-4

Pyke, K. D. (2018). Institutional betrayal: Inequity, discrimination, bullying, and retaliation in academia. *Sociological Perspectives, 61*(1), 5–13. https://doi.org/10.1177/0731121417743816

Quina, K., Garis, A. V., Stevenson, J., Garrido, M., Brown, J., Richman, R., Renzi, J., Fox, J., & Mitchell, K. (2008). Through the bullet-proof glass: Conducting research in prison settings. *Journal of Trauma & Dissociation, 8*(2), 123–139. https://doi.org/10.1300/J229v08n02_08

Ralph, L. (2012). What wounds enable: The politics of disability and violence in Chicago. *Disability Studies Quarterly, 32*(3). Advance online publication. https://doi.org/10.18061/dsq.v32i3.3270

Ralph, L. (2015). Becoming aggrieved: An alternative framework of care in Black Chicago. *The Russell Sage Foundation Journal of the Social Sciences: RSF, 1*(2), 31–41. https://doi.org/10.7758/RSF.2015.1.2.03

Ralph, L. (2020). *The torture letters: Reckoning with police violence.* The University of Chicago Press. https://doi.org/10.7208/chicago/9780226650128.001.0001

Ralph, L. (2022). *Police violence* [Paper presentation]. Stanford University Center for Advanced Study in the Behavioral Sciences (CASBS) Research Seminar Series, Stanford, CA, United States.

Ray, R., & Rosow, J. A. (2012). The two different worlds of Black and White fraternity men: Visibility and accountability as mechanisms of privilege. *Journal of Contemporary Ethnography, 41*(1), 66–94. https://doi.org/10.1177/0891241611431700

Ray, V. (2019). A theory of racialized organizations. *American Sociological Review, 84*(1), 26–53. https://doi.org/10.1177/0003122418822335

Ray, V. (2022). *On critical race theory: Why it matters and why you should care.* Random House.

Read, J., & Moncrieff, J. (2022). Depression: Why drugs and electricity are not the answer. *Psychological Medicine.* Advance online publication. https://doi.org/10.1017/S0033291721005031

Read, R. (2015a). State board proposes fine, ethics course for University of Oregon psychologist. *The Oregonian.* https://www.oregonlive.com/education/2015/09/state_board_proposes_5000_fine.html

Read, R. (2015b). Student who sued UO, claiming she was gang-raped by basketball players, settles suit for $800,000. *The Oregonian.* https://www.oregonlive.com/education/2015/08/student_receives_800000_settle.html

Reinhardt, K. M., Smith, C. P., & Freyd, J. J. (2016). Came to serve, left betrayed; MST and the trauma of betrayal. In L. S. Katz (Ed.), *Understanding and treating military sexual trauma* (pp. 61–78). Springer.

Reisch, M. (2005). Radical community organizing. In M. Weill (Ed.), *The handbook of community practice* (pp. 287–304). Sage.

Resick, P. A., & Schnicke, M. K. (1992). Cognitive processing therapy for sexual assault victims. *Journal of Consulting and Clinical Psychology, 60*(5), 748.

Richeson, J. A. (2020). Americans are determined to believe in Black progress: Whether it's happening or not. *The Atlantic.* https://www.theatlantic.com/magazine/archive/2020/09/the-mythology-of-racial-progress/614173/

Richie, B. (2012). *Arrested justice: Black women, violence, and America's prison nation.* New York University Press.

Richie, B. E. (2003). Gender entrapment and African-American women: An analysis of race, ethnicity, gender, and intimate violence. In D. F. Hawkins (Ed.), *Violent crime: Assessing race and ethnic differences* (pp. 198–210). Cambridge University Press. https://doi.org/10.1017/CBO9780511499456.013

Richie, B. E., & Eife, E. (2021). Black bodies at the dangerous intersection of gender violence and mass criminalization. *Journal of Aggression, Maltreatment & Trauma, 30*(7), 877–888. https://doi.org/10.1080/10926771.2019.1703063

Ritchie, A. (2017). *Invisible no more: Police violence against black women and women of color.* Beacon Press.

Roberts, D. (2022). *Torn apart: How the child welfare system destroys Black families and how abolition can build a safer world.* Basic Books.

Roberts, S., & Mortenson, E. (2022). Challenging the White = neutral framework in psychology. *Perspectives on Psychological Science.* Advance online publication. https://doi.org/10.1177/17456916221077117

Rose, B., & Brown, E. (2022). Healing through authentic connection: Utilizing relational cultural therapy with Black gay men. *Journal of LGBTQ Issues in Counseling, 16*(4), 406–421. https://doi.org/10.1080/26924951.2022.2067284

Rosenthal, L. (2016). Incorporating intersectionality into psychology: An opportunity to promote social justice and equity. *American Psychologist, 71*(6), 474–485. https://doi.org/10.1037/a0040323

Rosenthal, M. N., Smidt, A. M., & Freyd, J. J. (2016). Still second class: Sexual harassment of graduate students. *Psychology of Women Quarterly, 40*(3), 364–377. https://doi.org/10.1177/0361684316644838

Ross, B. Z., DeShields, W., Edwards, C., & Livingston, J. N. (2022). Behind Black women's passion: An examination of activism among Black women in America. *The Journal of Black Psychology, 48*(3–4), 428–447. https://doi.org/10.1177/00957984221084779

Rotella, K. N., Richeson, J. A., Chiao, J. Y., & Bean, M. G. (2013). Blinding trust: The effect of perceived group victimhood on intergroup trust. *Personality and Social Psychology Bulletin, 39*(1), 115–127. https://doi.org/10.1177/0146167212466114

Rubin, M., & Donkin, C. (2022). Exploratory hypothesis tests can be more compelling than confirmatory hypothesis tests. *Philosophical Psychology*. Advance online publication. https://doi.org/10.1080/09515089.2022.2113771

Rucker, J. M., & Richeson, J. A. (2021). Toward an understanding of structural racism: Implications for criminal justice. *Science, 374*(6565), 286–290. https://doi.org/10.1126/science.abj7779

Rucks-Ahidiana, Z. (2021). Theorizing gentrification as a process of racial capitalism. *City & Community*. Advance online publication. https://doi.org/10.1177/15356841211054790

Salam, M. (2019). What is toxic masculinity? *New York Times*. https://www.nytimes.com/2019/01/22/us/toxic-masculinity.html

Sall, K., & Littleton, H. (2022). Institutional betrayal: A mixed methods study of college women's experiences with on-campus help-seeking following rape. *Journal of Trauma & Dissociation*. Advance online publication. https://doi.org/10.1080/15299732.2022.2079795

Sarsour, L. (2020). *We are not here to be bystanders: A memoir of love and resistance*. 37 Ink/Simon & Schuster.

Schnurr, P. P., Chard, K. M., Ruzek, J. I., Chow, B. K., Resick, P. A., Foa, E. B., Marx, B. P., Friedman, M. J., Bovin, M. J., Caudle, K. L., Castillo, D., Curry, K. T., Hollifield, M., Huang, G. D., Chee, C. L., Astin, M. C., Dickstein, B., Renner, K., Clancy, C. P., . . . Shih, M. C. (2022). Comparison of prolonged exposure vs cognitive processing therapy for treatment of posttraumatic stress disorder among US veterans: A randomized clinical trial. *JAMA Network Open, 5*(1), Articles e2136921–e2136921. https://doi.org/10.1001/jamanetworkopen.2021.36921

Scott, J. W. (2005). Against eclecticism. *Differences: A Journal of Feminist Cultural Studies, 16*(3), 114–137. https://doi.org/10.1215/10407391-16-3-114

Selwyn, C. N., Lathan, E. C., Richie, F., Gigler, M. E., & Langhinrichsen-Rohling, J. (2021). Bitten by the system that cared for them: Towards a trauma-informed understanding of patients' healthcare engagement. *Journal of Trauma & Dissociation, 22*(5), 636–652. https://doi.org/10.1080/15299732.2020.1869657

Shaheed, J., Cooper, S. M., McBride, M., & Burnett, M. (2022). Intersectional activism among Black lesbian, gay, bisexual, transgender, and queer or questioning young adults: The roles of intragroup marginalization, identity, and community. *The Journal of Black Psychology, 48*(3–4), 360–391. https://doi.org/10.1177/00957984211069058

Shakur, A. (2020). *Assata: An autobiography*. Chicago Review Press.

Simmons, R. (2020). Russell Simmons speaks on sexual assault allegations, social responsibility, + more [Radio interview]. *The Breakfast Club*. YouTube. https://www.youtube.com/watch?v=uxzhsMkCCcM

Simone, N. (1977). Don't let me be misunderstood [Song]. On *Nina Simone album: Broadway-blues-ballads*. Philips.

Simone, N. (1978). The family [Song]. On *Nina Simone*. CTI Records.

Simone, N. (2008, November 4). *I wish I knew how it would feel to be free* [Video]. YouTube. https://www.youtube.com/watch?v=iSUlgOzARy4

Slatton, B. C., & Richard, A. L. (2020). Black women's experiences of sexual assault and disclosure: Insights from the margins. *Sociology Compass, 14*(6), Article e12792. https://doi.org/10.1111/soc4.12792

Smidt, A. M., Rosenthal, M. N., Smith, C. P., & Freyd, J. J. (2021). Out and in harm's way: Sexual minority students' psychological and physical health after institutional betrayal and sexual assault. *Journal of Child Sexual Abuse, 30*(1), 41–55. https://doi.org/10.1080/10538712.2019.1581867

Smith, C. P. (2017). First, do no harm: Institutional betrayal and trust in health care organizations. *Journal of Multidisciplinary Healthcare, 10,* 133–144. https://doi.org/10.2147/JMDH.S125885

Smith, C. P., Cunningham, S. A., & Freyd, J. J. (2016). Sexual violence, institutional betrayal, and psychological outcomes for LGB college students. *Translational Issues in Psychological Science, 2*(4), 351–360. https://doi.org/10.1037/tps0000094

Smith, C. P., & Freyd, J. J. (2013). Dangerous safe havens: Institutional betrayal exacerbates sexual trauma. *Journal of Traumatic Stress, 26*(1), 119–124. https://doi.org/10.1002/jts.21778

Smith, C. P., & Freyd, J. J. (2014). Institutional betrayal. *American Psychologist, 69*(6), 575–587. https://doi.org/10.1037/a0037564

Smith, C. P., & Freyd, J. J. (2017). Insult, then injury: Interpersonal and institutional betrayal linked to health and dissociation. *Journal of Aggression, Maltreatment & Trauma, 26*(10), 1117–1131. https://doi.org/10.1080/10926771.2017.1322654

Smith, C. P., Gómez, J. M., & Freyd, J. J. (2014). The psychology of judicial betrayal. *Roger Williams University Law Review, 19,* 451–475.

Smith, S. G., Chen, J., Basile, K. C., Gilbert, L. K., Merrick, M. T., Patel, N., Walling, M., & Jain, A. (2017). *The national intimate partner and sexual violence survey (NISVS): 2010–2012 state report.* National Center for Injury Prevention and Control, Centers for Disease Control and Prevention. https://www.ncbi.nlm.nih.gov/pmc/articles/PMC5810354/

Snowden, L. R., & Yamada, A. M. (2005). Cultural differences in access to care. *Annual Review of Clinical Psychology, 1,* 143–166. https://doi.org/10.1146/annurev.clinpsy.1.102803.143846

Speer, P. W., & Hughey, J. (1995). Community organizing: An ecological route to empowerment and power. *American Journal of Community Psychology, 23*(5), 729–748. https://doi.org/10.1007/BF02506989

Spencer, M. B., Dupree, D., & Hartmann, T. (1997). A phenomenological variant of ecological systems theory (PVEST): A self-organization perspective in context. *Development and Psychopathology, 9*(4), 817–833. https://doi.org/10.1017/S0954579497001454

Stabile, B., & Grant, A. L. (2022). *Women, power, and rape culture: The politics and policy of underrepresentation.* ABC CLIO.

Steady, F. C. (1981). The Black woman cross-culturally: An overview. In F. C. Steady (Ed.), *The Black woman cross-culturally* (pp. 7–42). Schenkman.

Steele, C. M. (1998). Stereotyping and its threat are real. *American Psychologist, 53*(6), 680–681. https://doi.org/10.1037/0003-066X.53.6.680

Stolberg, S. G. (2018). Kavanaugh is sworn in after close confirmation vote in Senate. *The New York Times.* https://www.nytimes.com/2018/10/06/us/politics/brett-kavanaugh-supreme-court.html

Strolovitch, D. Z. (2008). *Affirmative advocacy.* University of Chicago Press.

Stronks, K., Wieringa, N. F., & Hardon, A. (2013). Confronting diversity in the production of clinical evidence goes beyond merely including underrepresented groups in clinical trials. *Trials, 14*(1), Article 177. https://doi.org/10.1186/1745-6215-14-177

Sue, D. W. (1978). Eliminating cultural oppression in counseling: Toward a general theory. *Journal of Counseling Psychology, 25*(5), 419–428. https://doi.org/10.1037/0022-0167.25.5.419

Sue, D. W., Arredondo, P., & McDavis, R. J. (1992). Multicultural counseling competencies and standards: A call to the profession. *Journal of Counseling and Development, 70*(4), 477–486. https://doi.org/10.1002/j.1556-6676.1992.tb01642.x

Szasz, T. (1961). *The myth of mental illness: Foundations of a theory of personal conduct.* HarperCollins.

Szasz, T. (2011). The myth of mental illness: 50 years later. *The Psychiatrist, 35*(5), 179–182. https://doi.org/10.1192/pb.bp.110.031310

Szasz, T. S. (1960). The myth of mental illness. *American Psychologist, 15*(2), 113–118. https://doi.org/10.1037/h0046535

Talhami, G. H. (2008). America's early experience with the Muslim faith: The Nation of Islam. *Middle East Policy, 15*(3), 129–138. https://doi.org/10.1111/j.1475-4967.2008.00364.x

Tamaian, A., Klest, B., & Mutschler, C. (2017). Patient dissatisfaction and institutional betrayal in the Canadian medical system: A qualitative study. *Journal of Trauma & Dissociation, 18*(1), 38–57. https://doi.org/10.1080/15299732.2016.1181134

Tan, R. (2022). Meet the psychologist drawing from the Black church to reshape mental health care. *Washington Post.* https://www.washingtonpost.com/dc-md-va/2022/03/27/mental-health-black-baltimore-bryant/

Taylor, K. (2016). *From #BlackLivesMatter to Black liberation.* Haymarket Books.

Taylor, K. (2017). *How we get free: Black feminism and the Combahee River Collective.* Haymarket Books.

Taylor, R. J., Chatters, L. M., & Cross, C. J. (2021). Taking diversity seriously: Within-group heterogeneity in African American extended family support networks. *Journal of Marriage and Family, 83*(5), 1349–1372. https://doi.org/10.1111/jomf.12783

Taylor, S. R. (2011). *The body is not an apology: The power of radical self-love.* Berrett-Koehler Publishers.

Teo, T. (2008). From speculation to epistemological violence in psychology: A critical-hermeneutic reconstruction. *Theory & Psychology, 18*(1), 47–67. https://doi.org/10.1177/0959354307086922

Terborg-Penn, R. (1986). Black women in resistance: A cross-cultural perspective. In G. Y. Okhiro (Ed.), *In resistance: Studies in African, Caribbean and Afro-American history* (pp. 188–209). University of Massachusetts Press.

Tervalon, M., & Murray-García, J. (1998). Cultural humility versus cultural competence: A critical distinction in defining physician training outcomes in multicultural education. *Journal of Health Care for the Poor and Underserved, 9*(2), 117–125. https://doi.org/10.1353/hpu.2010.0233

Therapy for Black Girls. (2022). *Therapy for Black girls*. https://therapyforblackgirls.com/about/

Thompson, A. K. (2013, July 14). *Well . . . most of you read the book so that means you're familiar with Rich by now* [Status update]. Facebook. https://www.facebook.com/ahmir.thompson/posts/10151491382337051

Tillman, S., Bryant-Davis, T., Smith, K., & Marks, A. (2010). Shattering silence: Exploring barriers to disclosure for African American sexual assault survivors. *Trauma, Violence & Abuse, 11*(2), 59–70. https://doi.org/10.1177/1524838010363717

Tracey, T. J., Bludworth, J., & Glidden-Tracey, C. E. (2012). Are there parallel processes in psychotherapy supervision? An empirical examination. *Psychotherapy, 49*(3), 330–343. https://doi.org/10.1037/a0026246

Tuck, E. (2009). Suspending damage: A letter to communities. *Harvard Educational Review, 79*(3), 409–428. https://doi.org/10.17763/haer.79.3.n0016675661t3n15

Tummala-Narra, P. (2016). *Psychoanalytic theory and cultural competence in psychotherapy*. American Psychological Association. https://doi.org/10.1037/14800-000

Turner, E. A., Harrell, S. P., & Bryant-Davis, T. (2022). Black love, activism, and community (BLAC): The BLAC model of healing and resilience. *The Journal of Black Psychology, 48*(3–4), 547–568. https://doi.org/10.1177/00957984211018364

Turner, J. E. (1984). Foreword: Africana studies and epistemology; A discourse in the sociology of knowledge. In J. E. Turner (Ed.), *The next decade: Theoretical and research issues in Africana studies* (pp. v–xxv). Cornell University Africana Studies and Research Center.

Ullman, S. E., & Peter-Hagene, L. (2014). Social reactions to sexual assault disclosure, coping, perceived control, and PTSD symptoms in sexual assault victims. *Journal of Community Psychology, 42*(4), 495–508. https://doi.org/10.1002/jcop.21624

United Nations General Assembly. (1979). *Convention on the elimination of all forms of discrimination against women*. 85th Plenary Meeting, Geneva, Switzerland. https://www.un.org/womenwatch/daw/cedaw/text/econvention.htm

United Nations General Assembly. (1993). *Declaration on the elimination of violence against women*. 85th Plenary Meeting, Geneva Switzerland. https://www.un.org/en/genocideprevention/documents/atrocity-crimes/Doc.21_declaration%20elimination%20vaw.pdf

Valentino, L., & Vaisey, S. (2022). Culture and durable inequality. *Annual Review of Sociology*. Advance online publication. https://doi.org/10.1146/annurev-soc-030320-102739

van der Kolk, B. A. (2015). *The body keeps the score: Brain, mind, and body in the healing of trauma*. Penguin Books.

Volpe, V. V., Smith, N. A., Skinner, O. D., Lozada, F. T., Hope, E. C., & Del Toro, J. (2022). Centering the heterogeneity of Black adolescents' experiences: Guidance for within-group designs among African diasporic communities. *Journal of Research on Adolescence*. Advance online publication. https://doi.org/10.1111/jora.12742

Walker, A. (1982). *The color purple*. Harcourt Brace Jovanovich.

Walker, A. (1983). *In search of our mothers' gardens: Womanist prose*. Harcourt Brace Jovanovich.

Walker, M. (2010). What's a feminist therapist to do? Engaging the relational paradox in a post-feminist culture. *Women & Therapy, 34*(1–2), 38–58. https://doi.org/10.1080/02703149.2011.532689

Washington, H. A. (2006). *Medical apartheid: The dark history of medical experimentation on Black Americans from colonial times to the present*. Doubleday Books.

Watson-Singleton, N. N., Lewis, J. A., & Dworkin, E. R. (2021). Toward a socially just diversity science: Using intersectional mixed methods research to center multiply marginalized Black, Indigenous, and People of Color (BIPOC). *Cultural Diversity and Ethnic Minority Psychology*. Advance online publication. https://doi.org/10.1037/cdp0000477

Watts, R. J., Diemer, M. A., & Voight, A. M. (2011). Critical consciousness: Current status and future directions. *New Directions for Child and Adolescent Development, 2011*(134), 43–57. https://doi.org/10.1002/cd.310

We, As Ourselves. (2021). *We, as ourselves: Shaping the narrative of Black survivors*. https://weasourselves.org

Wells-Barnett, I. B. (1895/2021). *The red record: Tabulated statistics and alleged causes of lynching in the United States*. Harrow and Heston Classic Reprint. https://static1.squarespace.com/static/5b7ea2794cde7a79e7c00582/t/62549d226bd8051a1a6cda30/1649712420140/red+record.pdf

West, C. M. (2006). Sexual violence in the lives of African American women: Risk, response, and resilience. *Applied Research Forum: National Online Resource Center on Violence Against Women*, 1–10.

West, C. M., & Johnson, K. (2013). *Sexual violence in the lives of African American women*. VAWnet, a project of the National Resource Center on Domestic Violence.

Whitaker, R. (2010). *Anatomy of an epidemic: Magic bullets, psychiatric drugs, and the astonishing rise of mental illness in America*. Random House Digital.

White, J. L. (1970). Toward a Black psychology. *Ebony, 25*(11), 44–52.

White, M. E., & Satyen, L. (2015). Cross-cultural differences in intimate partner violence and depression: A systematic review. *Aggression and Violent Behavior, 24*, 120–130. https://doi.org/10.1016/j.avb.2015.05.005

Wiesner, C. R. (2022). "The first thing we cry about is violence": The National Black Women's Health Project and the Fight Against Rape and Battering. *Journal of Women's History, 34*(1), 71–92. https://doi.org/10.1353/jowh.2022.0001

Wilkins-Yel, K. G., Hyman, J., & Zounlome, N. O. O. (2019). Linking intersectional invisibility and hypervisibility to experiences of microaggressions among graduate women of color in STEM. *Journal of Vocational Behavior, 113*, 51–61. https://doi.org/10.1016/j.jvb.2018.10.018

Williams, F. B. (1987). The colored girl. In M. H. Washington (Ed.), *Invented lives: Narratives of Black women, 1860–1960* (pp. 150–159). Anchor.

Williams, P. (1991). *The alchemy of race and rights.* Harvard University Press.

Williams, P. J., Kaplan, C., & Mitra, D. (2021). Ask a feminist: Patricia Williams discusses rage and humor as an act of disobedience with Carla Kaplan and Durba Mitra. *Signs: Journal of Women in Culture and Society, 46*(4), 1073–1088. https://doi.org/10.1086/713366

Wilson, J., Gómez, J. M., Sher, S., Morgan, J., & Briggs, J. (2021). *On the record: A conversation on cultural betrayal trauma theory* [Video]. YouTube. https://www.youtube.com/watch?v=zeYcfff7O_s&t=6s

Winston, A. S. (2020). Why mainstream research will not end scientific racism in psychology. *Theory & Psychology, 30*(3), 425–430. https://doi.org/10.1177/0959354320925176

Wong, Y. J., Horn, A. J., & Chen, S. (2013). Perceived masculinity: The potential influence of race, racial essentialist beliefs, and stereotypes. *Psychology of Men & Masculinity, 14*(4), 452–464. https://doi.org/10.1037/a0030100

Woods, K. C., Buchanan, N. T., & Settles, I. H. (2009). Sexual harassment across the color line: Experiences and outcomes of cross- versus intraracial sexual harassment among Black women. *Cultural Diversity & Ethnic Minority Psychology, 15*(1), 67–76. https://doi.org/10.1037/a0013541

Wright, N. M., Smith, C. P., & Freyd, J. J. (2017). Experience of a lifetime: Study abroad, trauma, and institutional betrayal. *Journal of Aggression, Maltreatment & Trauma, 26*(1), 50–68. https://doi.org/10.1080/10926771.2016.1170088

Wrigley-Field, E. (2020). US racial inequality may be as deadly as COVID-19. *Proceedings of the National Academy of Sciences of the United States of America, 117*(36), 21854–21856. https://doi.org/10.1073/pnas.2014750117

Yi, J., Neville, H. A., Todd, N. R., & Mekawai, Y. (2022). Ignoring race and denying racism: A meta-analysis of the associations between colorblind racial ideology, anti-Blackness, and other variables antithetical to racial justice. *Journal of Counseling Psychology.* Advance online publication. https://doi.org/10.1037/cou0000618

Yip, T. (2020). *Addressing inequities in education during the COVID-19 pandemic: How education policy and schools can support historically and currently marginalized children and youth.* Society for Research in Child Development. https://www.

srcd.org/sites/default/files/resources/FINAL_AddressingInequalitiesVolume-092020.pdf

Zehr, H. (2002). *The little book of restorative justice*. Good Books.

Zehr, H. (2005). *Changing lenses: A new focus for crime and justice* (3rd ed.). Herald Press.

Zilioli, S., Gómez, J. M., Jiang, Y., & Rodríguez, J. (2022). Childhood socioeconomic status and cardiometabolic health: A test of the John Henryism hypothesis in African American elders. *The Journals of Gerontology: Series A, Biological Sciences & Medical Sciences, 77*(2), e56–e64. https://doi.org/10.1093/gerona/glab280

Zinzow, H. M., Littleton, H., Muscari, E., & Sall, K. (2021). Barriers to formal help-seeking following sexual violence: Review from within an ecological systems framework. *Victims & Offenders*. Advance online publication. https://doi.org/10.1080/15564886.2021.1978023

Zounlome, N. O., Wong, Y. J., Klann, E. M., David, J. L., & Stephens, N. J. (2019). "No one . . . saves Black girls": Black university women's understanding of sexual violence. *The Counseling Psychologist, 47*(6), 873–908. https://doi.org/10.1177/0011000019893654

Zounlome, N. O. O., Wong, Y. J., Klann, E. M., & David, J. L. (2021). "I'm already seen as a sexual predator from saying hello": Black men's perception of sexual violence. *Journal of Interpersonal Violence, 36*(19–20), NP10809–NP10830. https://doi.org/10.1177/0886260519877942

Zuberi, T., & Bonilla-Silva, E. (2021). *White logic, White methods*. Rowman & Littlefield.

Index

A

Aaliyah, 42
Ableism, 37, 42, 85
Absence, institutional cowardice as, 138
Abuse. *See also* Sexual abuse
   within family, 125–126
   race scholars' understanding of, 4
   responsibility for, 123, 125, 130
Abuse outcomes
   in CBTT, 55, 59
   postulates on, 61, 64, 65, 67
Accountability, 16, 150, 174
Acknowledgment of wrongdoing, 143
Acquaintance rape, 66
"Acting White" accusations of, 56, 65
Action plan, 100, 101
Activism
   co-optation of, 24
   for radical healing, 114, 118, 119
   and social justice research with CBTT, 72–73
Additive conceptualization of cultural betrayal, 38
Advocacy, 114, 158–159
Afrocentric feminist epistemologies, 15–16. *See also* Black feminism
Ageism, 37, 42
Agency
   in liberation health framework, 100
   and relational cultural theory, 96
   respect for, 90, 93, 104
Aggression, know-your-place, 160, 161
Agnotology, 161
Allyship, 151
Ambiguity, in trauma therapy, 91–92

American Medical Association, 159
American Psychiatric Association, 79
American Psychological Association (APA), x, 5, 85, 89, 116–117
Anger, 121–122
Anti-Black racism, 6, 24–25
   health consequences of, 26
   (intra)cultural trust developed due to, 48–49
   and sexual abuse, in CBTT, 23
   societal reckonings against, 7
   in United States, 25
Anti-Black violence, 4–5
Anti-Mexican racism, 37
Antiracist movement, 10, 28, 41
Antiracist research, on CBTT, 69–70
Antiracist work, coalition member selection based on, 153
Antiviolence movement, 151
Anxiety, about client's survival, 104–105
Anzaldúa, Gloria, 5
APA. *See* American Psychological Association
Apologizing, 123, 143, 148, 150, 153, 154
Apology to People of Color for APA's Role in Promoting, Perpetuating, and Failing to Challenge Racism, Racial Discrimination, and Human Hierarchy in U.S. (APA), 5
Artistic expressions and activities, 87, 119–120, 122
Asian/Asian American/Pacific Islander populations, 65
Assessments, for institutional courage, 139, 141

Association of Black Psychologists, 123
Assumptions, in CBTT, 68–69
Attachment theory, 50
Authenticity, 97, 117–119
Autonomy, respect for, 90, 93, 102–104, 123
Avery, Byllye, 122

B

Baldwin, James, 136, 174
Bearing witness, 91, 93, 106–107, 143
Behind-the-scenes advocacy, 158–159
Belkin Martinez, D., 98, 100
Benchmarks, for institutional change, 163–164
Benner, Chris, 153
Bent-Goodley, Tricia, xii
Betrayal blindness, 50–51
Betrayal trauma theory, xii, 50–51, 54, 57, 79
Between-group betrayal, 61, 63–65, 67
Biases
  awareness of own, 88
  in peer review system, 69–70
  working on, in therapeutic relationship, 108
Biden, Joe, 137
Biles, Simone, 56
Birth Detroit, 155
BITTEN framework, 147
Black boys
  in Black Lives Matter movement, 22–24
  as cultural betrayal sexual trauma survivors, 74
  false allegations against, 40–41
Black community
  CBTT for, 5
  collective sense of being in, 124–125
  harmful use of CBTT against, 48–50
  (intra)cultural trust in context of, 53
  in microsystem for trauma survivors, 51–52
  prioritization of sexual abuse in, 49
  privileging needs of, 57–58
  promoting gender equality in, 173
  radical healing in. See Radical healing
  "rape problem" discourse in, 4, 10, 30, 40–42
  sexual abuse in. See Sexual abuse in Black community
  sharing CBTT research with, 71
  social location of Black women and girls within, 39–40

Black feminism
  centering perspectives from, 15, 17–18
  and cultural betrayal trauma theory, 5, 23, 49, 72–73
  dialectics in, 72–73, 175
  on dimensions of change, 133
  dismantling White supremacy with, xi–xii, 8–9
  emotionality in, 18–19
  ethic of caring in, 135–136
  on intersectional oppression, 26
  knowledge validation process in, 15–16
  and medical model, 84
  as premise for research, 16–17
  researchers' and clinicians' understanding of, 4
  transformation in process in, 19
  worldview of, 17
Black girls. See Black women and girls
Black immigrant women, 43, 75
Black Latinas, 43, 75
Black Lives Matter Global Network Foundation, Inc., 7
Black Lives Matter movement, 22–24
Black men
  accountability for, 174
  in Black Lives Matter movement, 22–24
  cultural betrayal trauma perpetrated by. See Perpetrators of cultural betrayal sexual trauma
  discrimination faced by, 28
  false allegations against, 40–41
  (intra)cultural pressure to protect, 58
  oppression and power for, 27
  protection of, by Black women and girls, 44
  racism against, 41
  role, of in radical healing, 123–124
  secondary marginalization by, 39–40
Black Muslim women, 30, 43, 75
Blackness, 26, 37
Black people
  cultural betrayal trauma for, 57
  dehumanization of, 6, 145
  experiential understanding of harm for, 96
  oppression of, in United States, 22
  research supporting CBTT with, 66, 67
  use of medical model against, 82, 85
  validation of perspectives of, 155
Black psychology, 117
Black solidarity
  and anti-Black racism, 6
  in CBTT framework, 7
  and (intra)cultural pressure, 166

in largely White spaces, xii
and representational intersectionality, 29
and role of men in radical healing, 123–124
spaces for, 174
true, 20
violent silencing for, xiii
Black spaces, creating, 173
Black trans*women, 30, 43, 70, 75
Black women and girls
  centering experiences of. *See*
    Centralization of Black women and
    girls
  change making to positively impact, 174
  cultural betrayal sexual trauma
    perpetrated by, 74
  damage narrative for, 86
  diversifying population of, 30, 36–39
  equity in social justice efforts for, 171
  humanity of, 17, 81–82, 174–175
  incarcerated, 43–44, 75
  institutional courage that benefits,
    139–144
  as leaders of social justice movements,
    23–24
  power-over relationships for, 92–93
  privileging perspectives of, 171
  "rape problem" for, 41–42
  secondary marginalization for, 58–59
  social location of, within Black
    community, 39–40
  stifling of anger by, 121–122
  theory of multiplicity for, 32
  violent silencing of, 115
Body
  reclaiming the, 118–119
  respect for, 145–148
Bonilla-Silva, E., 26
"Both/and" dialectic, 175
Bronfenbrenner socioecological systems
  model, 51–53
brown, adrienne marie, 117, 144
Brown, L. S., 138
Bryant, Thema, xii, 5, 127
Bryant-Davis, T., 87, 119, 121
Buchanan, N. T., 70
Buggs, Shantel Gabrieal, 25
Burke, Tarana, 23, 58, 118, 146

C

California Black Women's Health Project
  Info, 116
Campus climate surveys, 151

CARA (Cardiovascular Disease and
  Cultural Betrayal Trauma in Black
  Middle Age and Older Adults Study),
  66
Cardiovascular Disease and Cultural
  Betrayal Trauma in Black Middle Age
  and Older Adults Study (CARA), 66
Caring
  by Black men, for radical healing, 124
  and emotionality in institutional change
    work, 135
  ethic of, 16, 18, 73, 135, 136, 166
Caring institutions, 136–137
CASBS (Center for Advanced Study in the
  Behavioral Sciences), xiv, 155
Cat-calling, 124
CBAs (community benefits agreements),
  156–157
CBMI-BAYA. *See* Cultural Betrayal
  Multidimensional Inventory for Black
  American Young Adults
CBMI-DSAYA (Cultural Betrayal
  Multidimensional Inventory for Desi/
  South Asian Young Adults), 64
CBTT. *See* Cultural betrayal trauma theory
Center for Advanced Study in the Behavioral
  Sciences (CASBS), xiv, 155
Center for Institutional Courage, 155
Centralization of Black women and girls,
  x–xii
  abolishing White Read with, 81
  in Black feminism, 15, 17–18
  in CBTT, 6, 11–12
  links between healing and harmful
    contexts, 11–12
  in social justice efforts, 170
Change, dimensions of, 133
Change agents, institutional courage for,
  165–167
Childhood sexual abuse survivors, xii, 50–51
City redevelopment processes, 156–159
Civil rights movement, 22, 24
Classism, 37, 42, 72
Client to clinician discrimination, 107–108
Client worldview, awareness of, 88
Coalitions, 30, 151–155
Cocreation, 81–82, 157–158, 170, 175
Cognitive flexibility, 92
Cognitive processing therapy (CPT), 103
Cohen, Cathy, 36, 39, 57
Cokley, K., 25
Cole, E. R., 30, 31, 70, 74

Collaboration. *See also* Power-with
  collaborative approaches
    with clients, 90
  community–lawyer, 156–159
  in liberation health framework, 100
  in relational cultural theory, 96
Collective determination, 165
Collective sense of being, 124–125
Collective *we*, rhetorical use of, 10, 154–155
Collectivism, 117–120
Collins, Patricia Hill, 9, 15–17, 26, 72, 73, 83–84, 127, 128, 133, 135, 136, 164, 172, 174
Comas-Díaz, L., 99
Combahee River Collective, xii, 27, 41, 81, 123, 169, 170
Comfort, White people's, 152
Common cultural betrayal, 62–64
Community. *See also* Black community
  collaborations between lawyers and, 156–159
  cultural betrayal trauma within, 120
  radical healing for change in, 118
  societal solutions for harms in, 172–173
  systemic racism in, 26
Community-based participatory research, 74
Community benefits agreements (CBAs), 156–157
Community care, x
Community healing, 120–124
  in groups, 122–124
  and individual healing practices, 118
  restorative justice, 120–122
  trust and support for, 173
Community Healing Network, 123
Community organizing, 156
Compassion, courageous, ix
Compassionate listening, 123
Complex trauma, 43, 93
Connection
  in knowledge generation, 16, 73
  relational cultural theory (RCT) for reconnection, 97–98, 120
  reconnection to community, 120
  and relational paradox, 97
  for trauma clinicians, 95
Consensus building, 171
Consent, lack of, 146
Contact sexual abuse, prevalence of, 43
Continuous assessments of institutional courage, 139, 141
Cooper, Anna Julia, xii, 3, 4
Coping strategies, 84

Correcting false statements, 144
Counterhypotheses, 60–65, 67
Courage, institutional. *See* Institutional courage
Courageous compassion, ix
COVID-19 pandemic, 4, 5, 22, 28
Cowardice, institutional, 135, 138, 153
CPT (cognitive processing therapy), 103
Crenshaw, Kimberlé, xii, 19, 27, 28, 39–41, 44, 47, 51, 67, 74, 81, 84, 102, 151
Criminal justice system, 26, 42
Critical consciousness
  artistic expressions and activities to promote, 119
  and cultural competency in trauma therapy, 94
  in liberation health framework, 98–100
  in psychological framework of radical healing, 117, 118
Critical race theory, 10, 17, 24, 51
Critical self-reflection, 91, 92
Cross-cultural counseling competencies, 88–89
Cross-racial groups, 151–152, 171–172
Cultural authenticity, 117–119
Cultural basis for oppression, 170
Cultural betrayal
  between-group betrayal vs., 61, 63–65, 67
  client experience in context of, 94
  in cultural betrayal trauma theory, 37–38, 56
  defined, 6, 56
  framework for understanding, ix–x
  future research on, 75
  and high betrayal, 61, 63, 65
  race scholars' understanding of, 4
Cultural Betrayal Multidimensional Inventory for Black American Young Adults (CBMI-BAYA)
  examining within-group variation with, 64
  quantitative evidence from, 66
  questionnaires within, 56, 57, 59, 60, 87
Cultural Betrayal Multidimensional Inventory for Desi/South Asian Young Adults (CBMI-DSAYA), 64
Cultural betrayal sexual harassment, 66, 67, 114, 149–150
Cultural betrayal sexual trauma
  CBTT as framework for examining, 6–7, 10
  conceptualizations of, 73–74
  criminal justice system on, 42
  defined, 6

developmental context for, 71
within the family, 125–126
growing awareness of, 166
high-profile perpetrators of, 7
impact of context on, 134
intersectional invisibility in studies of, 30
need for Black solidarity and need to acknowledge, 7
perpetrators of. *See* Perpetrators of cultural betrayal sexual trauma
persistence of, 137
RCT for reconnection after, 97–98
restorative justice lens for, 121
White people's perceptions of, 66
Cultural betrayal trauma
case examples of healing after, 128–129
in CBTT, 54, 55, 57
within community, 120
complexity of, 68
defined, 6, 57
Cultural betrayal trauma theory (CBTT), 47–76
about, 5–6
across diverse marginalized populations, 62, 64–65
as basis for research, 6
for Black feminist critical practice, 72–73
case example of, 67–68
cultural betrayal in, 56
cultural betrayal trauma in, 57
on culturally competent trauma therapy, 79–80
dismantling White supremacy with, xii–xiii
diversification of Black women and girls in, 37–38
empirical evidence supporting, 60–67
as frame for trauma therapy, 78
as framework for examining cultural betrayal sexual trauma, 10
as framework for understanding Black women and girls' experience, 6–7
future antiracist research on, 69–70
future intersectional research on, 70–71
on inequality within social justice movements, 23
on institutional change, 135–136
(intra)cultural pressure in, 57–59
(intra)cultural support in, 59
(intra)cultural trust in, 53–56
outcomes predicted by, 59–60
postulates of, 60–62
potential harmful use of, 48–49

qualitative evidence for, 67
quantitative evidence for, 66
on radical healing, 115–116
on relational paradox, 97
theoretical and methodological next steps for, 73–75
trauma in context in, 51–53
on violent silencing, 115–116
within Black populations, 66, 67
Cultural change, 11, 118
Cultural competency, 87–90
centralizing, in trauma therapy, 91, 94, 105–107
individual, 88–89
structural, 89–90
Cultural congruency, 87
Cultural context
Black men's understanding of, 124
in liberation health framework, 99, 101, 102
Cultural differences, respect for, 105–107
Cultural humility, 87
Cultural-level harms, societal solutions for addressing, 172–173
Culturally appropriate intervention strategies, 88–89
Culturally competent trauma therapy, 10, 77–112
abolishing the White Read with, 79–81
ambiguity, emotional intensity, and good and evil in, 91–92
bearing witness in, 91, 93
case examples of, 102–110
centralizing cultural competency in, 91, 94, 105–107
and client to clinician discrimination, 107–108
critical self-reflection in, 91, 92
cultural betrayal trauma theory on, 79–80
dimensions of harm and healing in, 86–87
holding hope in, 91, 93–94
with liberation health framework, 98–102, 108–110
medical model vs., 82–86
power-with collaborative approaches in, 91–93, 104–105
processes and practices in, 90–95
and radical healing, 113–114
recognizing the humanity of Black women and girls in, 81–82
and relational cultural theory, 96–98
replacing the medical model with, 79–81
respecting autonomy in, 102–104

self-care for practitioners of, 91, 94–95, 104–105
theoretical orientations for, 95–102
types of cultural competency, 87–90
Culturally responsive therapy, 103
Cultural outcomes
　in CBTT, 55, 59–60
　postulates on, 61, 64, 65, 67
Cultural racism, 26
Cultural values, 55, 88
Cummings, Scott L., 156–157, 161, 163
Cumulative conceptualization of cultural betrayal, 38

D

Damage narrative, 86
Dance Theatre of Harlem, xii, 155, 166
Danylchuk, Lynette S., 90–92
DARVO responses, 130
Davis, Angela, xi, 35, 150
Decision-making processes, transparent, 160
Deficit-based approach, 85–86
Dehumanization, of Black people, 6, 145
DEI (diversity, equity, and inclusion) efforts, 151–153
Delker, B. C., 95
Delva, Jorge, 165
Depression, sexual abuse and, 44
Developmental context, for cultural betrayal sexual abuse, 71
Diagnostic and Statistical Manual of Mental Disorders, Fifth Edition (DSM-5), 79, 83
Dialectics, in Black feminist thought, 72–73, 175
Dialogue, 16, 73
Disconnection, 91, 94, 96
Discrimination
　against Black women and girls, 81–82, 174
　client to clinician, 107–108
　double, 28
　internal, 65, 161
　in medical model, 84
　overt, 107–108
　structural intersectionality and, 28
　in therapy, 81–82, 107–108
Disguised presentation of trauma, 86
Dissociation, 6, 65, 66, 84–85
Distress, psychological, 82–85
Diverse marginalized populations, CBTT research with, 70, 75
Diversity, equity, and inclusion (DEI) efforts, 151–153

Diversity, within population of Black women and girls, 30, 36–39
Doctor, institutional betrayal by, 145
Doctor's office, institutional betrayal by, 146
Dominant culture, as macrosystem for trauma survivors, 52
Domination
　centering Black women and girls as rejection of, 17–18
　by clinician, 92–93
　and freedom fighting, 170
　matrix of, 175
　power without, 164–165
　in sexual abuse, 42–43
Double discrimination, 28
Dramatic arts, 119
Dreamstorming
　for equality and equity in process and outcome, 174
　expressing hope in, 170
　on health care, 148
　on nonprofit coalitions, 154–155
　for radical transformation, xi, 175
　for structural healing, 134
　on universities, 150–151
DSM-5 (Diagnostic and Statistical Manual of Mental Disorders, Fifth Edition), 79
Dugger, Preston Warren, III, 126
Durkee, M. I., 65

E

Education, popular, 98–99, 102
Elitist institutions, validation from, 164–165
Emotional Emancipation Circles, 123
Emotional intelligence, 92
Emotionality
　Black feminist perspective on, 18–19
　in culturally competent trauma therapy, 91–92
　in institutional change work, 135–138
Emotions, reclaiming, 121–122
Empirical evidence
　against medical model, 84–85
　supporting cultural betrayal trauma theory, 60–67
Empowerment, 16, 103, 118, 123
ENRICH (Experimental Study of Violence and Race in High School), 66
Epistemic injustice, 83–84
Epistemic oppression, 69–70, 84, 161
Epistemic violence, 5, 84

Equality
    CBTT research in movement toward, 69
    dreamstorming of, 150–151
    gender, 173
    in nonprofit coalitions, 152, 153
    in process and outcome, 159
Equal opportunity, 25
An Equal Place (Cummings), 156
Equity, in social justice efforts, 171–172
Essentialism, 69
Ethic of caring, 16, 18, 73, 135, 136, 166
Ethic of personal accountability, 16
Ethnopolitical psychology, 117
Eurocentric White male epistemology, 83–84
Evidence-based treatments, 79, 103
Evidence-informed therapies, 80
Excited delirium syndrome, 85, 159
Exosystem, for trauma survivors, 52
Exoticism, xii
Experiential knowledge base, 166
Experimental Study of Violence and Race in High School (ENRICH), 66
Expertise, 158
External harm, 31
Externalizing pathology, on trauma, 95

F

False allegations, in "rape problem" discourse, 30, 40
False statements, correcting/retracting, 144
Falsifiability, 29–30, 62
Family betrayal, 75
Family healing practices, 124–127
    case example, 129–130
    choices within families to pursue radical healing, 126–127
    healing from cultural betrayal sexual trauma occurring in, 125–126
Family-level harms, societal solutions for addressing, 172–173
Fear, 53, 146–148
Feedback, critical, 153
Feminism, coalition as tool in, 151.
    See also Black feminism; White feminist movement
Feminist therapy, 86, 96
First Annual NASEM Action Collaborative to Prevent and Address Sexual Harassment in Higher Ed Public Summit, 150
Fook, J., 99
Ford, Christine Blasey, 114–115

Four-column chart, for action plan in Liberation Health (LH) framework, 101
Freedom, 127–129
    case example of finding, 128–129
    dismantling oppression in fight for, 170
    dreamstorming about, 134
    radical healing for, 127–129
    as safe space within the self, 127–128
Freewriting, 92
    case examples of, 128–130
    to find a safe space within the self, 127–128
    for radical healing, 129–130
    in response to institutional betrayal, 154
Freire, Paolo, 98, 99, 155
French, Bryana H., 78, 114, 117
Freyd, Jennifer J., xii, 62, 79, 134, 139

G

Garza, Alicia, 23
Gaslighting, 163
Gendered racism, 28
Gender equality, 173
Gobin, Robyn L., 20, 67, 123
Gómez, Jennifer M., xiii, 23, 31, 40, 62, 64–67, 69, 79, 83, 94, 96, 101, 104, 108–109, 114, 119, 120, 123, 137, 139, 166, 167
Good and evil, coexistence of, 82, 91–92
Graduate education, societal solutions for, 173
Graduate Record Examinations, 25
Group healing, 122–124
Grzanka, Patrick, 29–31, 70, 71, 89, 98

H

Hallucinations, 65, 84–85
Hames-García, M. R., 32, 39
Hansen, H., 89
Harm
    Black experiential understanding of, 96
    dimensions of, 86–87
    potential to use CBTT for, 48–50
    structural change to address, 172–174
    in therapy, institutional courage to address, 139
    use of medical model to perpetrate, 82
Harm-to-healing process, 11–12, 119
Harrell, S. P., 26
Harris, Kamala, 137

Hatred, 122
Healing. *See also* Radical healing
  contextual harms linked to, 11–12
  dimensions of, 86–87
  in medical model, 83
  responses to disclosures of abuse that promote, 122–123
  strengths-based approach to, 60
  in trauma psychology, 175
  use of CBTT for, 48–50
Health care, 51, 59, 145–148
Helmers, Breanne, 66
Helplessness, 104–105
Herman, J., 86
Heterosexism, 37, 42
Hettler, B., 86–87
Hicken, M. T., 29, 30
Hierarchies of oppression, 36–38
High betrayal, 50
  case examples of healing after, 128–130
  cultural betrayal and, 61, 63, 65
  future CBTT research on, 75
  RCT for reconnection after, 97–98
Higher education, White mediocrity in, 160. *See also* Universities
Hill, Anita, 67, 114
Hill, Lauryn, 129
Holistic healing, 86
Homecoming, 127
Homework, 101
Homophobia, 36, 37, 42
hooks, bell, xii, 7–9, 18, 26–27, 53, 56, 113, 115, 125
Hope
  holding, 91, 93–94
  and inaction, 149
  radical, xiii–xiv, 116–119
  in small-wins model, 164
Howard Valdivia, R. L., 65
Humanity
  of Black male perpetrators, 122, 174
  of Black people, 6, 145
  of Black women and girls, 17, 81–82, 174–175
Humility, 157
Hurley, J., 126
Hurston, Zora Neale, 80

I

Identity matching, in therapy, 108
Imarisha, Walidah, 117
Immigrant women, 43, 75
Imposter syndrome, 18
Inadequacy, feelings of, 91–92
Incarcerated Black women, 43–44, 75
Individual cultural competency, 88–89
Individual experience, in popular education, 98
Individual healing, 19
  artistic expressions and activities for, 119–120
  contextual harms linked to, 11
  in medical model, 85–86
  radical healing practices, 118–120
  reclaiming the body, 118–119
  and structural change, 117–118
Individualized coping strategies, 84
Individualized harms, structural change to address, 172–174
Individualized therapy, 96, 97
Inequality
  CBTT research to dismantle, 71
  conflicts of, 151–153
  in field of psychology, 98
  in intersectionality framework for research, 30
  postulate on marginalization and, 61–63
  in social justice movements, 22–24
  structural change to address, 172–174
  and structural healing, 152
  and uneven power field, 161–163
Inequity, as barrier to healing, x
Injustice, epistemic, 83–84
Institutional betrayal, 75, 138, 139
  in health care, 145–147
  in nonprofit coalitions, 151–152
  self-assessments of potential for, 142
  at universities, 149–150
Institutional change, 11, 133–168
  avoiding barriers to, 159–167
  benchmarks for success related to, 163–164
  case examples of, 155–156
  community–lawyer collaborations for, 156–159
  cultural betrayal trauma theory on, 135–136
  emotionality in work of, 135–138
  in health care, 145–148
  and institutional betrayal/cowardice, 138
  institutional courage for, 139–144
  in nonprofit coalitions, 151–155
  pathways from betrayal to liberation, 144–155
  perseverance for, 165–167

power without domination for, 164–165
radical healing for, 118
and uneven field of power, 161–163
at universities, 149–151
White mediocrity as barrier to, 159–161
Institutional context, in liberation health framework, 101, 102
Institutional courage, 174
and behind-the-scenes advocacy, 158–159
case examples of, 155–156
for change agents, 4, 165–167
classes of, 139–144
defined, 139
in health care, 147–148
and liberation health framework, 108–110
in nonprofit coalitions, 153–154
small wins resulting from, 166
societal solutions that reward, 173
in universities, 150
Institutional cowardice, 135, 138, 153
Institutionalized self-caring, 95
Institutional-level harms, societal solutions for addressing, 172–173
Institutional oppression, 30
Institutional power, 5, 30
Institutions, caring, 136–137
Interactive conceptualization of cultural betrayal, 38
Internal discrimination, 65, 161
Internalized prejudice, 6, 86
Interpersonal context, in betrayal trauma theory, 50, 53
Interpersonal healing, 11, 19
Interpersonal trauma, downstream harm from, 86
Intersectional invisibility, 30
Intersectionality
case examples of, 31–32
in cultural betrayal trauma theory, 23, 37–38
political, 28, 31–32, 39
within psychology, 29–31
representational, 28–29, 32, 49, 58
structural, 28, 39, 74
Intersectionality theory, 27–31, 117
Intersectional oppression, 26–31
assumption of, in CBTT, 69
for Black women and girls, 22
client experience in context of, 94
by clinicians, 82
and cultural betrayal trauma theory, 5
erasure of survivors due to, 7, 10
institutional courage to address, 139

lack of research as manifestation of, 43–44
and need for structural healing, 134
persistence of, 137
public identification of, 137
and racism against Black men, 41
radical healing for survivors of, 114
"rape problem" discourse as manifestation of, 40–42
sexual abuse as manifestation of, 41–43
and stifling of anger, 121
as theme in Black feminism, 16
trauma researchers' understanding of, 4
at universities, 149
Intersectional research on CBTT, 70–71
Intimate terrorism, 125
(Intra)cultural pressure
abuse outcomes and, 65
awareness of, 166
in CBTT, 10, 55, 57–59
client experiences in context of, 94
disavowing cultural betrayal trauma due to, 48–49
outcomes associated with, 66
and perception of Black family, 125, 126
persistence of, 137
prejudice and, 66
responsibility to eradicate, 120
and violent silencing, 115
(Intra)Cultural Pressure and Support Questionnaire, 59
(Intra)cultural support
in CBTT, 59
client experiences in context of, 94
for community healing, 173
in Emotional Emancipation Circles, 123
within family, 125
for survivors, 68
(Intra)cultural trust
in CBTT, 7, 53–56
client experiences in context of, 94
for community healing, 173
cultural betrayal as violation of, 56
defined, 53
in Emotional Emancipation Circles, 123
and (intra)cultural pressure, 57
and (intra)cultural support, 59
postulate on, 61–64
for radical healing, 120
as result of anti-Black racism, 48–49
(Intra)Cultural Trust Questionnaire, 56
Islamophobia, 37
Isolation, 93, 94

J

Jane Doe, xvii, 109–110
Jefferson, Hakeem, 155
Journaling, 92, 95, 119, 122
Judicial system, in exosystem, 52

K

Kavanaugh, Brett, 114–115
Kelly, R., 7
Kerr, Shelly, 109, 110
King, M. L., Jr., 25, 116–117
Knowledge validation process, 15–16, 84
Know-your-place aggression, 160, 161

L

Ladson-Billings, Gloria, 8, 86
Lane County, Oregon, 155
Latent profile and class analyses, 74
Latino/a populations, 43, 65, 75
Law, intersectional oppression in, 27
Lawyers, collaborations with, 156–159
Leadership, 23–24, 165
Learning, from clients, 106–107
Leaving the family, 126–127
Lewis, J. K., 79, 83, 96
LGBTQ community, multiplicity of
  oppression in, 37
LH framework. *See* Liberation health
  framework
Liberation, 87, 134, 144–155
Liberation health (LH) framework, 80
  case example of, 108–110
  clinical application of, 100–102
  influences on, 98–99
  principles of, 99–100
  in trauma therapy, 91, 98–102
Liberation psychology, 98, 99, 102, 117
Listening, 123, 124, 171, 174
Livingston, Julie, 161
Longitudinal research, 75
Long-term transformation, 163
Lorde, Audre, xii, 19, 36–38, 49, 82, 160,
  171, 174
Los Angeles, Calif., 134–135, 156–159
Loyalty, racial, 44, 48, 57

M

Macrosystem, 52, 94, 118
Managerial discretion, 135

Manualized treatment, 90, 93, 103
Marginalization, 61–63, 74
Marginalization theory, 39, 58
Marginalized individuals
  adapting mainstream trauma research
    for, 51
  CBTT with, 6, 62, 64–65
  know-your-place aggression against,
    160
  protecting, in city redevelopment
    processes, 156–159
  scholarly literature produced by, 72
  silencing of, 5
  uneven power field for, 161–163
  use of medical model to harm, 82
Matrix of domination, 175
McAdoo, Harriette Pipes, 124
Measurable progress, 142, 163–164
Media, in exosystem for trauma survivors,
  52
Medical board, institutional betrayal by, 146
Medical model, 10–11, 82–86
  CBTT lens on, 79–80
  challenges to premises of, 83
  culturally competent trauma therapy to
    replace, 79–81
  deficit-based approach in, 85–86
  empirical evidence against, 84–85
  epistemic injustice, violence, and
    oppression inherent in, 83–84
  relational cultural theory vs., 96, 97
Medium betrayal, 65
Mental health, 4, 65, 85
Mental health care, systemic racism in, 26
Mentorship committees, 151
Mesosystem, for trauma survivors, 52
#MeToo movement, 7, 22–24, 149
Metzl, J. M., 89
Michigan Opera Theatre, 119
Microaggressions, 107
Microsystem, for trauma survivors, 51–52
Miller, J. B., 96
Mills, Charles W., 24, 38
Misogynoir, 24, 37
Mitchell, Arthur, xii, 166–167
Mitchell, Koritha, 120, 161
Mixed methods research, 74
Moraga, Cherríe, 5
Morlok, Jennifer, 109, 110
Motor City Singers Space community event,
  37, 115
Movement practices, for radical healing, 119
Multicultural Guidelines (APA), 89

Multiplicity, theory of, 32, 37, 59
Music, for radical healing, 119
Muslim women, 30, 43, 75
Mutual empowerment, 103
Mutuality, 92, 96

N

Narcissism, 167
Nassar, Larry, 56
Nationalism, 37, 43
Nature, radical healing in, 119
Needs of victim, 121, 123
Negative emotions, self-care and, 105
Nested group comparisons, 71
90by30 partnership, 155
Nonpathologizing frame, 17
   in betrayal trauma theory, 79
   in CBTT, 69
   in liberation health framework, 102
   in trauma therapy, 90
Nonprofit coalitions, 30, 151–155
"Notes for Yet Another Paper on Black Feminism, or, Will the Real Enemy Please Stand Up?" (Smith, Barbara), 7

O

Obama, Barack, 137
Objectionable behavior, defining, 58
"Objective reality," 25
Objectivity, 91, 136
Ondersma, Steven J., 103–104
On the Record (film), 28
Oppositional worldview, 125
Oppression
   of Black people, in United States, 22
   cultural basis for, 170
   dismantling, in fight for freedom, 170
   epistemic, 69–70, 84, 161
   hierarchies of, 36–38
   as individual-level problem, 134
   intersectional. *See* Intersectional oppression
   models of, 29
   power without, 164–165
   similarities in institutional and social, 30
   structural, 85
   subpersonhood to justify, 25
   systemic, 71, 99
   in therapy, persistence of, 137
   violent, rational responses to, 136
   by White women, 171

Oregon Board of Psychologist Examiners, 109–110
Outcomes
   in CBTT, 55
   postulates related to, 60–62, 64–67
   predicting, 59–60
Outsider-within perspective, 174–175
Overt discrimination, 107–108
Ownership, of sexist sexual abuse, 59

P

Pacific Islander populations, 65
Pain, 105, 167
Partnerships, shared identity as basis for, 167
Pastor, Manuel, 153
Patriarchy, dismantling, 173
Payton, Carolyn R., 135
Peaceful amplification, 116
Peer review system, 69–70
Peer supervision, 95
People of color and Indigenous individuals (POCIs), psychological framework of radical healing for, 116–117
Perpetrators of cultural betrayal sexual trauma
   Black women as, 74
   excusing behavior of, 124
   hatred of, 122
   high-profile, 7
   humanity of, 122, 174
   in microsystem of trauma survivor, 51
   protecting, 6–7, 66
   reducing men to caricatures of, 170
Perry, Imani, 69
Perseverance, 165–167
Personal accountability, ethic of, 16
Personal context, in liberation health framework, 101
Personal meaning, 127
Pharmaceutical drugs, 84
POCIs, psychological framework of radical healing for, 116–117
Poetry, for radical healing, 119
Police
   disclosure/reporting to, 6–7, 59
   in exosystem for trauma survivors, 52
   systemic racism in policing, 26
   violence perpetrated by, 22–23, 85, 159
Policy making
   city redevelopment, 157
   for institutional change, 135, 139
   by nonprofit coalitions, 151–152

Political intersectionality, 28, 31–32, 39
Popular education, 98–99, 102
Posttraumatic growth, 60, 73
Posttraumatic Growth Questionnaire, 60, 87
Posttraumatic stress, sexual abuse and, 44
Posttraumatic stress disorder (PTSD), 53, 64–66, 85, 103
Power
 abuse of, 148
 adopting strategies of those in, 161–163
 institutional, 5, 30
 institutional and social, 30
 intentional use of, 124
 intersectional views of oppression and, 27
 in nonprofit coalitions, 151
 in relationships with community partners, 157–158
 in sexual abuse, 42–43
 in therapeutic relationship, 108
 uneven field of, 161–163, 171
 without domination, 164–165
Power-over relationships, 92–93, 96, 105–107, 151, 152
Power-with collaborative approaches
 case examples of, 102–107
 and clinician self-care, 104–105
 and power-over case example, 105–107
 with professionals, 157–158
 in relational cultural theory, 96
 respecting autonomy in, 102–104
 in trauma therapy, 91–93
Prejudice
 internalized, 6, 86
 (intra)cultural pressure to protect from, 66
 self-discovery of own, 92
Premises postulates, CBTT, 60–63, 66, 67
Presenting problem, conceptualization of, 99, 100
Prestige, power through, 165
Prevalence postulates, CBTT, 60–63, 67
The Price of the Ticket (Baldwin), 136
Priorities
 aligning behavior with, 167
 institutional, 142
Prison industrial complex, 26
Privilege, 22–24, 27, 39
Problem, understanding, 143
Problem conceptualization, in LH framework, 99, 100
Problem statement, thickening, 100–101
Processing journals, 92, 95
Protective behaviors, 95

Psychological distress, 82–85
Psychological framework for radical healing, 116–117
Psychology field
 extending intersectionality within, 29–31
 social justice in, 31
PTSD. *See* Posttraumatic stress disorder

Q

Qualitative research, on CBTT, 67
Quantitative research, 29, 66

R

Race
 clinicians' understanding of, 4
 defined, 25
 privileging of, 37
Racial capitalism, 72
Racial contract, 24–25, 38, 52
Racial hierarchy, 162
Racialization, 25, 66
Racial loyalty, 44, 48, 57
Racial progress, narrative on, 137
Racism. *See also specific types*
 against Black men, 41
 against Black women and girls, 22. *See also* Intersectional oppression
 denial of, 5
 institutional courage to address, 139
 and medical model, 82
 and need for structural healing, 134
 privileging of, 37
 sex and class privilege in, 27
 sexual abuse and, 42
 society as "too racist" for CBTT, 50
 in structural intersectionality, 28
 as unifying oppression, 38
 in women's liberation movement, 137
Radical healing, 11, 94, 113–131
 artistic expressions and activities for, 119–120
 case examples of, 128–130
 choices within families to pursue, 126–127
 clinicians' understanding of need for, 4
 community practices for, 120–124
 from cultural betrayal sexual trauma occurring in the family, 125–126
 cultural betrayal trauma theory on, 115–116
 in families, 124–127
 for freedom, 127–129

freewriting for, 129–130
in groups, 122–124
individual practices for, 118–120
and liberation health framework, 98
psychological framework for, 116–117
reclaiming the body in, 118–119
restorative justice for, 120–122
and structural change, 117–118
from violent silencing, 114–116
Radical hope, xiii–xiv, 116–119
Radical social work, 98, 99, 102
Ralph, Laurence, 4
Rape, prevalence of, 43
Rape culture, 124
@RapedAtSpelman, 7
"rape problem" discourse in Black community, 4, 10, 30, 40–42
Rationality, 136
RCT. *See* Relational cultural theory
Reconciliation, 122, 154
Reductionism, xiii
Referential knowledge, 166
Relational cultural theory (RCT), 80, 91, 93, 96–98, 120
Relational paradox, 97
Remediation, 147
Reparations, 141, 148
Representational intersectionality, 28–29, 32, 49, 58
Representativeness, 72
Resistance, 16
artistic expressions and activities to promote, 119
in community healing practices, 124
in psychological framework of radical healing, 117, 118
safe space within self for, 127
Resource commitment, to institutional courage, 141
Respect
for agency, 90, 93, 104
for autonomy, 90, 93, 102–104, 123
for the body, 145–148
for cultural differences, 105–107
power through, 165
for strengths, 123, 125
Responsibility, for abuse, 123, 125, 130
Restorative justice, 120–122, 130
Retaliation, 149, 150
Retracting false statements, 144
Richeson, Jennifer A., 149
Right, importance of being, 106–107

Role of Psychology and APA in Dismantling Systemic Racism Against People of Color in U.S. (APA), 5
Rotating betrayal blindness, 50–51

S

Safe spaces, 127–128
#SayHerName campaign, 23
Scholarly literature, by marginalized individuals, 72
Scott, Joan Wallach, 68
Secondary marginalization, 36
by Black men, 39–40
as cultural betrayal, 56
defined, 39
erasure of survivors due to, 7, 10, 41
(intra)cultural pressure related to, 58–59
and privileging of Black men in civil rights movement, 24
responsibility to eradicate, 120
and sexual abuse of Black women and girls, 42
shared power and absence of, 165
within social justice movements, 23
Secondary prevention program, 106–107
Segregation, power without, 165
Self, xiii, 118, 127–128
Self-affirmations, 119
Self-assessments of institutional courage, 142
Self-care, 91, 94–95, 104–105, 119
Self-definition, 51, 117, 127
Self-determination, 90, 166
Self-knowledge, 117–119
Self-reflection, 91, 92
Self-valuation, 127
Sex, distinction between sexual abuse and, 43
Sexism
for Black women and girls, 22. *See also* Intersectional oppression
and cultural betrayal trauma theory, 37–38, 74
within family, 125, 126
institutional courage to address, 139
race and class privilege in, 27
sexual abuse and, 42
in structural intersectionality, 28
and violent silencing, 115
Sexist sexual abuse, 7, 58–59
Sex trafficking, 43

Sexual abuse
  and anti-Black racism, 23
  in antiracist movement, 41
  childhood, xii, 50–51
  contact, 43
  as cultural betrayal trauma, 57
  cultural context for, 124
  and depression, 44
  distinguishing sex from, 43
  as manifestation of intersectional
    oppression, 41–43
  prioritization of, in Black community, 49
  sexist, 7, 58–59
  silencing victims of, 114–115
  White supremacy as cause of, 151,
    153–154
Sexual abuse in Black community. *See also*
    Cultural betrayal sexual trauma
  complexity of, xiii
  as complex problem, 48
  defined, 42–43
  and intersectional oppression, 22
  outcomes of, 44
  prevalence of, 43–44
Sexual abuse policy, working group on,
    151–155
"Sexual contract," 58–59
Sexual harassment, 66, 67, 109, 114,
    149–150
Sexual health concerns, 44
Sexualization, 42, 124
Sexual politics, 16
Sexual violence problem, public
    identification of, 137
Shared identity, partnerships due to, 167
Shen, Rinku, xi
Silence, as institutional cowardice, 153
Similarities, research on, 30, 74
Simmons, Russell, 7, 28–29, 39–40
Simone, Nina, xiii, 126–128
Site fights, 157
Six Dimensions of Wellness model, 86–87
Skills-based work, in therapy, 104
Slavery, 26
Small-wins model, 164, 166
Smith, Barbara, 7
Smith, C. P., 139
Social context, in LH framework, 99, 100
Social contract, 25
Social identity threats, 56
Social justice
  and activism, 72–73
  allyship for, 151
  approaches to healing from, 86
  CBTT research for, 71
  in field of psychology, 31
  inequity and inequality in, 22–24,
    171–172
  and liberation health framework, 102,
    108–110
  and relational cultural theory, 98
Social oppression, 30
Social power, 31
Social support, for radical healing, 119.
  See also (Intra)cultural support
Social work, radical, 98, 99, 102
Societal change
  community–lawyer collaborations for,
    156–159
  radical healing for, 118
Societal-level harms, addressing, 172–173
Societal trauma, 53, 55
Sociocultural context, 51–53, 92
Sociopolitical analysis, 98
Solidarity. *See also* Black solidarity
  equality as condition of, 172
  for nonprofit coalitions, 153
  shared power for, 165
Soul, as truest form of self, xiii
Spirituality, 119
Stanford University, xiv, 155
Stereotypes, 121
Stokes, Karen, 109, 110
Storytelling, for radical healing, 122–123
Strengths, respect for, 123, 125
Strengths-based approach to healing, 60,
    70, 117–119
Structural change, 11
  to address individualized harms, 172–174
  benchmark for successful, 163–164
  institutional courage for, 68
  and radical healing, 117–118
  in trauma psychology, 175
Structural cultural competency, 89–90
Structural healing, 11, 19, 134, 152, 161
Structural humility, 90
Structural intersectionality, 28, 39, 40, 74
Structural oppression, 85
Structural racism
  assumption of, in CBTT, 69
  Black feminist and critical race
    perspectives on, 17
  and cultural betrayal trauma theory, 5
  defined, 26
  eradicating, x
  (intra)cultural trust as protection from, 56

and liberation psychology, 99
persistence of, 137
trauma researchers' understanding of, 4
and White mediocrity, 160
and White supremacy, 152
Study on Suicidality, Disclosure, and Healing (SUID study), 66, 67
Subpersonhood, 25
Substance use, 44
Success, benchmarks for, 163–164
Sue, Derald W., 87, 88
Suicidal behavior, 44, 174
SUID Heal (Study on Suicidality, Disclosure, and Healing), 66, 67
Supervision, 95
Support. *See also* (Intra)cultural support
from clinicians, 93
for radical healing, 119
Survival, anxiety about client's, 104–105
System-centered language, 70
Systemic bias, in peer review system, 69–70
Systemic change
barriers to, 159–167
behind-the-scenes advocacy for, 158–159
benchmarks of success for, 163–164
and power without oppression, 164–165
in radical social work, 99
uneven power field and, 161–163
White mediocrity and, 159–161
Systemic harms, addressing, 139
Systemic oppression, 71, 99
Systemic racism, 26

T

Takeaway therapy, 101
Talking with the heart, 16
Taylor, Keeanga-Yamahtta, 3, 6, 7, 12, 38, 123, 170
Teens, respecting cultural difference from, 105–107
Theatrical arts, for radical healing, 119
Theoretical orientation, for trauma therapy, 95–102
Theory-driven research, 48
Therapeutic relationship, 80, 97, 108
Therapeutic settings, CBTT research in, 74–75
Thomas, Clarence, 67, 114
Time horizon, for structural change, 163
Torres Rivera, E., 99
"Toxic femininity," 39

Transformative social justice, 31
Transparency, of decision-making processes, 160
Transphobia, 37, 70
Trans*women, 30, 43, 70, 75
Trauma. *See also specific types*
bearing witness to, 91, 93
in CBTT context, 51–53
clinicians' understanding of, 4
complex, 43, 93
race scholars' understanding of, 4
traditional model of, 54
Trauma-informed care, 90–91, 158
Trauma narratives, 103
Trauma psychology, 175
Trauma-related distress, 84
Trauma therapy practices, 90–95, 103. *See also* culturally competent trauma therapy
ambiguity in, 91–92
bearing witness, 91, 93
coexistence of good and evil in, 91–92
critical self-reflection, 91, 92
cultural competency, 91, 94
emotional intensity of, 91–92
holding hope, 91, 93–94
power-with collaborative approaches, 91–93
and self-care for practitioners, 91, 94–95
Triangulating the problem, in LH framework, 101
Trust, earning, 167. *See also* (Intra)cultural trust
Truth-telling, 153–154

U

Uncertainty, 91–92
Uneven power field, 161–163, 171
Unilateral hatred, 122
Unilateral success, 163–164
"The Unique Harm of Sexual Abuse in the Black Community" (Gómez), 101, 166
Universality, xi–xii
Universities
cultural betrayal sexual trauma within, 68
institutional betrayal by, 138
institutional change at, 149–151
institutional inaction for, 135
systemic racism in, 26
White mediocrity at, 160
University of Oregon, 108–109
U.S. Capitol insurrection, 137

V

Validation
  of Black perspectives, 155
  from clinicians, 93
  from elitist institutions, 164–165
  knowledge validation process, 15–16, 84
Victim-blaming, 146
Victims
  impact of institutional betrayal on, 138
  (intra)cultural support for, 59
  needs of, 121, 123
Violence
  anti-Black, in society, 4–5
  within Black family, 126
  epistemic, 5, 84
  as individual-level problem, 134
  police perpetrated, 22–23, 85, 159
  in theory of structural intersectionality, 40
Violence and Discrimination Questionnaire, 57
Violent oppression, rational responses to, 136
Violent racial injustice, 22
Violent silencing, xii–xiii, 6
  anger in response to, 121–122
  CBTT framework for studying, 10
  and centering of Black men in civil rights movement, 24
  growing awareness of, 166
  and health of Black women and girls, 44
  institutional courage to address, 139
  as (intra)cultural pressure, 58
  need for Black solidarity and, 7
  and perception of Black family, 125, 126
  persistence of, 137
  radical healing from, 114–116
  responsibility to eradicate, 120
  at universities, 149
Vulnerability, 116

W

Walker, Alice, xii, 17, 138
Walker, M., 96–97
We, As Ourselves campaign, 155
We, rhetorical use of, 10, 154–155
Whistleblowers, cherishing, 143
White comparison groups, 74
White domination, rejecting, 17–18
White European humanism, 24
White feminist movement, 10, 22, 26, 28
White mediocrity, 152, 159–161
White men, rape of Black women and girls by, 42
Whiteness, 4, 5, 155
White people
  concern about comfort of, 152
  in cross-racial social justice groups, 171–172
  discrimination against clinicians of color by, 107–108
  medical pathologizing of Black people by, 85
  oppression perpetrated by, 137–138
  perceptions of cultural betrayal sexual trauma by, 66
  use of collective we by, 154–155
  validation of Black experiences by, 8
White Read, 8, 79–81, 125, 166
White supremacy
  as cause of sexual abuse, 151, 153–154
  clinicians' understanding of, 4
  critical race perspective on, 24–25
  and definition of objectionable behavior, 58
  dismantling, xi–xiii, 8–9
  and diversity of Black women and girls, 38
  and inequality in social justice movements, 23–24
  meaning of term, 152, 153
  in medical model, 10–11, 17
  power by domination in, 165
  in racial contract theory, 38
  rape discourse rooted in, 41
  structural solutions to, 173
  transdisciplinary understanding of, 154
  and use of CBTT for healing, 49–50
  and validation of Black experiences by White people, 8
  and violent silencing, 115, 116
  and White mediocrity, 160
White women
  cross-racial groups including, 151–155
  cultural betrayal of Black women by, 56
  discrimination faced by, 28
  institutional betrayal in health care perpetrated by, 145–146
  in #MeToo movement, 22–24
  oppression and power for, 27, 171
  political intersectionality and, 31–32
  and "rape problem" discourse, 30, 40
Wiesner, C. R., 116
Wilkins, R., 126
Williams, F. B., 22
Williams, Patricia, 21
Wisdom through experience, 16

Within-group variation
  CBMI-BAYA in research on, 66
  CBTT postulate on, 61–64
  intersectional approaches to studying, 70–71
Women, in antiviolence movement, 151
Women's liberation movement, 137
Women's March, 30
Worldview
  awareness of client's, 88
  in Liberation Health (LH) framework, 101
  in liberation health framework, 100
  oppositional, 125
  transformative deconstruction of, 101
  for trauma therapy clinicians, 90
Wrongdoing, acknowledging, 143

Y

Young adults, CBTT research with, 62–65
Younge, Sinead N., 124
YouTube, 115

Z

Zilioli, Samuele, 66

About the Author

Jennifer M. Gómez, PhD, board member and chair of the Research Advisory Committee at the Center for Institutional Courage, is an assistant professor at Boston University School of Social Work and Center for Innovation in Social Work and Health. She is also a member of the Scientific Committee at the International Society for the Study of Trauma and Dissociation (ISSTD) and the American Psychological Association (APA) Presidential Task Force for Culturally Informed Trauma and Grief Kits. Additionally, she is a guest coeditor of two special issues in the *Journal of Trauma & Dissociation: Discrimination, Violence, & Healing in Marginalized Communities* (2021) and *Self-Injury & Suicidality: The Impact of Trauma and Dissociation* (2015). Finally, she is a former fellow at the Center for Advanced Study in the Behavioral Sciences (CASBS) at Stanford University (2021–22), National Academy of Sciences (NAS) Kavli Fellow (2019), and Ford Fellow (2015–16, 2018–19).

Having published over 100 peer-reviewed journal articles, book chapters, other scholarly writings, professional development documents, and pieces for the general public in the areas of violence and inequality, Dr. Gómez created cultural betrayal trauma theory (CBTT) as a Black feminist theoretical framework for empirically examining violence and mental, physical, behavioral, and cultural health outcomes for Black and other marginalized youth, young adults, and elders within the impactful context of structural inequality.

Her work has already advanced thinking in violence research, with invitations to share her research and its implications as a plenary speaker at the ISSTD International Conference (2021) and the Canadian Psychological Association 83rd Annual National Convention (2022), panelist at the Stanford University CASBS' Social Science for a World In Crisis Series (2021), invited speaker at the National Academies of Sciences, Engineering, and Medicine (NASEM) Action Collaborative on Preventing Sexual Harassment in Higher

Education Public Summit (2019, 2020), and invited speaker at University of Toronto (2019, 2021) and University of Michigan (2019, 2021), among others.

Dr. Gómez's work has had a demonstrative public impact, with over 638,000 readers of her 2019 article detailing CBTT and sexual abuse in the Black community in *The Conversation*.